Transitions in Segmented Labor Markets

Göttinger Studien zur Entwicklungsökonomik
Göttingen Studies in Development Economics
Herausgegeben von/Edited by Hermann Sautter

Band 14

PETER LANG
Frankfurt am Main · Berlin · Bern · Bruxelles · New York · Oxford · Wien

Silke Woltermann

Transitions in Segmented Labor Markets

The Case of Brazil

PETER LANG
Europäischer Verlag der Wissenschaften

Bibliographic Information published by Die Deutsche Bibliothek
Die Deutsche Bibliothek lists this publication in the Deutsche Nationalbibliografie; detailed bibliographic data is available in the internet at <http://dnb.ddb.de>.

Zugl.: Göttingen, Univ., Diss., 2004

Gratefully acknowledging the support of the
Ibero-America-Institut for Economic Research
at the University of Göttingen.

D 7
ISSN 1439-3395
ISBN 3-631-53162-1
US-ISBN 0-8204-7380-4

www.peterlang.de

Editor's Preface

Informal labor relations are widespread in labor markets of developing countries. But they are also increasing in the industrialized world, as global economic interaction increases and wage rates are exposed to international competition. Comparable to temporary work or part-time work, informal employment is often regarded as an inferior labor relation. In this thesis, the author uses Brazilian labor market data to show that informal employment in Brazil has more dimensions and cannot be regarded solely as an unfavorable occupational relationship.

The author takes two approaches to investigate the effects of informal employment on the development of Brazilian workers' labor histories. In a first approach, it is shown that informal employment, in spite of its negative reputation, has a positive impact on labor allocation into formal employment. For many professions in Brazil, there exist no vocational training courses and most of the learning in these professions is learning-by-doing in informal work relations. Employers as well as employees may gain from the informal contract: Workers may acquire skills and experience, enhancing their chances to enter formal employment. Employers pay lower wages to workers with unknown skills and productivity and so decrease the possible costs that are involved in the risk of hiring a worker with low productivity. To test the hypothesis that informal occupation serves as a stepping stone to formal employment for some groups of workers, transition rates into formality are estimated for workers with different labor market histories. The estimation results show indeed that informal employment increases the chances to enter formality for women searching on-the-job and for unemployed males who exited informal employment.

In a second approach, the author takes a closer look at the search process itself. Unlike the heavily studied effects of unemployment insurance benefits and qualification programs on the job search process, the importance of job search methods has only recently attracted more attention. A special focus of this thesis lies on the impact of search methods on exit rates into formal employment. It is argued that vacancies in different labor market sectors (formal/ informal) are promoted via different channels and that part of the labor market segmentation originates from lack of information on vacancies in the formal sector. Some search methods are more effective to find a job in the formal sector; other channels will rather lead to self-employment. This assumption implies that labor market policies can model labor market transitions by designing customized job-matching programs. Job placement or job matching could improve labor search processes by facilitating access to labor market information that otherwise may be hard to obtain for unemployed workers. To design an efficient job-placement service, a careful analysis of possible focus groups is essential to maximize efficiency. The design of public job placement assistance might improve the individual welfare by promoting search methods shifting more workers into formal employment.

To obtain more information about the search process, first, the influence of an individual's labor history on the choice of search methods is tested. Second, the effect of different search methods on transitions into formal employment is investigated. The results reveal that individuals reporting to have contacted the public job-placement agency tend to transit into informal employment. This indicates that the design of the public employment service has potential for improvement.

In a world where precarious work relationships appear with increasing frequency and are seemingly robust to all attempts to eradicate them, it is important to analyze their effects to be able to formulate appropriate labor market policies. By shedding light on the positive impacts of informal employment on the labor histories of less skilled workers the author provides a differentiated and valuable angle of view on the role of informal employment.

Göttingen, June 2004

Prof. Dr. Hermann Sautter

Author's Preface

Writing a thesis is something strange. Before you start, you already know what will happen. At least, you think you know. About the trial and error phase to define the subject of research. All the ups and downs your colleagues already told you about. And you think that now you know about all this, it couldn't possibly be that bad anymore. But then you experience that it does not matter if you know, it will happen all the same. All the loops you do while assuming and hoping that the things you try do not end in a loop. The downs you knew that would appear still leave you there. So why doing all this, anyway? Well, there are these moments when something works out (and this something that worked out may be increasingly small as time goes on) that leave you feeling really good. When you meet great people you would never have met in other circumstances and when you see your project grow ...

Writing this preface makes me remember all the circumstances and chances that came along, and all the people involved who contributed each in his or her own way and without whom I would never have been able to finish this project.

My first thanks go to my supervisor Prof. Hermann Sautter for accepting me as a doctoral student and leaving me so much freedom in the choice of my subject! O.K., he did not let me do my project on India, but once Brazil had been settled we arranged well! Prof. Walter Zucchini accompanied most of the econometric part of the thesis (all remaining errors and flaws are entirely mine) and was always there to most patiently discuss all my urgent questions. Prof. Stephan Klasen provided a working contract, lot's of helpful comments and a reduced workload just when I needed it most. And I am glad the members of his chair endured me during the final phase of the thesis and made me have a good time in Göttingen until the end!

Special thanks go to all the great people who just integrated me during my stay at IPEA in Rio de Janeiro, especially to Kiko Corseuil, Daniel dos Santos and Prof. Eduardo Pontual Ribeiro! They not only let me have a good time full of scientific input and great discussions about life, Brasil(!) and everything but became great friends who made me love Brazil, like Dani and Bruno Milanez and Alexandre Kappaun and his family and so many more. Special thanks to Daniel dos Santos who ignited the first sparks of inspiration for a new direction of research over some beers in Ipanema! The major part of research in Brazil has been financed by a DAAD Research Grant which is gratefully acknowledged.

At the economics department in Göttingen, Tim Krieger and Prof. Andreas Hauffler literally pushed me to write my first paper and to apply for IZA-Summer School. My colleague and friend Kai Stukenbrock was always there, not only for invaluable LaTeX support (kept up until the writing of this preface) but also for taking the edge out of all the other peculiarities of working at the department. Andreas Stadie, Analía Schlosser, Marloes Zijl and Marcelo Pessoa never tired to discuss lots of econometrics and provided even more mental support! I met Ken Harttgen at the department and over time he grew to be a very special friend who gave me lots of back up until the end (not only while climbing!).

None of my friends has been around for a longer time than Anke Scholz. She simply knows what is going on and knows about it all and is just there whatever happens even living somewhere else for most of the time. And this is just good to know.

I am grateful to Uta and Redelf, not only for the many cooked meals and all the 100% non-economic diversion, and to Leo for almost unconditional warmth and tons of cat hair. The kids' clowns and the jugglers gladly managed to take my thoughts off the thesis and put my small problems into perspective. Special thanks to Gert Liebenehm for helping out in a very difficult situation.

A big thank you to all the other people who somehow helped me directly or indirectly to finish my thesis but who have not been mentioned here!

But most probably nothing of this would have been without my parents who gave me lots of freedom and trusted in me, even if I did not always recognized it at first glance. Thanks to them and to my sisters Jana Marie and Miriam for just being one crazy family!

Silke Woltermann
Göttingen, June 2004

Contents

List of Figures

List of Tables

List of Abbreviations

BNDES	Banco Nacional de Desenvolvimento Econômico e Social
CGT	Confederação Geral dos Trabalhadores
CLT	Codigo dos Leis do Trabalhador
CNA	Confederação Nacional da Agricultura e Pecuária
CNC	Confederação Nacional do Comércio
CNF	Confederação Nacional das Instituções Financeiras
CNI	Confederação Nacional da Indústria
CUT	Central Única dos Trabalhadores
CODEFAT	Conselho Deliberativo do Fundo de Amparo ao Trabalhador
EOPP	Employment Opportunity Pilot Project
FAT	Fundo de Amparo ao Trabalhador
FGTS	Fundo de Garantia por Tempo de Servico
FS	Força Sindical
GDP	Gross Domestic Product
GPV	Gross Present Value
IBGE	Instituto Brasileiro de Geografia e Estatistica
IDB	Inter-American Development Bank
ILO	International Labor Organization
MA	Ministério de Agricultura
MPAS	Ministério da Previdência Social
MTE	Ministério de Trabalho e Emprego
NPV	Net Present Value
OECD	Organization for Economic Cooperation and Development
PME	Pesquisa Mensal de Emprego
PIS/PASEP	Programa de Integração Social/Programa de Formação do Patrimônio do Servidor Público
PLANFOR	Plano Nacional de Educação Profissional
PNAD	Pesquisa Nacional por Amostra de Domicílios
PREALC	Programa Regional del Empleo para America Latina y el Caribe
PROGER	Programa Nacional de Geração de Renda e Emprego

SDS	Social Democracia Sindical
SEBRAE	Serviço Brasileiro de Apoio ás Micro e Pequenas Empresas
SENAC	Serviço Nacional de Aprendizagem Comercial
SENAI	Serviço Nacional de Aprendizagem Industrial
SENAR	Serviço Nacional de Aprendizagem Rural
SENAT	Serviço Nacional de Aprendizagem do Transporte
SESC	Serviço Social do Comercio
SESI	Serviço Social da Indústria
SEST	Serviço Social do Transporte
SINE	Sistema Nacional de Emprego

Part I

Informal Employment Revisited Theoretical Concepts and Stylized Facts From Brazil

Chapter 1

Introduction

The employment relationship is one of the fundamental relationships in our lives. Labor generates income and people spend most of their waking time working, learning or searching for a job. The labor market is the central market within an economy where labor force is offered and sought for. Next to the material functions of allocating labor into the most productive positions, the labor market also has an important social function, as labor services cannot be separated from the individuals offering them. The well-being of the individual is based on the position of the person in the labor market, on the income obtained and on the non-pecuniary conditions of work. In a recent public opinion survey by Latinobarometer (2001), covering 17 Latin American countries, labor market problems and especially unemployment (20% of the respondents) were the most often reported answers on the question "What is the most pressing issue in the region?". Next to unemployment, employment stability and low wages were other "pressing issues" reported, all three problems accounting together for about 40% of the responses. A person's income is generated by labor, and even benefits like the unemployment insurance benefits and also pensions are often based on the income an individual gained. In a macroeconomic view, the rate of unemployment is one of the indicators of the well-being of a society (Di Tella, MacCulloch, and Oswald 2003; Oswald 1997; Winkelmann and Winkelmann 1998).

The efficiency of the labor market in allocating labor in productive positions is therefore an important issue: if assumed that wages reflect productivity of a worker, the worker will be better off the more productive he is. As people are not goods or capital to be dislocated easily, and labor market information is not distributed equally and not always available, the labor market function is often distorted. Because of the social functions of the labor market, many countries have chosen to implement regulations to install minimum working standards to increase security and well-being of the workers. Security systems have been installed to prevent unemployed workers from falling below the poverty line. Many states use active labor market policy instruments to improve the allocative function and by this the flexibility of the labor market, introducing public job placement centers, qualification courses and a labor market information system.

In many countries, like in Brazil, a segmented labor market can be observed. Next to employment in jobs with good working conditions, job and social security and decent wages, there exists a second labor market segment lacking these criteria, especially the entitlement to legally enforce labor market regulations and to benefit from social security and unemployment insurance benefits. But the existence of precarious work is not only a phenomenon of developing countries. During the last decades industrialized countries have also experienced a process of increasing precarious work-relations (Schneider 2002). The German sociologist Beck (1999) even named the recent developments in the German labor market the *Brazilianization of the labor market.*

Many papers have been written on the processes by which some individuals get decent work while others end up in less favorable working conditions. Much less attention has been paid to the functions of the secondary segment for the allocative process of work, and on the role that the choice of search methods may play for the allocation of workers into the primary or secondary segment.

The existence of informal work can have different effects on the stream of income and the well-being of an individual. The most obviously negative direct effects of informal work result from the characteristics generally related to this type of work relation: poor working conditions, low wages and no social or legal protection. On the other hand, informal employment very often represents a source of income for those people who would not be able to find work in the formal segment of the labor market. By taking up informal employment, they have the possibility to generate some income. In this sense, informal jobs are valuable for the well-being of those who would otherwise be unemployed and without access to resources. Besides these direct advantages and disadvantages of informal employment, informal employment may also have an influence on the future employment states of an individual. Labor market theory gives no clear indication whether having been informally employed may or may not enhance the chances to find formal employment with better working conditions and a better wage in the future. In countries like Brazil, where a quarter of the economically active population is informally employed, it is quite important for the economic and social development of the country to know about the role of informal employment within the allocation and development of the labor force. Besides this, informal employment, as any precarious working relationship, affects the well-being of individuals and its effects therefore deserve to be thoroughly investigated.

In **Part Two** of this thesis, I will therefore investigate the mobility of workers between the different segments of the Brazilian labor market. The focus here lies on the transitions into formal employment, and the three groups of individuals of special interest are those individuals who are currently informally employed or who held an informal job before and are now searching, and the newcomers to the labor market, those individuals who have not been economically active before.

I will test several hypothesis concerning the transitions of informally employed workers, job searchers and newcomers into formal employment. My **first hypothesis** is that, unlike the prediction of the dualistic labor market economists, informal employment in Brazil does not lead to a "scarring" of workers in a way that they may not find formal work again once they have worked for some time in their informal jobs. The "scarring" may hold for some groups of workers, but an individual's labor history does not generally lead to persistence in the same occupational state. My **second hypothesis** is that informal employment serves as a stepping stone to formality for individuals without direct access to formal employment. I argue that much vocational training is performed on-the-job while workers are informally employed. So, informal labor experience may also serve as a positive signal to formal employers, indicating that the individual acquired skills in that profession. These considerations directly lead to my third hypothesis. Work experience leads to the accumulation of skills useful for a certain profession. These skills are usually not learned within the first days of employment, so the effect of learning should increase over time[1], and the spell of the employment should therefore be a signal for formal employers. My **third hypothesis** therefore is: the informal employment spell has a positive impact on the transition probability into formality. The group of newcomers serves as a control group for both latter hypotheses as members of this group have not acquired any skills relevant for a profession. The results of Part Two are of relevance for the design of active labor market policies and the integration of informal employment relationships into public policy considerations.

Until now, the allocative function of informal employment as a stepping stone into formal employment in segmented labor markets has not been investigated. The closest related studies to this subject are studies on the impact of temporary or part-time work on the transition into permanent full-time jobs (Van Den Berg, Holm, and Ours 1999; Van Den Berg, Heyma, and

[1]The learning curve is assumed to be increasing with time, but with a decreasing slope. Even a maximum is thinkable.

Zijl 2003; Booth, Francesconi, and Frank 2002; Guell-Rotllan and Petrongolo 2000). While temporary or part-time jobs are legitimately considered as less favorable employment relationships as they usually lack training possibilities and career options, they are nonetheless to be considered as formal jobs. Individuals working in these kinds of jobs may not be offered the same promotion options and training, but their employers still pay contributions to the social security system and these workers are protected by the labor legislation and have access to unemployment benefits in case of dismissal. Informally employed Brazilian workers do not experience the same working conditions as their formal colleagues. They are neither eligible for unemployment benefits and other social security benefits, nor are they protected by the labor legislation. They have no claim to the set wages negotiated by the unions. Still I argue that the precarious labor relationship of informal employment does have a positive function in the Brazilian labor market helping to allocate workers into formality. A possible explanation is that in Brazil, much of the vocational training is performed as on-the-job training within the informal segment of the economy due to the lack of public or official professional training courses. As long as this is the case, informal employment has an important function of allocating those into formality who would never get there without the possibility of gathering working experience and thereby professional skills.

In **Part Three** of this thesis, I turn to the job search process itself. I argue that next to the question of inter-segment mobility, the way in which these transitions are performed has an impact on the efficiency of the labor market. Unemployed workers have different options how to search for their next job. They may for example directly contact potential employers, answer vacancy advertisements, or visit the public employment service for help. Different search channels may work more or less efficiently in a general way, or yield good results for jobs in one segment but not for jobs in the other segment. Some channels may be useful or accessible only for certain groups of individuals. Within the group of search channels, only the efficiency of the public employment service has been thoroughly investigated in various studies.[2] The other search channels have not attracted that much attention, though. And none of the studies considers segmented labor markets, as most of the research in this area focusses on industrialized countries and the rising share of precarious work in this group of countries only recently started to shift into the awareness of labor economists. In Part Three, I try to find answers to the above questions of efficiency of different search channels used by Brazilian unemployed workers. I split up the effects for formal and informal employment and I take into account the different characteristics of groups of workers. The

[2]See, for example, the studies of Addison and Portugal (2002), Böheim and Taylor (2002), Cardoso (2000), Gregg and Wadsworth (1996), Ramos and de Freitas (1998). The role of the public employment service is also discussed in greater detail in Section 11.2.

results from this part of my thesis are used to identify possibly problematic subgroups within the group of unemployed. The speed and efficiency of the matching process on the labor market can be improved by focussing active labor market policies like the public employment service and the labor market information system towards these target groups.

The focus of my study lies on dependent employment, both formal and informal. Self employment is not considered because of the very large heterogeneity within this group. The sample of workers used for the estimations in Part Two is additionally limited to individuals aged between 15 and 29 and with schooling levels of primary school or less, as a special focus lies on the comparison between transition rates of newcomers versus former informally employed individuals.

The thesis is structured as follows: In this first part, I will give an overview about how different labor market approaches try to explain the origin and persistence of labor market segmentation. I focus on approaches within the neoclassical framework and approaches formulated by dual labor market economists Although I present the ideas and concepts of these two strains of thought in labor economics separately from each other, I already want to point out that the main aim of this thesis is not to validate or falsify either of these theories. Instead, they are presented in Part One to show the different explanations of the origin of labor market segmentation and informality. In Part Two and Part Three the theoretical approaches are used to identify the determinants of transition directions between the segments indicated by the different theories. The presented theoretical considerations serve to determine the variables of the econometric analysis performed in these parts of the thesis. I will therefore not present all approaches in great depth in Part One, but only use the overview as a base for theoretical discussions and econometric model building in the following parts. This overview is followed by a section containing stylized facts of the Brazilian labor market to show the problems of this specific segmented labor market and give the reader an idea why the investigations undertaken are of interest. This first part also contains a section about the features of the database used for the econometric estimation to avoid repetitions in the latter parts.

Part Two of this thesis deals with the mobility of workers between the different labor market segments, with a focus on the transitions between formal and informal employment. After giving a more detailed motivation for this area of investigation, I present additional details on education and vocational training and other information about Brazil important for the following discussion. The factors and individual characteristics affecting transitions between segments and from unemployment into work identified in the theoretical chapter of Part One are discussed in more detail in Chapter 7 in Part Two. The implications found in the different theoretical approaches within the neoclassical framework as well as in the dualistic approaches are discussed and possible directions of effects of the different factors like education and work experience are identified. These findings are then used to formulate the econometric model used to estimate the impact of these factors for the sample of Brazilian workers and unemployed. To perform the estimations I use a competing risks framework and formulate Cox proportional hazard rate functions for the different groups of workers considered. In Chapter 9 I discuss the results of my estimations and show the hazard rate contributions for different groups of workers. I also discuss possible policy implications resulting from the findings.

Having dealt with the existence of inter-segment mobility and identified important factors for the different groups of workers, I then investigate the matching process itself in Part Three of this thesis. As in Part Two, I start with a detailed motivation for the subject of research of this part and some more details of the Brazilian labor market important for the matching procedures like active labor market policies, labor market key-numbers and job search methods in Brazil. In the following chapter, I use approaches from search theory and findings from the neoclassical and dualistic approaches already shortly presented in the theoretical Chapter 2 to identify possible factors of impact for the efficiency of the different search channels. In Chapter 14 I use these theoretical implications to build the econometric model. In this case I formulate multinomial logistic regressions to estimate the impact of different factors for the transitions into different labor market states and segments. As in the previous part, personal characteristics as well as labor history variables are included in the estimation. The regression results are reported and discussed in Chapter 15, and possible policy implications are presented.

The Appendix following Part Three contains more general information about the data samples used, and more detailed results of the empirical investigations for the interested reader. The bibliography for all three parts of this thesis is also located at the end of the thesis.

Chapter 2

Theoretical Concepts of Segmented Labor Markets

2.1 Informal Work in the Labor Theory

The well-known ILO-Study on the structure of the labor market in Kenya (ILO 1972) was the first emphasizing the unregistered small-scale activities of rural migrants and urban dwellers as a particular phenomenon providing employment and thereby means of living. One year later, Hart (1973) introduced the term 'informal sector' and the concept of the informal sector entered development theory. Since then many studies on the broad subject of 'informality' have been performed. A bibliography on studies concerning informality in Latin America and the Caribbean presented by the Programa Regional del Empleo para América Latina y el Caribe PREALC, ILO (1991) in the early nineties already lists about 400 papers.

From the beginning the phenomenon covered by terms like 'informality', 'informal sector' or 'non-structured sector' has been a diffuse one. The ILO-Study, (ILO 1972), uses seven criteria to define informal work: ease of entry, unregulated and competitive markets, reliance on indigenous resources, family ownership of enterprises, small scale of operation, labor intensive and adopted technology, skills acquired outside the formal school system. Because of the heterogeneity of the labor markets in developing countries, several attempts have been made to adapt the sometimes quite complex criteria and to allow for statistical treatment.[1] Most of the criteria for informality concern the self-

[1] For a discussion of different classifications and criteria see, for example, Charmes (1990) and Thomas (1992). For some authors the ease of entry into the informal labor market segment is the crucial feature, see Fields (1990).

employment or micro-company-part of the informal economy. Even classification criteria for this kind of informal activity change from country to country. In some countries the payment of taxes on revenues is a sign of formality; in other countries this tax is not collected and can therefore not be considered as a criterion for formality. Sometimes registration with the municipality serves as an indicator for formal business, but sometimes no registration is required or performed. The same blurriness of the criteria holds for informal employment. Sometimes labor cards are issued and workers possessing one are classified formal workers. But what happens if the same worker receives part of his wage registered on his labor card and the other part of the wage on the side, not registered? Apart from the difficulties of classifying informal occupation the different groups of micro-entrepreneurship, self-employment, pseudo-self-employment and dependent informal employment are not at all homogeneous. Several studies show that the group of informally self-employed behaves quite differently from other groups such as the informally dependent employed (Maloney 1997).

In the first basic neoclassical labor market model with clearing markets and wage as sole regulative mechanism, the existence of informal work cannot be explained. When informal occupation first came into the focus of labor economists, it was therefore classified as a transitional phenomenon occurring in developing countries' labor markets on the way to industrialization. When absolute and relative numbers of informally occupied workers rose over the years instead rather than declined, other approaches emerged to explain this part of the labor market. Confronted with the shortcoming of the neoclassical power to explain informality it was then claimed that informality could be explained by this theoretical framework making some assumptions, implying that informal labor markets were just a special case within the neoclassical framework.

In my dissertation I will focus on informal employment, meaning dependent employment within a firm or company. This group of workers is easily identified in Brazil via the non-possession of a signed labor card.[2] In the rest of this chapter I will give a short introduction on how the existence of informal employment and the labor allocation into different sectors is explained within the neoclassical context and within the dual labor markets framework.[3] This chapter will also serve as a base for analyzing the Brazilian labor market in the next chapter and the further discussion in the following parts of this thesis. I will therefore focus on recent research directly concerning the Brazilian labor market in the subsequent chapter. Additionally, more detailed theoretical dis-

[2]See Section 3.3 for more details on the Brazilian labor market and informal employment.
[3]See for example McNabb (1987) for detailed information on this topic.

cussions will take place in the theoretical chapters of the following parts of my dissertation, focussing on the specific issues of these parts.

2.2 Segmentation in the Neoclassical Labor Market Theory

2.2.1 The Basic Neoclassical Labor Market Model

The Theory of General Equilibrium is the fundamental theory in the neoclassical paradigm, starting with the first formulations by Walras at the end of the nineteenth century. Assuming perfect markets without information asymmetry and regulative restrictions, all interactions on a market will lead to an equilibrium; no regulation by outside institutions is necessary. The assumptions that individuals act rational, have a defined set of preferences, have free choice of how and when to interact and tend to maximize their utility, serve as the basis for all economic activity. By comparing utility gains and costs, decisions are made and resources are allocated in their most productive use. The most productive use for individuals is the one that yields highest utility; companies are assumed to maximize profits. All relevant market information is available at zero costs for all parties active in the specified market. Prices of the goods traded are determined by supply and demand, the central regulating mechanism is the market. The market price itself is the mechanism to establish the equilibrium in the market, the way individuals and firms achieve this equilibrium is by competition.

Within the early neoclassical framework the labor market is considered as a market like all the other markets for goods, the asset 'labor' is assumed to follow the same laws like any tradable good. This also implies the idea that all processes on the labor market can be controlled by changing the wage rate, being the price for the traded good on that particular market. This leads to the following assumptions about the behavior of the individuals within this simplified partial equilibrium model of the labor market:

- There is perfect competition in the labor market, neither entry barriers nor restrictions impede competition.
- All individuals offering their labor on a special labor market are homogenous, e.g. they have the same productivity and can easily be substituted. There is no discrimination.

- Individuals are completely mobile, they immediately transit into the new optimal working relationships if market conditions change. This includes regional and sectoral mobility as well as qualifications.
- Wages are completely flexible and adjust instantaneously if there are changes in labor demand.
- All individuals participating in the labor market have perfect information about the present and future labor conditions, e.g. changing intensities of economic activities, vacancies, wages etc..
- Employers are able to sell their profit-maximizing output at any time.

It is assumed that there are I households offering labor l_i, $i = 1, ..., I$, and J firms demanding for labor l_j, $j = 1, ..., J$. According to the assumptions stated above, households maximize their utility conditioned on their income from labor, and firms maximize their profits conditioned on the price of the factor labor, the wage w:

$$\begin{aligned} \text{labor supply} &= l_i = l_i(w), \\ \text{labor demand} &= l_j = l_j(w). \end{aligned}$$

Income other than that generated by labor is ignored in this approach. The overall supply and demand of labor then are:

$$\begin{aligned} L_i(w) &= \sum_{i=1}^{I} l_i(w), \\ L_j(w) &= \sum_{j=1}^{J} l_j(w). \end{aligned}$$

The equilibrium on the labor market is established when labor supply and labor demand equal each other:

$$L_i(w) = L_j(w). \tag{2.1}$$

Generally, labor supply L_i is assumed to increase with increasing wage rate, while labor demand L_j decreases with increasing wages rates.

Individuals maximize their utility, derived only from labor income in this simple example, by comparing the utility of the income of the last unit of work supplied with the cost of the unit of leisure time foregone by working. The optimal supply of labor is the one where the marginal utility of income equals the marginal cost of foregone leisure time.

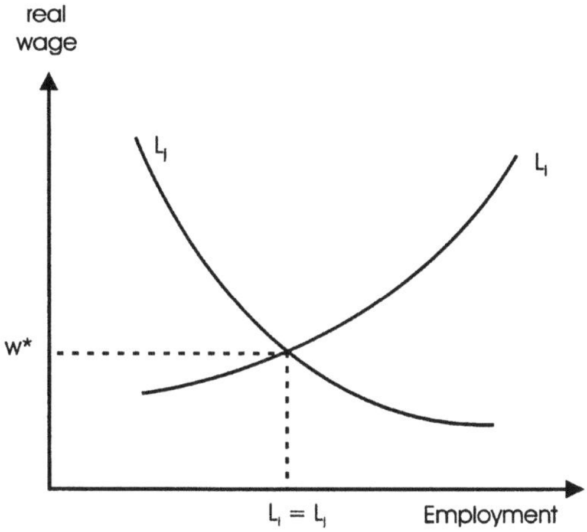

Source: Ehrenberg and Smith (1991), p. 44.

Figure 2.1: Neoclassic demand and supply in the labor market.

Assuming that firms can produce their output choosing any combination of labor and capital, and that the productivity of both factors is determined by a given production function for that company, then wages are the only variable control mechanism. Firms then maximize their profits when the productivity of the last contracted worker, the marginal productivity, equals the marginal costs of labor, the wage rate.

If labor supply and labor demand are not equal, an adaption mechanism is triggered, leading to a change in the wage rate in direction of the equilibrium wage rate. The assumed perfect competition on both sides of the labor market and the completely flexible wages allow immediate changes of the wage rate followed by the adaption of the supply and demand of labor. This adaption mechanism continues until a stable equilibrium is again reached. In this equilibrium there are, per definition, no workers supplying work at exactly that wage rate but not finding work. Similarly, there are no firms offering jobs at the equilibrium wage rate and not finding workers. In this framework no involuntary unemployment is possible; all existing unemployment is voluntary. The observed unemployment in real labor markets is caused by wage rates above the market clearing wage rate. According to this very simplified model of neoclassical labor market theory this frictional unemployment should be of short duration, as the adaption mechanism would soon lead to changes in the wage rate, leading to a new equilibrium. Ehrenberg and Smith (1991) explain persistent unemployment in this model setting by rigid wage rates caused by exogenous reasons like set wages negotiated by the unions or institutional labor market regulations like minimum wages or working hour regulations.[4]

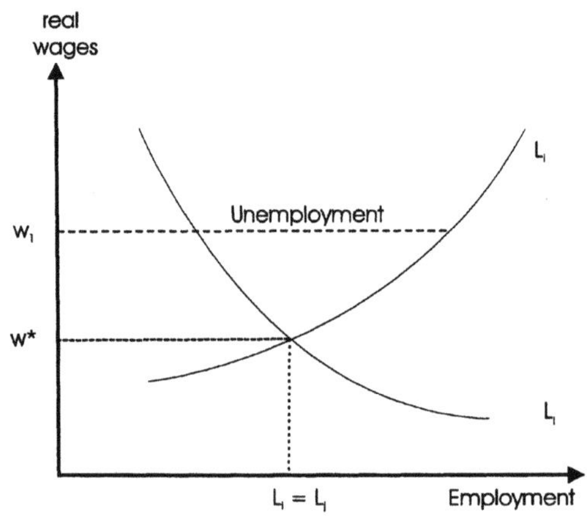

Source: Ehrenberg and Smith (1991), p. 53.

Figure 2.2: Unemployment in the neoclassic labor market.

Next to the difficulties of explaining unemployment endogenously, the basic neoclassical framework also does not explain the existence of labor market segmentation.[5] As all individuals supplying labor are considered homogeneous,

[4]Empirically the role of unions concerning the level and rigidity of wages is less evident; see the overview on the empirical findings in Ehrenberg and Smith (1991). For detailed survey on the abundant literature on the theoretical and empirical impact of minimum wages on employment and the distribution of wages, see Brown (1999). Heckman and Pagés (2000) gather evidence on the impact of job security regulations on the level and distribution of employment in Latin America. Their findings are that job security regulations reduce employment and increase inequality across workers.

[5]Next to the lack of explanatory power regarding unemployment and labor market segmentation, there is a more general critique on the neoclassical assumptions concerning the modelling of the labor market and the General Equilibrium Theory. I will not provide a general overview about this critique within this thesis. See Sesselmeier and Blauermel (1997) for a comprehensive overview over the critique. The points relevant to labor market segmen-

there is no endogenous way to explain why some of them get jobs with good working conditions, while others end up in precarious working relationships. In the seventies some of the assumptions of the basic neoclassical model were relaxed to incorporate the possibility of labor market segmentation.

2.2.2 Neoclassical Approaches to Segmentation

Three of the above assumptions of the neoclassical labor market theory are especially important in the context of explaining labor market segmentation and unemployment. One is the assumption of homogeneity of workers and the other ones are the assumptions of flexible wages and free choice of working time.

Beginning with the latter two assumptions, both flexible wages and free choice of working time are necessary for a frictionless adjusting labor market, as well as the possibility of smooth substitution of capital and labor in the production process. Regulations like minimum wages and maximum working hours or the definition of full- and part-time jobs add rigidities to labor market adjustment and have therefore frequently been criticized by neoclassical labor economists. They have been identified as reasons for unemployment, especially rigid wages like those negotiated by the unions were considered to be above the market clearing level, therefore creating incentives for more people to look for a job as the labor demand side is able to absorb. Efficiency wages are another factor contributing to wage levels above the market-clearing rate.

The assumed homogeneity of the workers proved to be an even larger issue. Of course, in the real world labor markets, perfect homogeneity of the workers cannot be observed. But the earning differences that can be observed are sometimes of such a magnitude that they cannot be neglected, and the assumption of a homogenous workforce is a too strong simplification. In response to these facts different approaches have been developed trying to explain differences in earnings and discrimination, both properties of segmented labor markets. Both the Human Capital Theory and theories of discrimination try to endogenize heterogeneity of the labor force.

The Human Capital Theory

The modern foundations of the Human Capital Theory were developed in works by Schultz (1961), Mincer (1962), Oi (1962) and Becker (1964) at the

---

tation and unemployment will be dealt with in the following section and in the theoretical sections of the other parts of this thesis.

beginning of the sixties of the last century. The problematic assumption of complete homogeneity of the factor labor is relaxed by allowing for heterogeneity in one dimension: the level of individual investment in human capital is allowed to differ. Investment in human capital is defined as all activities effecting the future productivity of a worker. It is composed of the direct costs for education and qualification, and of the opportunity costs for forgone or reduced income during the time of qualification. Differences in earnings, working conditions and job security then result from the different stocks of human capital of the workers. The level of education is seen as one of the most important characteristics determining the productivity and thereby the wage a worker can obtain on the labor market. Employers consider productivity to be a function of education and offer wages according to the amount of education obtained (Schultz 1961).

Investment in human capital follows the same lines as the other neoclassic optimization processes: an individual will invest in achieving more human capital until the marginal costs of obtaining more qualification equal the present value of marginal returns. According to the basic neoclassic paradigm the wage equals the marginal productivity; the wage will therefore increase with increasing productivity.

Within the neoclassical labor market theory the productivity of a worker depends on the education this worker has obtained. The human capital theory regards education as an investment: an individual is paying now to become more skilled, the skills increase his productivity and make him eligible for higher paid jobs. Education thus increases future earnings and the investment turns profitable when the discounted future earnings exceed the price to be paid for the education. Empirically, a strong link can be observed between education and earnings.[6] More formally, education increases the individual's future marginal product and hence the future income. If this income at time t, B_t, is assumed to be the only benefit from education, ignoring utility derived for example from the process of learning itself or from the status accompanying a higher paid job, a simple model is obtained. The gross present value (GPV) of one additional year of education, given an interest rate of r, can then be written as:

$$GPV = \frac{B_1}{1+r} + \frac{B_2}{(1+r)^2} + \ldots + \frac{B_n}{(1+r)^n}, \quad t = 1, \ldots, n. \tag{2.2}$$

[6]For a detailed causal modelling of the return to education and a selective survey of empirical studies on the subject see Card (1999).

Letting C_0 be the cost of one additional year of education, including the forgone wages, the net present value (NPV) is:

$$NPV = \sum_{t=0}^{n} \frac{B_t}{(1+r)^t} - C_0, \quad t = 1, \ldots, n. \tag{2.3}$$

According to this approach, an individual keeps acquiring education until his GPV exceeds the cost for education, and the NPV equals zero (marginal cost of education equals the marginal value of an additional year of schooling).

Critiques of the human capital theory, for example Spence (1973), argue that there is high correlation between education and productivity, but that education is not causal for productivity. Individuals with better abilities simply self-select into higher education, but their productivity is not increased by education beyond the basic level. Education may therefore serve as a signal for productivity, but a certain level of education does not necessarily imply proportional productivity.

If a certain level of education is no guarantee for a minimum productivity, the neoclassical assumption of complete information does not hold anymore. There is an information disequilibrium in the labor market impeding optimal market clearing. At one market side, workers are (probably) aware of their abilities, employers screen for signals to decrease their information deficit. This is the precondition for the signaling theory developed by Spence (1973). The screening approach (Chiswick 1973; Borjas and Goldberg 1978) and the 'sheepskin effect'-hypothesis (Hungerford and Solon 1987; Belman and Heywood 1991) argue that years of education where a diploma is earned yield wage premiums that are not explained by the human capital theory.

As the human capital theory is endogenizing education and professional qualification, the marginal product theory had to be modified: instead of wages being equal to the marginal productivity of the worker, now, in the optimum, the discounted present value of the firm's future returns equals the discounted present value of future earnings and qualification costs. This implies that the wage is not necessarily equal to the present marginal product any more. The human capital theory thus explains the structure of wages, complementing the theory of marginal productivity explaining the level of wages (Sesselmeier and Blauermel 1997). Within this theoretical framework it is of no importance for the outcome who is making the investments in human capital. Apart from the individual himself, the state or employers are possible investors. Usually the state, and to some extend the individuals, are financing the basic schooling, while employers rather invest in specialized on-the-job training for their workers. Schooling is generally thought to increase the productivity of a person in many different occupations, while the specialized on-the-job training often only increases the productivity within the particular firm. This differentiation is useful for determining who profits from additional qualification and who therefore should pay for it. In addition this provides an explanation for the payment of wages above the market wage: the more an employer invests in a worker, the higher is the loss in case the worker quits. To reduce fluctuation of highly specialized workers employers often pay above-market wages.

Oi (1962) points out that labor costs, generally regarded as variable costs, may also show fixed components. Examples for fixed elements are screening and contracting costs, severance payments, as well as expenditures for on-the-job training. A quasi-fixed production factor is then classified as a factor generating both fixed and variable costs. Assuming perfect competition in the labor market, wage rates and marginal productivity would only be equal if labor would be a variable production factor. If on-the-job training is to be regarded as a fixed cost element, then product sales have to provide an additional rent to cover these period-specific fixed labor costs. The fixed cost element leads to a rigidity in the labor market as firms tend to keep workers associated with the fixed costs for a longer time during recessions than other, less-skilled workers. On the other hand side, firms will wait longer and be more risk averse to contract a worker who will generate fixed costs. So according to Oi (1962), only unskilled labor can be regarded as a variable production factor.

The human capital theory serves to explain the structure of wages in an economy by allowing for heterogeneity concerning the human capital accumulated by workers. Nevertheless, differences in earnings can be observed for individuals with identical productive characteristics. These differences in wages cannot be explained by different human capital stocks; other approaches had to be found. Additionally, the human capital theory only focusses on the labor supply side and neglects impacts from the labor demand side. An investment in human capital may always be preferable to individuals, but in a more general macroeconomic view, the investment in human capital may not always lead to better results, because the demand for certain types of human capital may be finite and not all individuals may be able to realize higher earnings. These kinds of restrictions from the labor demand side are not integrated in the human capital approach.

Principle-Agent-Situations: Efficiency Wages

A further attempt to explain wage rigidities, and hence unemployment, has been made by introducing the concept of efficiency wages. This concept is intended to explain why wages do not adjust downwards even in the presence of unemployed workers willing to work for a lower than the currently paid wage. Works in this area refer to the causal relationship between a workers productivity and the wage he earns as postulated by the human capital theory. Efficiency wages can be interpreted within the framework of the principal-agent theory (Weiss 1980), because employers often can neither determine nor control completely the productivity of their workers. They can set minimum requirements, but it is hard to determine how high productivity could really be. What can be observed though is a positive correlation between productivity and wages. This leads to the assumption that a reduction of wages will reduce productivity and thereby increase labor costs (Yellen 1984). Figure 2.3 shows the effort level $E(w)$ of a randomly selected worker as a function of the wage rate w.

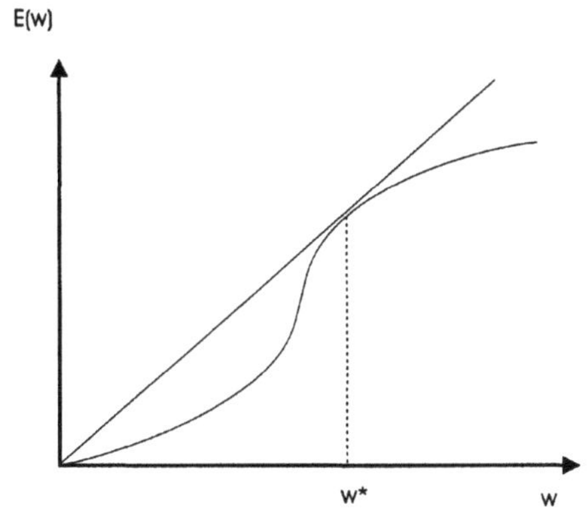

Source: Weiss (1990), p. 20.

Figure 2.3: Worker's effort level as a function of the wage.

The optimal (efficiency) wage rate w^* for the employer results where a ray from the origin touches the effort function, as this is the maximum of $E(w)/w$, the maximum effort level per wage paid.

Employers are primarily interested to maximize their profits, so if all other parameters of the labor force, like working hours and non-wage labor costs are assumed fixed, they will chose wages that minimize labor cost per efficiency unit instead of minimizing labor costs per worker. By paying these so-called efficiency wages, employers then maximize their profits. If the productivity of a worker drops more than 50 % when his wage drops by half, then an employer will prefer to pay the higher wage, thereby reducing labor costs per efficiency unit. An efficiency wage w^* set by the employer higher than the market clearing wage may then cause unemployment, as shown in Figure 2.4.

While the labor supply curve L^S behaves normally, observe the backward bent labor demand curve L^D for wages lower than the market clearing wage.

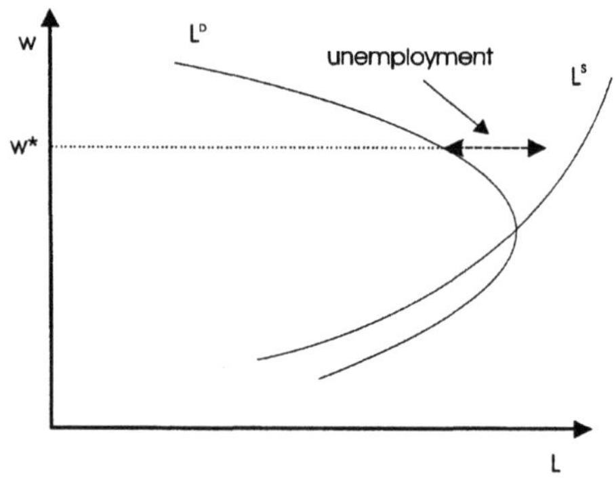

Source: Weiss (1990), p. 20.

Figure 2.4: Labor demand curve L^D in the efficiency wage framework.

So, contrary to the Human Capital Theory, productivity here can be increased by paying higher real wages, not only by investing in education. Economists working within the field of efficiency wages focussed on different hypotheses about the advantages efficiency wages would bring to the employers. The first straightforward explanation on this subject stems from (Leibenstein 1963) who worked on labor markets in developing countries. He argues that higher wages lead to improved nutrition and living conditions of rural workers, and by this improve health and therefore lead to higher productivity. Stiglitz (1976), Weiss (1980) and Malcomson (1981) name a reduction of adverse selection as the main advantage for the employers: higher wages than the market clearing wage attract higher qualified workers. Workers signalling that they would work for lower wages are turned away by employers as this is taken as a sign for lower productivity. The payment of efficiency wages also increases the costs of quitting for the worker; firms can so reduce labor turnover by paying wages above the market clearing level. The higher aggregate unemployment rate caused by rigid wages additionally increases the opportunity costs of quitting. Especially firms who need skilled workers and offer on-the-job training will profit from the lower job rotation by reduced training costs and more experienced and productive workers (Salop 1979; Stiglitz 1974; Schlicht 1978). Paying wages above the market-clearing level also prevents workers from shirking as the cost of being fired is increased[7]. Akerlof (1982) and, to some extend, Solow (1979) take a different approach from the sociological side, arguing that social conventions

[7]See for example Shapiro and Stiglitz (1984) and Foster and Wan (1984)

and moral considerations lead to higher wages and increased productivity: in his partial gift exchange model, Akerlof (1982) argues that a group's working norms and effort may raise above the enforceable level when employers pay wages above the required minimum level. Akerlof takes this argumentation to classify labor markets into primary and secondary markets. In the theoretical model he develops, it is endogenously determined whether a specific labor market falls into the primary or secondary segment. The market is a primary one if the gift exchange component of labor input and wages is sizeable and wages therefore are not market-clearing. In secondary markets, the gift exchange component does not have an impact and wages are market-clearing in these markets. A critique of the gift exchange approach is that in reality the contrary behavior of workers is also observable: instead of increasing their productivity, workers keep productivity deliberately at a lower level than necessary, especially when working in piecework, and new entrants in production teams are soon introduced into these lower "generally accepted" productivity levels (Sesselmeier and Blauermel 1997).

The differences to the neoclassic approaches presented above are, next to the assumed asymmetrical information about worker's productivity, that wages are not determined anymore via the market process. The efficiency wages, by definition higher than the market clearing wages, are set by employers. By choosing the efficiency wage level, employers have an influence on the marginal productivity of workers, maintaining the neoclassical assumption that the wage rate equals the marginal value product of the labor. Adjustment in case of changes on the demand side of the market here takes place by variations of the labor demand curve, e.g. hirings or firings, and not by adjusting real wages.

Efficiency wage approaches offer an explanation why jobs in certain labor markets may be rationed and wages may be set persistently above the market clearing level by the demand side of the market. These non-clearing labor markets may exist within an economy along with other labor markets behaving according to the neoclassic paradigm. In labor markets with rigid wages and unemployment, the lower skilled and therefore less productive workers may end up finding no work paying efficiency wages. They will therefore compete for the jobs in labor markets where the wage-productivity correlation is weak or nonexistent (Akerlof and Yellen 1986). In these labor markets only market wages are paid, and they are usually classified by a larger demand for unskilled labor, high job-insecurity and poor working conditions. This is especially the case for industrial production with chain work and high labor division, where the machinery determines the productivity of the worker and almost no specific skills are needed. In these cases an efficiency wage would not increase productivity and therefore not lower the efficiency unit costs.

Still, efficiency wages do not explain why some workers educated within the same profession are formally employed and some end up in an informal employment relationship. In order to close this gap, insider-outsider approaches and theories of discrimination have been developed.

Insider-Outsider Approaches

The efficiency theory explained persistent unemployment as a result of a principal-agent problem between employer and employees resulting in higher than market-clearing wages. The insider-outsider approach considers the conflict between two other parties of the labor market, namely employed and unemployed workers, as the source of unemployment (Lindbeck and Snower 1988; Lindbeck and Snower 2001). Three groups of individuals are distinguished on the labor supply side:

- insiders, who are already employed in the company and have received full training,
- entrants: recently employed workers still receiving training, and
- outsiders: unemployed workers looking for a job.

Workers already employed by a company, the insiders, are interested in keeping outsiders out, mainly to prevent wage slips (Sesselmeier and Blauermel 1997). Insiders are able to build certain barriers for outsiders, as they have a stronger position than the outsiders. The power of the insiders stems from the investment the employers have already undertaken for them: employers have already paid hiring costs in form of screening applications, setting up assessment centers and performing all kinds of administrative tasks, as registering the employee with the social security systems and the like. In addition employers may have invested in general and firm-specific training of the insiders. These costs would have to be paid again if insiders were fired and replaced by newcomers, thereby increasing the fluctuation cost. Furthermore, it is assumed that the firing process itself is also costly, for example in the form of severance payments. As entrants are still in the training process, it is assumed that the training costs are lower, but all other costs are the same in case of dismissal.

Besides the costs mentioned above, insiders may produce additional costs if the company hires outsiders for lower wages. As at least part of the firm-specific knowledge is assumed to be passed on by informal on-the-job training, the company has to rely on the cooperation of insiders and entrants. If insiders threaten with non-cooperation, the company is faced with more costs in the form of a lower productivity of the entrants. This holds equally for the general production process where cooperation may significantly enhance productivity, and a threat of non-cooperation with entrants increases production costs. Within the insider-outsider approach it is therefore an advantage for the company to keep insiders and pay them a higher wage, even in the presence of unemployment and lower wage bids from outsiders. Outsiders do not have these opportunities to exert pressure on a company's cost curve. By maintaining these internal structures and keeping outsiders out, wages may seem to be rigid, and vacancies are not necessarily filled with the best qualified applicant but rather with an insider who has to move from his former post.

Theories of Discrimination

The theories of discrimination are closely related to the human capital theory, but they also incorporate elements of the labor demand side, trying to solve the shortcomings of the human capital theory in this respect. This includes the incorporation of personal characteristics like sex, age, ethnicity and the like into the analysis of contracting decisions and differing wages. Different sources of discrimination have been hypothesized, ranging from personal prejudice to statistical pre-judgement.

According to the human capital theory, employers should be indifferent which person to employ if individuals have the same productive characteristics, as they are expected to be equally productive. If individuals with identical productive characteristics systematically receive differing wages for supplying equal services because they belong to different demographic groups, then labor market discrimination exists (Ehrenberg and Smith 1991). Next to wage discrimination, occupational discrimination may also be observed when individuals of a specified group do not have access to the same job, job-level or career options as their colleagues with identical characteristics. Apart from racial discrimination, gender discrimination is also frequently observed in the labor market. The problem with defining discrimination is that it is almost impossible to determine when two individuals are identical in their productive characteristics. Additionally, it is difficult to assess the preferences of individuals, so that occupational segregation is not necessarily caused by discrimination. This holds especially in areas of "female-dominated" or "male-dominated" occupations.

Becker (1957) laid the foundations of the theory of discrimination, focussing on racial discrimination in the labor market. In this personal-prejudice model, Becker (1957) models two societies, one black and one white, each consisting of workers and capitalists. White capitalists are assumed to prefer white workers, paying white workers a premium if contact with black workers can be avoided. The model turned out not to be stable because it relies on employers maximizing their utility by satisfying their prejudicial preferences instead of the usually assumed profit maximization. As the model is set up in a perfect-competition environment, firms are price-takers and have to maximize profits to survive in the market. But profit maximization would, in the long run, lead to a reduction in premiums and by this to an end of discrimination. So this type of discrimination only works in a non-perfect-competition market.

In contrast to the Becker-model basing on perfect competition, the theories of statistical discrimination base on imperfect information, see for example Aigner and Cain (1977) and Spence (1973). Within Spence's approach, known as the Signalling Approach, no individual characteristics are used to distinguish between individuals with seemingly identical properties. As an employer cannot judge the productivity of an unknown worker, he uses characteristics of the group the individual belongs to as signals to estimate individual productivity. It is not the human capital a worker accumulated that determines his productivity, but the signals attributed to the social group. Signals may be education and diplomas obtained, work experience, vocational training or qualification programs, ethnical origin, sex, age, or length of the unemployment spell. Statistical discrimination here can be regarded as a part of the screening problem that arises when the individual characteristics used to assess productivity are not perfect predictors. So this method of productivity evaluation succumbs to the same problems as the basic neoclassic model: although the group of workers is broken up into smaller groups allowed to differ in several properties, now the employer generalizes within these smaller groups and makes assumptions on the probability of good and bad characteristics. There is still room for discrimination in this approach, even with the complete absence of personal prejudices (Gottfries and McCormick 1995; Leblanc 1995).

In general, the discrimination theories help to explain some differences in wages that cannot be explained by the human capital theory. But discrimination in the hiring and firing process, or concerning career-options, is less well explained by the discrimination theories, leaving room for future research.

Neoclassic Conclusions Concerning Segmented Labor Markets

Within the very simple neoclassic framework presented at the beginning of this chapter, the existence of informal, precarious working relationships and wage differences are the result of individual decisions of investment in human capital on the labor supply side. Concluding from this, all informal work relationships are created on a voluntary base. Workers in these precarious occupational states opted for less investment in human capital as it seems less favorable to them. This also means that informal, secondary work should be found only among those workers that are low skilled within their specified labor market.

Efficiency wage and discrimination theories can also explain persistent differences in earnings for certain groups of individuals. Economists working in this field introduce factors of the labor demand side which they claim to have been missing within the neoclassical approach; factors like preferences of employers or their use of group signals may lead to the payment of lower wages for members of certain groups of workers.

However, even the considerations concerning the demand side of the labor market base mainly on characteristics of the supply side agents. Persistent structural job scarcity or other labor demand side properties causing unemployment of long-term differences in earnings and job conditions can, until now, not be explained within the neoclassical framework. Next to these considerations, there are more fundamental critiques of the neoclassical labor market theory, see Sesselmeier and Blauermel (1997) for an overview. I focus here on the parts concerning the explanation of informal employment and labor market segmentation.

There exist a large number of empirical studies testing the assumptions and results of the presented approaches. I refrain from presenting these studies here but in Chapter 2.4 I will report the results of various empirical studies testing the validity of neoclassical versus dualistic approaches .

2.3 Dual Labor Market Theory

2.3.1 The Basic Ideas

The Dual Labor Market Theory emerged in the late 1960's and early 1970's as an alternative approach to the neoclassical view of the labor markets. Works in this new approach described the labor market as consisting of two segments in spite of just one uniform market: the high-wage segment (also named the primary sector) offering high wages, job security, good working conditions and good returns on human capital variables such as education and work-experience. The low-wage segment (secondary sector) offers jobs with far less favorite characteristics: besides the lower wages, jobs are often unstable and social security networks are missing. The jobs in the primary segment are scarce, not every individual wishing to work there is able to obtain a job, even if qualified for the work. Workers who do not find a job in the high-wage segment usually end up in the secondary segment. In this framework, the high-wage labor market does not clear while the low-wage labor market is assumed to take in the labor surplus.

Dualistic labor market theories were fruitful in various ways: with their broader approach and their opposition to neoclassic concepts they opened new fields for economic research. Neoclassic economists felt an urge to respond; they started testing for labor market segmentation and incorporated various elements of the segmentation theories in their own approaches, enriching neoclassical models in this area. The way to set up the models was the key difference between neoclassical and dualistic labor economists. While the neoclassical models started from the general idea of a perfect labor market and later on relaxed strong assumptions and deductively explain specified problems from within this general theory, dualists started by observing labor market problems and tried to explore them empirically to inductively derive theoretical explanations. This is also the reason why there is not the one well-defined theoretical framework within the dualistic area. Dualistic labor economists worked on many different labor market phenomena, including but not particularly emphasizing unemployment. The main differences to the neoclassic assumptions can be summarized as follows (Sesselmeier and Blauermel 1997):

- The focus of the analysis of labor market agents is less biased towards the supply side.
- The effects of institutional, social, historical and juridical factors are included in the explanation of persistent disequilibria in the labor market.
- The wage rate is not regarded as the only or dominant regulating mechanism for labor allocation.
- The existence of a market-clearing wage rate leading to full employment is questioned.
- The efficiency of wage differences for reducing structural scarcity and mobility rigidities is doubted.
- The validity of the marginal productivity as the unique decision variable for the labor demand side is questioned.

In the dualistic view, the structure and requirements of the primary segment containing formal employment and the secondary segment containing informal occupation evolve in very different ways thereby almost excluding mobility between these segments. The different working conditions and rules of each of the two segments have an impact on the working habits and skills of the workers employed in the respective segments, resulting in a declining employability in the 'other' segment. The longer a worker is employed in one of the segments, the more decreases his probability of transiting to a job in the other segment (Gordon 1972; Doeringer and Piore 1971). This more balanced treatment of the labor supply and demand sides allows frictions to originate not only from the supply but also from the demand side.

2.3.2 Concepts of Segmentation

Primary and Secondary Labor Markets

Doeringer and Piore (1971) and Piore (1972) formulate an institutionalistic approach of labor market segmentation that provides a basis for the works of many other dual labor economists. Their model describes a labor market that is segmented in a high-wage, good working conditions primary segment and a low-wage, poor working conditions secondary segment with the properties described above. The basis for this segmentation is a dualism in the markets for goods: there are two producing sectors, a *core economy* with cycle-independent, standardized mass production, and a *peripheral economy*. The *core economy* provides secure employment and is characterized by capital-intensive production and an oligopolistic structure. In contrast, the *peripheral economy* mainly comprises small and medium sized enterprizes producing labor-intensive goods that can neither be produced in a standardized way nor by mass-production. Demand for goods produced in the *peripheral economy* is volatile, acting as a buffer for the *core sector*. Piore (1972) starts his theoretical reflections with Adam Smith's constatation that increasing labor division increases productivity, but that the degree of labor division is proportional to the size of the market of the goods produced. Piore then extends his model by introducing additional factors influencing the degree of labor division: the standardization of production and the stability and predictability of the demand. Piore recurs in his argumentation to a sociologically founded differentiation of employers into different classes.

In a later paper Piore (1975) further refines this structure by dividing these segments into upper and lower subsegments. In addition to the characteristics of the primary segment, the upper subsegment requires characteristics including formal qualifications regarding educational and vocational formation, enabling the individuals to be creative, responsible and flexible. Jobs in the upper subsegment of the primary segment are mainly professional and management jobs. In contrast, jobs in the lower subsegment require characteristics like loyalty, working discipline and tolerance concerning monotonous tasks. Following Piore and Doeringer, the secondary segment then simply absorbs all those individuals who do not satisfy the criteria to find a job in the primary segment. By introducing this division into subsegments, Piore allows for additional heterogeneity within the original two segments.

Internal and External Labor Markets

The above mentioned segmentation of the labor market into a primary and a secondary partial labor market is the common segmentation assumed when talking about dual labor markets. In their early paper on labor market segmentation, Doeringer and Piore (1971) used two theoretical concepts of segmentation as a basis for their empirical study: next to the already discussed primary and secondary labor markets, they differentiate between internal and external labor markets. Internal labor markets are characterized by wage determination processes that do not follow neoclassical ideas. For an example, wages in the craft labor markets in industrialized countries are usually negotiated by unions; the same applies to wages for many of the professions in industrial production. Doeringer and Piore classify these labor partial markets as internal labor markets, because their wage setting mechanism depends on internal structures like organizational forms of employers and employees, and less on the neoclassically assumed market forces. In this approach, wages in the internal market are the result of negotiations between groups of individuals and not between an individual applicant and an individual employer. The external labor market in Doeringer's and Piore's concept is a labor market with a wage determination mechanism depending on market forces, like the ones assumed in the neoclassical approach. Internal labor markets can only form in the presence of institutions and rules on both the labor demand and the labor supply side. The institutions create rules that stabilize the internal labor market. They fix wages, at least over a period of one or two years, they introduce severance payments and minimum wages. This stability reduces transaction costs on both sides of the labor market. Access to the internal labor markets is no longer via the wage negotiation but via so called ports of entry, determined by the internal structures and rules of the specific market. Parts of the labor market, like the crafts segment, may have special incentives to build internal labor markets, as in these partial labor markets special firm specific skills and special customs evolved, sometimes over the course of several centuries. Concerning the firm specific skills Doeringer and Piore (1971) recur implicitly to the human capital theory, equally distinguishing between "general traits" and "task-specific traits". By "traits", they subsume not only skills necessary to perform the productive actions but also characteristics like punctuality and reliability. Within the internal labor markets approach, the firm-specific "traits" are passed on to the entrants via informal on-the-job learning, while the general "traits" are taught in formal training. But senior workers will only pass on their knowledge if they do not have to fear dismissal and replacement by younger, cheaper workers later on. The structure of internal labor markets therefore eliminates the wage competition to assure the informal knowledge transfer as a central part of internal training. The formation of firm or labor market segment-specific rules leads to a common identity of the members of the concerned group, making the group more stable because all members of the group, including the employers, are expected to comply to these rules.

In contrast to the neoclassical labor market approaches developed up to then, the internal labor market concept explicitly includes the behavior of human beings. Sociological and psychological factors enter the analysis as well as economic considerations. The approach was subsequently refined by various economists, and served as a base for a neoclassical approach on internal and external labor markets at the beginning of the eighties.

Critiques to this approach have been that Doeringer and Piore developed the approach on the base of labor market data from the USA (Sesselmeier and Blauermel 1997; Franz 2003). Later work on this subject, performed on data from the USA and West Germany, lead to doubt being voiced that this concept might be easily transferred to countries with labor market segments that do not look back on a century-old tradition, or the existence of long-established unions. Furthermore, the approach concentrates on explaining the dichotomy of the labor market but does not yield any explanation for the origin of employment or the existence of unemployment.

Within the dual labor market framework, wage determination and labor allocation are often considered to follow mechanisms where human capital factors play a less significant role. Within this theory frame employers screen potential new employees for several characteristics. One of the characteristics is education, but it is only one of several criteria. The characteristics serve as proxies for the ability of the worker, but contrary to the human capital approach, the relationship between education and productivity is not regarded as a causal one. Other characteristics are previous work experience, whether a person has been recommended to the employer etc.. The employment decision may also be explained in part by the theory of internal labor markets. Internal labor markets may exist within a company, or within a certain group of economically active individuals. The usually assumed market rules do not hold inside internal markets and worker selection follows a different mechanism in this market.

Human capital theory indicates that further investment in education and training leads to access to better jobs with higher wages. While certainly no dual labor market economist would dispute that better trained workers are likely to earn more money, they claim that segmentation between segments is rigid. This implies that investment in education may lead to higher wages but does not allow the individual to transit from informal to formal employment. The argument underlying this assumption is the influence of the different working conditions and structures within the different segments on the behavior and performance of the worker. The workplace conditions mould the worker in a permanent way, they scar him so that he gets less valuable for the employers of the other segment. This is especially claimed for informally employed workers. A more detailed discussion of the role of education and training and the scarring hypothesis can be found in Chapter 7.2.

2.3.3 Unemployment in Segmented Labor Markets

Because of their higher wage and better working conditions, jobs in the primary segment are assumed to be more desirable for workers. So workers try to find jobs in this segment, and those who do not manage to find work there will take a job in the secondary segment. The labor market in the high-wage segment does not clear, so some individuals end up in the low-wage segment, the latter being implicitly assumed to provide infinite vacancies for everybody who wants to work. How can unemployment emerge in this setting?

Piore (1975) attributes unemployment to the prevailing job-insecurity and poor working conditions in the secondary segment: As hiring and firing costs are comparatively low or nonexistent, at least in the low-skilled jobs, employers tend to lay off workers quite easily. This implies that most of the unemployed were formerly working in the low-wage segment. In contrast, employers in the high-wage segment are assumed to invest in the qualification and performance of their workers and therefore tend to keep these workers in order to secure their investment. The rent that has to be included in the efficiency wages to prevent workers from shirking and absenteeism may be the lower the more stable a job appears to its occupant, and the longer its stream of future income seems to be secure. Another argument to explain the lower job rotation in the primary segment is the higher investment in production capital that requires a certain number of workers to produce efficiently. Stable employment is essential for a stable production.

In the classic models of rural-urban migration, first formulated by Todaro (1969) and Harris and Todaro (1970), workers migrate from the traditional agricultural sector with low and flexible wages to the modern urban sector where significantly higher wages are paid. Migration is a response to the wage gap between these sectors, the decision to migrate is made on the basis of the difference in expected wages, that is the formal sector wage multiplied by the probability to find a job in the formal segment. As wages in the modern sector are assumed to be rigid, the number of vacancies in this sector is finite, not all migrants are able to find a formal job with a high wage. Those who fail to find employment end up either unemployed and searching or with employment in the lower paying informal urban sector. This fact lead subsequently Bulow and Summers (1986) to argue that all unemployment in the dual-market-context is waiting unemployment: individuals queuing up for jobs in the primary segment. In this case all workers unemployed have a higher utility by waiting for a high-wage job than by taking up a job in the secondary segment. This will naturally occur in an efficiency-wage model of a segmented labor market, as future rents from higher wages will compensate for loss of income during the time of searching and waiting. By taking up a low-wage job these rents would be lost. Additionally, the existence of an unemployment insurance will keep more former high-wage workers waiting for another job in the primary segment, as the opportunity costs of job searching are reduced by the benefits.

2.4 Some Empirical Evidence

The dual labor market approach has been criticized for not providing a theoretical base for its assumptions. Some of the critiques, see for example Cain (1976), argued that the results obtained could also be obtained by a neoclassical analysis. With the development of new theoretical concepts like the imperfect-information-theory and efficiency wage models, the dual labor market theory returned to the focus of attention during the 80ies (Dickens and Lang 1988). Additionally, new econometric estimation techniques allowed for testing parts of the assumptions made by dual labor market economists. Even declared proponents of the neoclassical labor market theory started working on segmented labor market approaches.[8] McDonald and Solow (1985) and Bulow and Summers (1986) with their theoretical works are some examples. Heckman and Hotz (1986) tested the dual market hypothesis on the wage differences of Panamanian males. The results Heckman and Hotz obtained did not allow them to reject the model, but they claimed that test methods were not appropriate and came to the conclusion that the dual market theory was untestable. This argument, that the dual labor market approach could not be

[8]The concept of labor market segmentation does not necessarily imply that there cannot be more than two segments in the labor market: "We do not propose that the labor market consists of exactly two distinct segments, only that dualism is a useful simplification." (Dickens and Lang 1988).

tested, had already been put forward in an earlier paper by Heckman and Sedlacek (1985). They claimed that the dual labor markets model only provided a more parsimonious model of the wage distribution than the neoclassical model with just a single market. They tested their hypothesis and succeeded, showing as a side effect that it is possible to test the dual labor markets model. The difficulty rather was to test for market clearing itself, but this is a problem for single market theories as well as for dual market theories and is therefore no critique uniquely aimed at the dualistic approach (Dickens and Lang 1988).

While the neoclassical approach explains the wage differences between individuals by their different characteristics, the dual labor market theory is able to explain wage differences of individuals with similar characteristics. This helps to understand why the high wages observed in the primary segment are persistent in spite of unemployment and the presence of qualified workers in the secondary segment waiting for a job in the primary segment. Within the dual labor market approach the wage distribution is assumed to follow different patterns in each of the segments. Variables like education, job-experience or labor history do not have the same impact on the income distribution of workers in the primary and secondary segment, allowing for the wages to differ. Within the neoclassical framework, the coefficients of these variables are implicitly assumed to be the same for all individuals, as they are estimated for the one and only wage equation valid for every person entering the estimation. In contrast, Dickens and Lang (1985) estimate a segmented labor markets model using two different wage equations, one for each segment, and an additional switching function, determining the sector in which an individual is employed. The three equations are then estimated together. Their results confirm the predictions of the dual labor market model. This model-setting additionally allows to test for the single market approach, and Dickens and Lang report that the model had to be rejected. As these results may also originate from the fact that two wage equations capture more non-linearities than a model with just one wage equation, Dickens and Lang (1987) develop a single-market model including higher-order variables and allowing for heteroscedastic error terms to compensate for the advantages of the dual labor market model. Nevertheless, they still find that the dual labor market model yields by far the better estimates for the wage distribution.

These results indicate that the dual labor market model outperforms single-market models in approximating the empirical wage distributions. The labor market does not necessarily have to be split up in only two segments; dualism just proved to be a workable simplification (Dickens and Lang 1988).

Several studies have been performed on wage differentials, based on the efficiency wage approach and focussing mainly on interindustry wage differentials

(Bulow and Summers 1986; Dickens and Katz 1987; Krueger and Summers 1988). All these studies find remarkable wage differentials that are correlated over long periods of time (decades up to almost a century). It seems therefore implausible to assume temporary disequilibria as a reason for the differentials. If market clearing is assumed then either workers in the primary segment must be particularly skilled, or employers in this segment must pay some compensation such as efficiency wages. A market-clearing model consistent with these findings would be that some workers have skills that are only useful in the high-wage segment. This result nonetheless is conform to the dual-markets assumption that workers in the different segments develop different skills only useful in that specific segment. Additionally, Chahad, Orellano, and Picchetti (2001) observe that job rotation in the primary segment is considerably lower than in the low-wage segment, allowing one to conclude that workers in the former segment receive rents. This can also be observed in Brazil, where workers in the formal segment show high persistence compared to informally employed workers. A more detailed discussion of the Brazilian case can be found in Chapter 6 of this thesis.

While much of the discussion of the validity of models centered on explaining wage differentials, another important question is the degree of rigidity of the prevailing segmentation. This more recent question is addressed by some authors performing tests of labor market segmentation and wage differentials. Maloney (1999) started to work on the Mexican labor market and found that different segments can be observed. He differentiates between formal dependent work and informal labor, focussing on self-employment within the latter group. He observes that these two segments are not rigidly separated, workers transit between segments in both directions. Navarro-Lozano (2002) comes to the same result, also using Mexican labor market data. Still, the question of the degree of segmentation is not easy to answer as the criteria for segmentation are not sharply defined. There are no clear cut levels of transition rates between segments indicating whether a labor market is segmented or not.

Having given a short survey on the concepts of labor market segmentation in both the neoclassical and the dualistic labor market theory and major empirical findings in that context, I will now turn to a description of the Brazilian labor market and its institutions and regulations in the following chapter.

Chapter 3

The Brazilian Labor Market

3.1 The Brazilian Labor Market in the Last Two Decades

The development of the structure of the Brazilian labor market has been heavily influenced by various macroeconomic shocks during the last two decades. For a better understanding of the current state of the labor market, I begin with a short introduction to the economic history of the last two decades.[1]

The debt crisis triggered by Mexico's debt default in 1982 also lead to major inflation rates in Brazil, leading the country into many attempts to comply with heterodox stabilization programs intended to contain inflation and to stabilize the economy. The first of these plans was the Cruzado Plan in 1986. For a short while this stabilized inflation and to created a positive impulse for the economy but it did not deal with the excess demand problem which was the basic source for inflation at that time. Within a short time price controls failed to work, and inflation soared to even higher levels. Other, less successful, stabilization plans followed and ended in hyperinflation at the beginning of the nineties. In 1990 Brazil also started a trade liberalization, reducing external tariffs by about two thirds and ending a long period of import substitution. However, all these measures did not reduce inflation until, in 1994, Fernando Henrique Cardoso, then finance minister, implemented the Plano Real (Sachs and Zini 1996). He severely cut government spending and introduced a nominal exchange rate anchor. Together with the trade liberalization policy, these policies exposed

[1]Fox, Amadeo, and Camargo (1994) and Urani (1998) provide detailed overviews about the macroeconomic shocks and their impacts on the Brazilian labor market. See also Hoek (2002).

Brazilian firms producing export goods to the rough competition in the world market. Without subsidies, facing very low external tariffs and an extremely overvalued exchange rate, conditions grew adverse. These policies not only affected the export sector of the economy, but also paved the way for imported goods for just the same reasons that impeded exports. With the plummeting of production the labor market was subjected to extreme pressure. A large proportion of the workforce moved out of the manufacturing sector. In fact formal employment in the manufacturing sector started to decline when the Plano Cruzado failed in the mid-eighties. From the start of the Plano Cruzado until the late nineties unemployment rose to some extent, but the share of informal employment in the manufacturing sector rose by about a third, being more than seven percent of the total labor force, while formal employment in this segment dropped from 20 % to 10 % in the same period. Most of the workers affected by the strict economic stabilization policies were simply too poor to afford being unemployed.

Figure 3.1 shows the evolution of labor in formal and informal services, and formal and informal manufacturing, in the period from 1982-2000. The values for informal services and manufacturing contain both dependent employees and self-employed individuals.

Informal jobs are characterized by the lack of a labor card, see also Section 3.3 for a definition of informal employment in Brazil. Many workers dismissed in the manufacturing sector found work in the informal services segment, while informal manufacturing stayed at a stable employment level. But unemployment also rose (see Figure 3.2), and overall labor force participation sunk during these years.

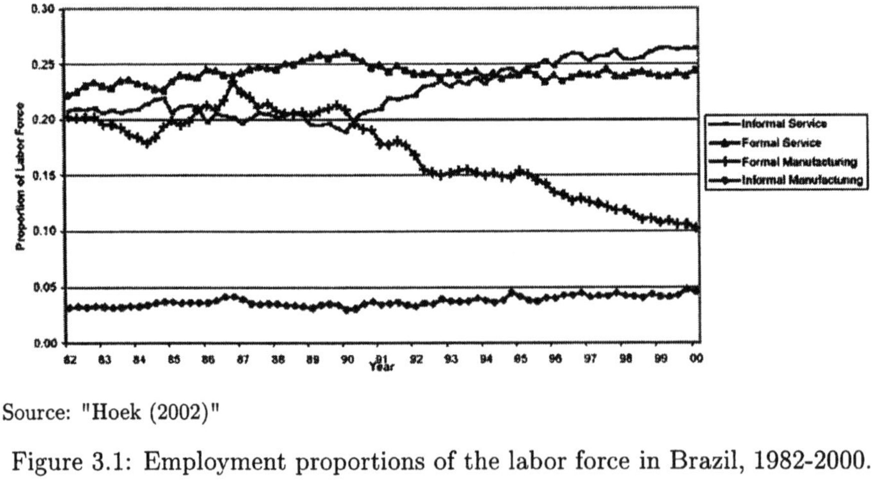

Source: "Hoek (2002)"

Figure 3.1: Employment proportions of the labor force in Brazil, 1982-2000.

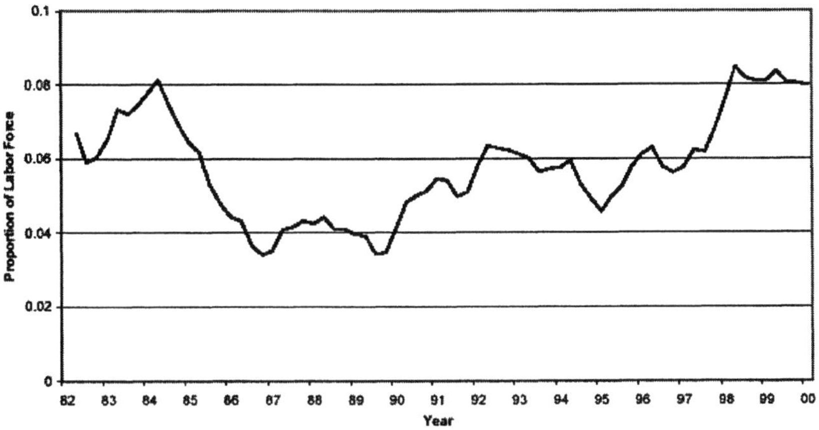

Source: "Hoek (2002)"

Figure 3.2: Unemployment rate in Brazil, 1982-2000.

In the following sections, different aspects of the Brazilian labor market, like the level of regulations, the wage structure, job rotation and unemployment will be treated in more detail to provide an overview of the characteristics of this huge labor market. Some of the aspects will be discussed in even greater detail later in the thesis.

3.2 The Institutional Background

There are two major sources containing laws and regulations concerning labor relations in Brazil (Lyra 1999). The constitution regulates the major principles determining the rights of Brazilian workers: the minimum wage, daily working hours, the unemployment insurance, the thirteenth wage bill, holidays and others.[2]

Detailed regulations are contained in the Labor Legislation Code, Codigo dos Leis do Trabalhador (CLT). This code dates from 1943 and has undergone substantial changes since its first enactment. The principal regulation for the questions of concern in this thesis is that the legislation forces employers to issue labor cards to their employees. The possession of a labor card distinguishes a formal worker from an informal one. By law all employed workers are entitled to a labor card, and labor legislation is valid for all employed

[2]See Paragraph 7 and subsequent paragraphs of the Brazilian Constitution.

workers. In practice employees with a labor card are in a far better position to enforce their rights stated in the labor legislation than those without labor cards, the informally employed ones. Labor cards entitle workers to collect unemployment benefits during an unemployment spell.[3]

Much earlier, and replacing the Law of Stability, the Fundo de Garantia por Tempo de Servico (FGTS) was established by Law N° 5.107 in September 1966. The system of this fund includes individual accounts for each worker, into which the employer pays 8% of the monthly salary every month. The rate of interest paid on these savings is 3% per year. By this payment, about one monthly salary is accumulated within each working year, if the worker remains employed over this period. Workers have the right to receive the amount saved in their account in three cases: (1) when they get fired without just cause; (2) when they plan to buy or build a house; (3) when they retire (their families receive the savings in case of the death of the worker). It is obvious that only the formally employed can participate in this program. In case of dismissal without just cause the company has to pay a fine to the worker that amounts to 40% of the savings accumulated in the account of the worker.

Workers with a formal labor contract are, at least theoretically, hard to dismiss. Camargo (1997) studies the positive and negative effects of the Brazilian labor legislation on labor market flexibility. He finds a very detailed set of laws and provisions and a huge incentive for employees to file complaints upon dismissal. As court appeals are lengthy processes and it can take years for a sentence to be pronounced, employers have strong incentives not to comply with the labor legislation. Originally intended as a fund to help workers to save for and finance their own houses, workers are also entitled to the money accumulated in their FGTS-account in case of unjustified dismissal. In practice formal workers generally receive the FGTS-savings, even if dismissal took place for a just reason, or even if the worker asked to be dismissed, because labor courts usually act in favor of the worker in this point. To avoid costly legal proceedings employers therefore very often agree to pretend to dismiss the worker without just cause. Camargo (1997) and Paes De Barros, Corseuil, and Foguel (1999) argue that the increased incentive to collect the FGTS-savings leads to higher labor market volatility. But when Paes De Barros, Corseuil, and Gonzaga (999b) empirically test their hypothesis by estimating the impact of the 1988 constitutional change which brought significant increments in separation payments, they do not find evidence for increased fluctuations on the labor market.

Most of the formal workers get a medical insurance paid by their employer, while employers usually do not pay contributions for medical insurance, pen-

[3]If they meet some specific conditions such as a minimum time of employment etc..

sions and social security for their informal workers. Formal workers are in a better position to enforce the wages negotiated by the unions, and in fact they sue their employers quite frequently to enforce their rights Camargo (1997). Informal workers are not protected from immediate dismissal and thus find themselves in a much weaker position to enforce their rights.

3.3 Informal Employment and Self-Employment

In spite of the precise regulations found in the Brazilian labor legislation, informal employment is a very common form of working relationship. Informality is defined quite differently in different countries, but still Brazil is one of the countries with the highest rate of informal employment in Latin America. Ramos (2002) studies the evolution of informality over the last decade and finds a constantly rising degree of informality (regarding informal employment and self-employment as the same) from around 40% in 1991 up to a peak of 51% of the economically active population in 2000 and a slight decrease to 50% in 2001. Carneiro (1997) reports the same and relates the increase in informality to excessive government intervention in the productive system. Figure 3.3 shows the participation of the economically active population in the different labor market segments in the year 1999. Less than half of the economically active population held formal labor contracts (42.7%), while informal employment accounted for 24.7%. Self-employment was a source of income for 23.5% of the individuals and 9.1% were searching for a job.

Unlike in some other countries, the definition of informal employment in Brazil is rather simple: all workers being employed but not holding a labor card are classified as informally employed. Employers issuing labor cards must offer their workers labor contracts complying with the labor laws. Formal workers profit from set wages and they can collect unemployment insurance benefits (if fulfilling the necessary conditions). Informal workers are not eligible to these rights, and in case of dismissal they lack resources to maintain living standards and to perform an efficient job search. While contributions to the social security or the pension fund are deducted directly from the wages paid to formal workers, informally employed workers may contribute voluntarily, but most of them do not. The resulting lack of protection and resources in case of emergencies or old age often leads to impoverishment. It is therefore a major concern to increase formal employment and so to provide protection and access to security systems to a larger proportion of workers.

In 1999, about 25% of the urban occupied labor force was employed informally. About 45% held formal labor contracts, and nearly all of the remaining

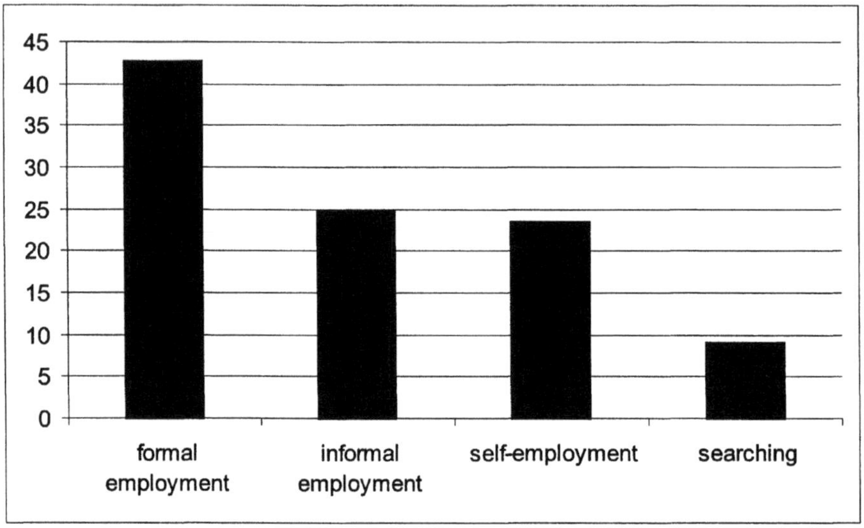

Source: "Monthly Labor Survey (PME) (1999), own calculations"

Figure 3.3: Labor market segments in Brazil.

economically active individuals fell in the category 'self employed'. This labor market structure was by no means rigid and there was mobility of workers between sectors in both directions.

3.4 Wages and Labor-Related Costs

Paes De Barros, Corseuil, and Leite (2000) and Ferreira and Barros (1999) show that informal labor in Brazil is usually lower paid than similar formal labor. Kassouf (1998) estimates wage differentials between the formal and the informal sector in Brazil and reports that about 20% of the observed differential is caused by segmentation of the labor market. Informally employed workers have no possibility to enforce the wages negotiated by the unions. Wages in Brazil are already concentrated at the lower end of scale, Figure 3.4 shows the overall wage distribution in Brazil.

The unions are involved in the wage negotiations in most industrial and service sectors, and many formal workers profit from that (Carneiro and Henley 1998). The effect of the unions though is not equal for all groups of formal workers. Arbache (1999) studies the impact of an increase in unionization on the wage distribution of unionized and other formal workers and finds that

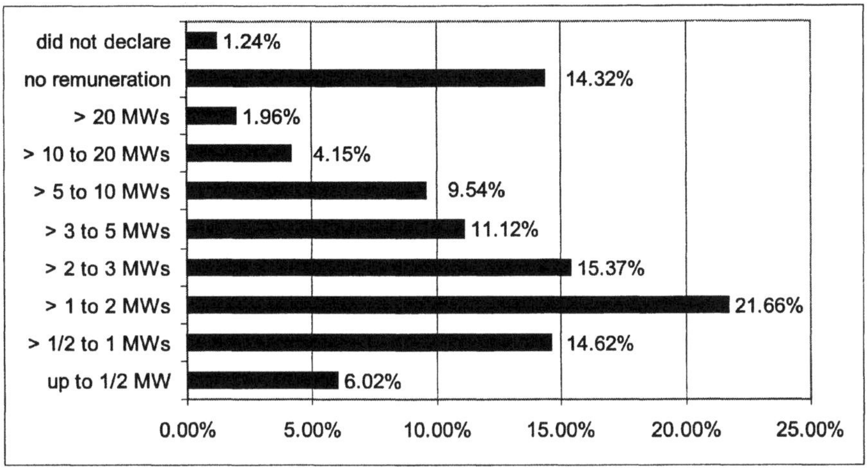

Source: National Household Survey PNAD (1999), own calculations.
Sample: Working individuals aged 10 years or more
MW = minimum wage

Figure 3.4: Monthly wages in Brazil 1999 in multiples of minimum wages.

unionization contributes to an increased inequality among union members, as well as between them and others. Menezes Filho et al. (2002) report negative impacts on employment, average wages and productivity when unionization rates rise above a level of 50% of the employees. Wages for informal employment are often orientated at the minimum wage, which is taken as a guideline for wages (Amadeo, Gill, and Neri 2002). In fact most wages in the informal segment are equal to or multiples of the minimum wage (Neri, Gonzaga, and Camargo 2001). Workers with no or low skills may still find low paid jobs in the informal sector contrary to the formal one. Employers compensate for less productivity by paying lower wages. Fajnzylber (2001) studies the effect of changes in the minimum wage on pay and employment for formal and informal Brazilian workers. He finds that low-income workers are generally more affected by a rise in the minimum wage, and within this group, the informally employed are most likely to lose their jobs. This contradicts the hypothesis that the informal segment serves as a buffer segment for those who do not find jobs in the formal segment (IDB 2003).

Informal employment is taken up by many individuals who did not manage to find formal employment. In the informal segment of the labor market entrance and exit costs for both employee and employer are substantially lower than in the formal segment.

Entry costs are lower, because employers do not face the registration of the worker with the social security system and medical insurance. Labor cost itself is usually lower, too, because no contributions are made to the social security and the medical insurance. Another factor important to employers is the prospect of an easy dismissal of informally employed workers, as employers do not face firing costs in form of severance payments (Amadeo, Gill, and Neri 2002). In contrast, formally employed workers automatically accumulate money in a compulsory savings fund, the Fundo de Garantia, FGTS. Each month 8% of their wage is deducted from their wage and flows directly into the FGTS, so that over the span of a year, about one monthly wage is saved.

3.5 Unemployment

Unemployment in Brazil has always existed next to informal employment, although numbers up to the mid-nineties have been rather low compared to OECD-averages in the same period. However, during the second half of the last decade, unemployment rates have increased and now exceed the standardized OECD values around 7% for 1999 (OECD 1999). As remarked in the new IDB-Labor Market Study on Latin America (IDB 2003), high levels of unemployment indicate a problem in the labor market, but low levels of unemployment not necessarily signal a well-working labor market. This is the case in Brazil, where many people are simply too poor to remain unemployed, "unemployment is a luxury only few can afford" (Bienefeld and Godfrey (1975), p.6). Most of those not able to find a job in the formal segment take up employment, or become self-employed, in the informal segment.

Unemployment in Brazil is measured according to standards used by international organizations like the IDB (IDB 2003). A person is considered unemployed during a reference period if he (i) did not work, (ii) had been available for work, and (iii) had been searching for a job. The age range considered for the calculation of the unemployment rate is from 10 to 60 years.

During the last years both the proportion of those employed in the informal segment and the proportion of unemployed have been increasing. See Figure 3.5 for the rate of total open unemployment, and rates split up by sex from 1997 to 2001, and Figure 3.6 for the unemployment rates of the year 1999 used for the investigations in Part II and III of this dissertation.

Female unemployment constantly lies above male employment, a fact that does not reflect the female labor force participation in the overall economically

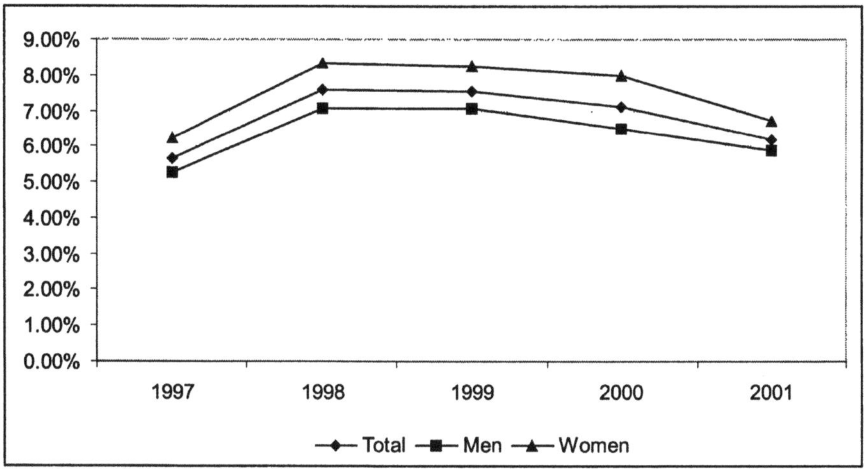

Source: "PME, Monthly Labor Survey (PME) (1999)."

Figure 3.5: Open unemployment rates in Brazil, 1997 – 2001, split up by sex.

active population. Soares and Izaki (2002) study female labor force participation during the last decades and find an increase of participation from 39% in 1977 to 58% in 2001 for women aged between 16 and 60 years. Male participation in this age frame shifted from 88% to 87% in the same period. Soares and Izaki (2002) find evidence that the strong increase in female participation is mainly fed by an increase of the entry of married women into the labor force.

3.6 Job Rotation and Labor Market Flexibility

The extent of labor market flexibility in Brazil has been much in discussion (Corseuil, Ribeiro, and Santos 2002). One group of labor economists claims that rigidity is quite high because of high non-wage labor costs impeding the creation of new jobs. This includes the limited possibilities of companies to negotiate wages directly with the applicants, as for some sectors, the employers negotiate wages with the unions and the outcome then is set for the companies (Camargo 1997). Another criticized feature is the severance payment that employers have to pay when dismissing employees without just cause, and a labor legislation favoring workers' interests (Camargo 1997). Opponents to this opinion argue that the rigidity only holds for formal employment and even there, the above mentioned arguments are not generally valid. High non-wage labor costs in the formal segment are circumvented by many employers

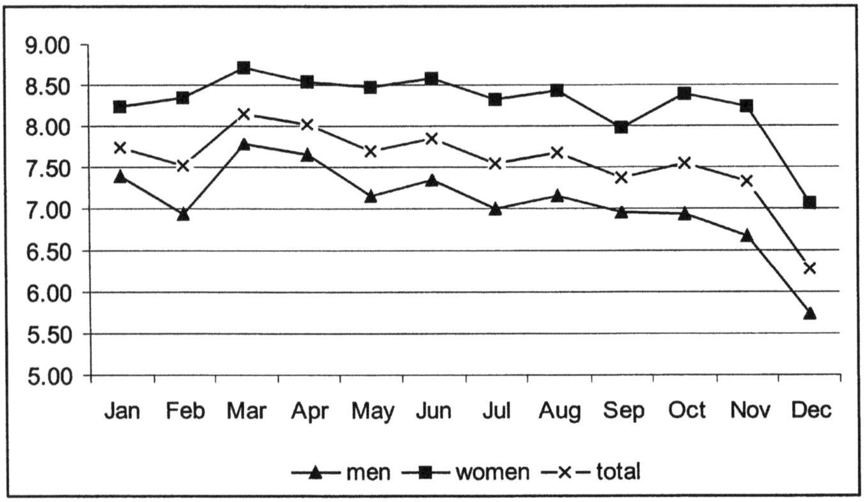

Source: "PME, Monthly Labor Survey (PME) (1999)."

Figure 3.6: Open unemployment rates total and by sex in 1999.

offering informal employment or even jobs that are only partly formal (Hoek 2002).[4] The high severance payments very often are not paid either, as those workers trying to claim their FGTS savings often negotiate with the employer and renounce the 40% fine to be paid by the employer (see Section 3.2 for more details on the FGTS regulations).

Looking at some labor market figures, labor turnover in Brazil indeed looks quite high: Chahad, Orellano, and Picchetti (2001) report that 47.3% of the formal workers in 1989 held their job for less than two years, and that this figure did not improve very much during the nineties. In comparison, labor market studies on labor rotation in OECD countries report that the proportion of workers employed less than two years is less than 25% of the overall labor force. Even countries with very deregulated labor markets like the U.S.A. show lower labor turnover rates. The fact that the Brazilian population is relatively young compared to those of OECD countries may be one reason for the high rate of short labor relationships: the number of labor market entrants is comparably larger. Nevertheless this fact does not account for the overall magnitude of rotation. Additionally, Corseuil, Ribeiro, and Santos (2002) show

[4]In the case of partial formal employment, only a part of the wage the employee receives is registered on the labor card, and the non-wage labor costs are contributed only for this part.

that about 40% of the overall reallocation of labor results from companies going out of business and other companies being created.

The high level of job rotation means that workers and employers do not build very close bonds; on average mutual commitment is weak. As a consequence, the accumulation of human capital during the work spell is low, as both parties anticipate short contract durations. The incentive for employers to offer training for their employees, be it company-specific or general, is low. Employees, on the other hand side, are equally weakly interested in acquiring firm-specific knowledge, as it does not pay off in short term. This behavior leads to relatively low firing costs for the employers considering the level of firm specific skills loss in case of dismissal. In fact the usual response of companies during times of recession is the dismissal of a large part of their work force. Still, workers will acquire skills to some extend while working for a company, even when there are no training programs. Chahad, Orellano, and Picchetti (2001) show that the probability that a worker with a formal contract resigns or gets dismissed decreases with the length of his work spell within the company. Transaction costs on both sides grow as the acquired specific human capital begins to pay off for the worker and also gets more valuable for the employer. Additionally, the severance payment to be paid by the employer increases over the work spell and so increases the incentive for the employer to keep the worker after a certain point of time. This mechanism has the advantage of decreasing excessive rotation, but it may gain a negative momentum when firing costs grow so much that they impede firing unproductive workers and hinder necessary restructuring of companies. In the Brazilian case it can be observed that labor turnover is high within the group of low skilled workers and especially within the informally employed (Chahad, Orellano, and Picchetti 2001). Most of the formal workers trying to collect their FGTS savings by asking for dismissal also come from the low skilled group. They usually do not have any career options in this or another company, and their firing costs are rather low as they did not accumulate much skills. This phenomenon may be one of the reasons of high labor turnover in Brazil: a relatively high percentage of workers is unskilled and does not accumulate much human capital while working. If they hold labor cards and therefore have to contribute to the FGTS, after a certain period the utility of collecting the FGTS savings will be higher than the utility of keeping this formal contract in the future. This behavior leads to a vicious circle: the high time preference rate of low skilled workers increases their speed of job rotation. By lowering the duration of the employment spell in each firm, the accumulation of human capital is heavily impeded, hindering these workers from acquiring more skills, and finding employment relationships with longer duration and better payment.

3.7 Labor Market Policies

3.7.1 Active Labor Market Policies

The National Employment System SINE

In Brazil, several public programs have been implemented to assist labor allocation. The only one of them active in the area of job-placement, the National System for Employment (SINE), was created in 1974 to enhance active labor market policies. SINE agencies have been established in most of Brazilian cities, but coverage in rural areas is still poor. Core tasks of the SINE are the organization of qualification and training programs, and providing assistance in job placement and job matching both to the employed and unemployed. Another important function of the SINE is the operational support of the unemployment insurance (which did not exist at the time of the implementation of SINE). Law N° 8.019/90, article 13, and subsequently, law N° 8.900/94 and law N° 7.998/90 legislate that the unemployment insurance shall assist job search by offering counselling, job-placement and vocational training. These services shall be offered decentralized by SINE offices, receiving administrative, technical and financial support by the Ministry of Labor, MTE. SINE also administers parts of the unemployment insurance, like the benefit payments.

Evaluation of the program by the Brazilian Ministry of Labor (MTE 1999) has shown very poor performance of most agencies and in all three main activities, due to missing technical support and antiquated administrative instruments. A difficult funding concept adds to the problems (SINE is financed from a federal fund, but money is first transferred to state funds before reaching the agencies, as the states are responsible for the administration of the SINE). This turns administrative and operative processes very slow and leaves the SINE politically quite vulnerable. The net of SINE agencies is still weak and just being implemented in remoter areas. In some regions, job-placement rates are as low as 5% of people requesting to be placed.[5] Recently, SINE has been returning to the focus of interest. An improvement of services and infrastructure is discussed. Furthermore, there have been proposals to link the payment of unemployment insurance benefits to the proof of job search conduct and participation in qualification programs (Chahad 2000b).

In practice unemployment insurance benefits may be collected in three different locations: at a federal bank, at the local representation of the MTE or at a SINE office. As SINE offices in some regions are still quite rare, and walking

[5]The SINE and evaluation of its services are presented in more detail in Section 12.2.1 in Part III of this thesis.

up to the representative of the MTE may be stigmatizing, most unemployed prefer to collect their benefits at the local branch of the federal bank. Many people hold personal banking accounts at branches of the federal banks and stigma of going there is low. These facts lead to a rather low rate of public frequentation at the SINE agencies, diminishing considerably the probability of motivating unemployed to take advantage of job counselling and available labor market information or of participating in qualification programs. Combined with the poor execution of services, frequentation of the SINE agencies is understandably low.

Vocational Training

In 1945 the SENAI was established to provide professional training for Brazilians of all educational levels.[6] During the second part of the 90s, a public program for vocational training was set up, namely the Plano Nacional de Educação Profissional (PLANFOR). The objective of this program is to coordinate and restructure the different institutions active in the field of training and qualification programs in order to improve access to these programs to underprivileged groups like young unemployed, female heads of household, low-skilled workers, handicapped, and unemployed persons.

Promotion of self-employment and the creation of small enterprises

To complete the list of active labor market policies, the Brazilian government also set up a program to promote self-employment and the creation of small enterprises: Programa Nacional de Geração de Renda e Emprego (PROGER). This program facilitates access to micro-credits and offers help with the paperwork for registration. Additionally, training courses are held on basic managerial skills like book keeping.

3.7.2 Passive Labor Market Policies

The Unemployment Insurance and the Fundo de Amparo ao Trabalhador (FAT)

In the Constitution of 1967, under Title III (Economic and Political Order) the implementation of an unemployment insurance is mentioned for the first

[6] See Section 6.1.2 for a more detailed description of the different institutions offering vocational training and qualification programs.

time. Its realization, though, only came two decades later, when the first unemployment insurance system in Brazil was installed in 1986.

As a part of the Plano Cruzado a second program was launched in 1986 that comes closer to the known system of unemployment insurance in European and North American countries. During the constitutional changes in 1988 the Fundo de Amparo ao Trabalhador (FAT) was created and major reforms of the former unemployment insurance systems were implemented. More legislative changes occurred in 1990, when the access to benefits was broadened by lowering the required number of months of work from 36 within the last 48 months to 15 within the last 24 months. Waiting time for repeated application was lowered from 18 to 16 months and the value of benefits was increased. Benefits were raised in 1994 by another law that raised the maximum payment period from three to five months. In 1990, the council CODEFAT was created to administer the financial resources of the FAT (Theodoro 2002). The council is formed by a representant of each of the following ministries: the Ministry of Labor and Employment, the Ministry of Social Security (MPAS), the Ministry of Agriculture (MA), and one representant of the National Bank for Economic and Social Development (BNDES). The labor supply side is represented in the council by a member of each of the four big unions (FS, CGT, CUT and SDS), and employers are represented by a member of each of the employers organizations of industry, the financial institutes, commerce and agriculture (CNI, CNF, CNC, CNA).

To qualify for benefits from this program workers actually have to be formally employed during the last six months and at least six months during the last 36 months. Their dismissal has to be without just cause. They receive benefits according to the length of time of their employment: if they have been employed from six to eleven months they will receive three months of benefits. From twelve to twenty-three months they will receive four months of benefits, and from twenty-four months of formal employment workers will receive benefits for the maximum length of five months. The size of the benefit is limited and is calculated on the basis of the three last wages received prior to dismissal. The minimum value of benefit a worker can get is 1 minimum wage, the maximum value is 1.87 minimum wages. At the time of writing a minimum wage equivalents 151 R$ (about 70 US$) per month. Once the benefits have been paid, there is a waiting time of sixteen months before the worker may again claim benefits from this program.

All benefits paid by this program come from the PIS/PASEP fund. In a strict sense the unemployment insurance program does not constitute an insurance. The PIS/PASEP fund is financed by a tax that every formalized company has to pay on its revenues.[7] The tax is not related to the number of workers nor to the pay bill size of the company. There are no individual contributions effected by the workers neither does the program represent a risk distribution among all contracted workers and their employers, contributions are paid only by companies, which roll-over these costs to their product prices. This means that in fact the program is financed by all consumers in Brazil.

The program consumes about 0.4% of the GDP. The average value of benefits is 1.5 minimum wages, around 75% of employees dismissed without just cause are covered.

If the social protection of unemployed workers is a public goal, the objective of any program implemented for this reason should be to cover the largest possible part of eligible, e.g. contracted workers. As eligibility for unemployment benefits is connected to the possession of a work card, it should be in the public interest to increase the number of formally contracted workers. The eligibility for unemployment benefits is a possible incentive for workers to look for a formal work. If demand for formal work increases, companies should increase the supply of such labor contracts. However, investigations have not presented evidence to support the development of such an increase. Cunningham (1997) took advantage of the increase of benefits in 1994 to study the impact of benefits on the reentry of unemployed into the formal labor market segment. The results showed no increase of the ratio of formal work after unemployment. Chahad and Fernandez (2000) studied the impact of the implementation of the unemployment insurance in 1986 on the choice of formal or informal work and could not find increased transition. Low benefit ceilings and short length of payments may be one reason for this low incentive effect. As the also working-card related social insurance is considered to provide a rather poor service, too, the general attractiveness of formal work may be not that high.

Some studies reveal evidence that unemployment insurance increases both participation in the workforce and occurrence of unemployment (Holen 1977). Atkinson and Micklewright (1991) and Holmlund (1998) provide surveys on the performance of unemployment insurance systems and the unwanted effects of prolonged and increased unemployment provoked by these systems. Chahad and Fernandez (2000) estimate the impact of the unemployment insurance on the Brazilian rate of unemployment. Contrary to the above studies, they find that the rate of unemployment would have been higher had there been no insurance system. They also find that most recipients of unemployment insurance benefits transit into inactivity, especially among non-heads of household.

[7]See Gill, Dar, and Thomas (1999) and Chahad (2000a) for a detailed discussion of the financing structure of the Brazilian unemployment insurance.

Labor market data collected by the CODEFAT focussing on repeated request of unemployment benefits do not present evidence of increased rotation. According to members of the CODEFAT, the observed rotation is a normal one resulting from workers changing into better jobs or quitting jobs to stay inactive.

Other investigations for Brazil showing increased job rotation attribute this fact to the design of the FGTS (Camargo 1997; Amadeo and Camargo 1997). As workers only have access to the money saved in their FGTS account if they are dismissed, the argumentation in these studies is that workers deliberately try to get dismissed. Originally created to increase job security and to prolong the time spent in one job by fining employers when dismissing, this same mechanism seems to have a counter productive effect on workers incentives. (Chahad, Orellano, and Picchetti 2001) estimate the impact of both unemployment insurance and FGTS on labor turnover rates but do not find significant impacts.

In summary, unemployment benefits in Brazil do not influence the rate of rotation neither positively nor negatively, and the effect of the FGTS seems to be ambiguous on labor turnover rates as well.

Chapter 4

The Database

The data used throughout this thesis are taken from a pool of all Monthly Employment Surveys (PME) collected by the Brazilian Institute for Geography and Statistics (IBGE) in 1999. Each monthly data set of the PME contains about 100,000 observations collected in the seven major metropolitan areas in Brazil: Belo Horizonte, Curitiba, Porto Alegre, Recife, Rio de Janeiro, Salvador da Bahia and São Paulo.

A special methodology of data collection is implemented within the PME: The members of a household are interviewed in four consecutive months. This process is repeated after an interval of eight months. One quarter of the questioned households surveyed every month are entrants, replacing those that already have been questioned for four months. So every monthly survey is composed of four different lots of households: one quarter is interviewed for the first time, one for the second, one for the third and the last one for the fourth time. This structure allows me to investigate workers transitions from one labor market state to another. It does not allow one to follow the labor history of one individual over a prolonged period of time with monthly values for the covariates. This fact limits the investigation in some aspects, as persons who have been unemployed and found a job again in the time before the sample is taken are missing in the sample of unemployed and searching workers. Short-time unemployed have a lower probability to enter the sample as those unemployed for a longer time as a person who has been unemployed for just one or two months is less likely to have been so just in the months of survey. Because of the rotating design of the PME survey it is unfortunately not possible to correct for this sample bias. The results in the following parts of this thesis therefore have to be interpreted in the light of this shortcoming: they are rather useful to interpret the behavior of individuals unemployed for a longer period.

The PME-panel data contain information about the current labor market status of each observed individual, and distinguish between formal and informal employment, self-employment, searching or inactivity. For those currently unemployed, the previous labor market state is also registered, using the above categories with the exception of newcomers in the category searching. The PME-questionnaire also contains a question about the possession of a labor card, allowing one to distinguish between formally and informally employed workers, a very important feature for the analysis of transitions between the different labor market states. The usual information on the individual level, like sex, age, educational background and position in the household, is also recorded. Information about wages is only available for those individuals working at the time of the survey, not for those unemployed. In addition to the individual data, the PME-Survey allows to calculate income at the household level.[1] To adjust for inflation, I use deflators for the wage data, as proposed by Corseuil and Foguel (2002).

In this first part of the thesis, the basic underlying theoretical concepts for the two empirical parts to come were presented. A general description of the structure of the Brazilian labor market and an outline of the used labor market survey data were added to provide a base for the following parts. Theoretical aspects as well as those aspects of the Brazilian labor market structure and the data that are only relevant for one of the two investigations following are presented in the respective part of the thesis.

[1] Income from capital assets or property is not included.

Part II

The Allocative Power of Informality

Chapter 5

Introduction

5.1 Motivation and Aim of Part II

Informal employment is usually associated with less favorable working conditions, lower wages and less job security compared to employment in the formal sector. The possible positive functions of informal employment have received far less attention. The positive effect that is mainly mentioned is the buffer function of informal employment and of informal activity in general for dismissed and otherwise unemployed workers in times of economic recession (see for example the overview by Tokman (1990) or, for the Brazilian case, Carneiro (1997)). This view is also promoted theoretically by the rural-urban migration models based on Harris and Todaro (1970) and the considerations of many labor-market-dualists (Dickens and Lang 1988) where the informal sector is regarded as a completely flexible and clearing labor market taking in all surplus labor. Discussions of the buffer function emphasize the social effect of avoiding poverty; positive affects for the allocation of labor are not expected.

Informal employment is mainly a phenomenon of developing countries, while in many industrialized countries, temporary or part-time occupations constitute the main alternatives for otherwise unemployed individuals. Neither of these two forms of labor contracts has a high reputation in the population. In fact, they are sometimes regarded as precarious work forms (Van Den Berg, Heyma, and Zijl 2003). Recent studies show that these types of occupation present stepping stones for unemployed and newcomers, especially for certain groups like women or the long-time-unemployed, and some governments promote the transition of unemployed workers and newcomers into these types of contracts.[1] I argue in this part of my thesis that informal employment, besides being a source of income for low- and non-skilled workers, can have a positive impact on the allocation of labor into formality . In countries where most vocational training is provided on-the-job, without officially organized and recognized training programs and certificates, informal employment may serve as a port of first entry to the labor market.

Brazil, like many developing countries, does not have a homogeneously organized vocational training system for most non-academic jobs. There are schools for some jobs like physiotherapy or electricians requiring intensive training, but most training for an occupation in the blue collar, menial or crafts professions is done informally on the job. Individuals entering the labor market for the first time therefore do not have the possibility of signalling their knowledge or ability in the field they would like to work in.

I argue that part of the informal sector in Brazil is not merely an expression of missing public control mechanisms and bad performance of the labor legislation but a way for employers to deal with uncertain characteristics of the future performance of unexperienced workers. Newcomers who cannot find a job in the formal sector will spend a time being informally employed before they acquire enough work experience measured by time to find access to formal occupations. Within informal employment relationships, employers may compensate for the lack of information on an individual's future performance by cutting down labor costs. This usually results in a lower wage, no employer's contributions to the social security, medical insurance or FGTS, and the refusal to issue a labor card. By reducing labor costs employers balance their risk of employing workers with unknown rate of performance, and workers who cannot find formal employment immediately can gain working experience which may help them to transit to formality later.

Departing from the above considerations, I formulate three hypotheses: First: at least for a part of the non-academic professions there is no complete fragmentation of the labor market. Second: mobility depends on the characteristics of the worker, especially on the possibility of signalling ability to potential formal employers. Work experience gained in informal employment may constitute such a signal. Informal employment may therefore be considered as a stepping stone into formality. Third: the previous time of employment in an informal occupation might be a signal about the quality of a worker, especially when other signalling possibilities are lacking.

To check these hypotheses, I investigate the impact of characteristics like labor history, education and personal characteristics on the transition into for-

[1] See Section 5.2 for an overview about the literature on stepping stones in the labor market.

mal employment. The sample used consists of individuals having completed primary school (first eight years of education), excluding individuals with more education. By concentrating on this group, I focus on individuals with enough educational background to exercise an occupation in the blue collar, menial or crafts professions. I exclude all academic professions as they require degrees in superior education and vocational training is therefore inherent.

The empirical investigation is performed in three steps. First, I obtain transition rates for currently employed as well as unemployed and searching individuals. There are four current occupational states considered: formal employment, informal employment, self–employment and searching. The estimations for these four occupational groups are performed separately to be able to observe the impact of the covariates on the different groups. In a next step, I only consider searching individuals to obtain estimates for the impact of labor history onto the transition rates into formality. In this sample, four different states are considered within the category of labor history: former formal employment, former informal employment, former self–employment and newcomers (first–time entries into the labor market) next to the other covariates. In a last step, transition rates for the different labor history groups are estimated separately. This allows me to observe differences in the impact of the educational level or the individual characteristics on groups of searching workers with different former occupational experiences.

Econometric estimation is performed by using a competing risks hazard model with semi-parametric Cox proportional hazard regressions. The data are taken from the Monthly Labor Market Survey (PME) of the Brazilian Institute for Geography and Statistics (IBGE).

This part of the thesis is structured in the following way: in the remaining two sections of this chapter, an overview about the related literature on labor market stepping–stones is given and the used samples are described. A description of labor market transitions, education and vocational training in Brazil follows in Chapter 6. In Chapter 7, theoretical implications concerning the transition into formality are derived both from the human capital theory and from dual labor market approaches. The relevant factors and the direction of their impact are identified. In Section 8.1 of Chapter 8, the econometric handling of the theoretically derived factors as covariates in the estimation is described. The competing risks framework and the estimation of semi-parametric proportional hazard models are explained in the following sections of Chapter 8. The results of the estimations are presented and interpreted in detail in Chapter 9, and in Chapter 10 conclusions are drawn.

5.2 Labor Market Stepping Stones in the Literature

Labor market transitions in industrialized countries have been studied in abundance, but mainly from unemployment to formal employment. Addison and Portugal (2003), for example, study the determinants of unemployment duration of Portuguese workers, considering transitions from unemployment into employment or inactivity. Sometimes formal employment has been split up into part-time and full employment or into temporary and permanent employment. Transitions in segmented labor markets have been less well researched, especially those of developing countries, little empirical research has been performed on the transition between formal and informal employment. New types of labor relations and labor market structures of industrialized countries have attracted more attention. Part-time work, temporary work contracts and different forms of precarious jobs are now increasingly competing with the traditional permanent full-time-employment. Van Den Berg, Holm, and Ours (1999) investigate the impact of accepting a low-paid medical assistant job on future career options of medical studies graduates and find a significantly positive impact. Several studies have been studying the impact of part-time work (O'Reilly and Bothfeld (2002), and others) or of temporary employment (Booth, Francesconi, and Frank 2002; Guell-Rotllan and Petrongolo 2000) on the future labor market performance of workers in industrialized countries. Similar to informal employment, temporary and part-time work are considered to be atypical labor forms with a generally lower reputation and few career opportunities (Van Den Berg, Heyma, and Zijl 2003). O'Reilly and Bothfeld (2002) find weak evidence for part-time work leading to full-time employment for British and German workers. Focussing on temporary contracts in the British labor market, Booth, Francesconi, and Frank (2002) find clear evidence that temporary jobs are a stepping stone to permanent work. Guell-Rotllan and Petrongolo (2000) report for the Spanish case that some employers offering temporary employment use this form of contract to screen the newly employed. Their estimates indicate that some temporary contracts are transformed into permanent hirings long before the legal limits of the contracts are reached. This result supports my hypothesis that so-called "bad jobs" are sometimes used as a screening device by the employers and that they therefore increase the probability of finding a "good job". Also using Spanish data, Dolado, García-Serrano, and Jimeno (2002) investigate the effects of liberalizing and promoting temporary contracts in a dual labor market framework. The authors focus more on comparing the new situation with the one before the changes in the Employment Protection Legislation than on the effects of temporary work on the transition into permanent work. Blanchard and Landier (2002) and Holmlund and Storrie (2002) follow similar lines of research and obtain comparable results for French and Swedish labor market data. Although none of these studies directly investigates the impact of temporary work on the transition into permanent work, all show that temporary jobs are more volatile and show lower human capital accumulation, facts that are also observed for informal employment. I therefore argue that the models used to evaluate temporary jobs are suitable for the evaluation of informal employment as well.

To my knowledge, substantially less research has been performed on the function of informal employment within the professional training process and on transitions into formal employment on labor market data of developing countries. In the recent literature, Calderón-Madrid (2000) comes close to my research topic investigating labor mobility between formal and informal employment in the Mexican labor market. He finds that participation in training courses helped informally employed individuals to leave the segment between 1991 and 1994 but not during 1995 and 1998. The missing effect in the second period may be explained by the sharp recession that hit Mexico in 1995. Still, the participation in training courses is not the same as the impact of informal employment being a source of labor experience itself and providing on-the-job training. However, the methodological framework used to evaluate these labor forms seems appropriate for the evaluation of informal employment.

Concluding from the presented literature, there is some evidence that for workers in industrialized countries, "bad jobs", like temporary contracts, are stepping stones into "good jobs" like permanent or full-time employment. Furthermore, temporary jobs show similarly volatile patterns and present comparable advantages and disadvantages as informal employment, so the hypothesis of informal work being a stepping stone to formal work seems reasonable. Informal employment as a stepping stone has so far not explicitly been considered in the literature; this thesis aims to contribute to closing this gap.

5.3 The Data

The data used for the empirical tests of my hypotheses are taken from the Monthly Labor Survey, PME (Monthly Labor Survey (PME) 1999). For more general information on this data set please refer to Chapter 4 in Part One. In the following analysis, several different samples were used to estimate hazard rates for on-the-job transitions, for the group of unemployed, and for the different subgroups of unemployed workers. The sample used to estimate on-the-job transition rates contains 65,678 individuals. In the first month, 41% were formally employed, 27% were informally employed, 23.5% were self-employed and

8.5% were searching for a job. The sample for the estimation of the hazard rates of searching individuals into the different occupational states contained 3881 observations. Of these, 33.5% of the workers had held formal jobs before unemployment, 44.5% were informally employed, 14.5% were searching work for the first time and 7.5% were self-employed.

As I am especially interested in the function of informal employment as a signal to the employer and as a substitute for professional training, I restrict the sample used for the following estimations. Most of the professions without organized professional education or vocational training are in the crafts, blue collar or menial jobs. These require at most an educational level of primary school concluded, but also allow the entrance of workers without any education. So the sample is restricted to individuals with primary school completed or less. Primary school in Brazil includes eight years of schooling, but some of the individuals in the sample may have had more years because of repeated school years.

Also, most of the professions providing informal as well as formal employment fall into the areas of occupation in the crafts, blue collar, and menial jobs. For a complete list of selected professions and rates of formal and informal employment in these professions refer to Table A.2 in the appendix. I control for the formerly exercised and the new professions by selecting only those professions for which no formal professional training is offered but formal as well as informal employment can be encountered, so there is a real option for workers to transit into formality.

In testing if informal employment might be a stepping stone to formal employment, the behavior of newcomers is of special interest. As most newcomers enter the labor market before the age of 30, I include only individuals aged between 15 and 29 years in the sample. An age of twenty-nine years may seem advanced, but the data show that there are some individuals of that age classified as newcomers in the sample.

In the following chapter, the role of education and vocational training as well as the role of the individual labor history on labor market transitions of Brazilian workers are discussed and result obtained in empirical studies on this subject are presented before I turn to the theoretical aspects of labor market transitions in Chapter 7.

Chapter 6

Education, Vocational Training, and Inter-Segment Transitions in Brazil

6.1 Professional Education and Training

6.1.1 Basic Education

Although 'the informal sector' in Brazil is very heterogeneous in terms of the quality and remuneration of positions, it clearly offers relatively more low-paid and low-skill job opportunities.[1] Individuals with a higher educational level are more likely to hold formal jobs while those with low levels of basic education tend to be more likely to take up informal employment (Soares, Carvalho, and Kipnis 2003). Soares, Carvalho, and Kipnis (2003) evaluate the basic educational system in Brazil and find that it produces high levels of drop-outs and many young people only finish primary school. For 1999, they report that only 22% of young adults aged between 18 and 25 years had completed secondary education (high school); 46% dropped out from high school. Of the remaining 32% 21% were still enrolled in high school and 11% in primary school. Consequently, these low levels of education are then reflected in equally low labor force participation rates in formal employment. Soares, Carvalho, and Kipnis (2003) find that of the young male adults in the above mentioned age range, and with educational levels lower than high school diploma, only 39% were formally employed. The rate for females was even lower at 36%. For

[1]See Section 3.4 for more information and references on wage differentials between labor market segments in Brazil.

those with high school diploma, levels rose to 68% for male and to 65% for female young adults. Improving the educational levels most certainly will lead to an increase of formal work in the long run.

6.1.2 Vocational Training and Professional Education

Since 1942, the National Industrial Training Service (SENAI) has offered training for qualified and semi-qualified workers.[2] Initially the vocational training courses offered by SENAI were aimed at the needs of young individuals who had finished the first level of primary school (four years). At the beginning, apart from special professional education, SENAI also offered general courses complementary to primary education. But over time, SENAI substituted these courses for courses customized for some of the most important branches of the industry, as the large companies were able to pay for these courses (Salm 1998). Today SENAI focusses almost completely on specialized courses for employees of large firms, and the employees of these firms are admitted with priority. With this change in the structure of offered programs, the educational necessities of the majority of the population are no longer met. The new focus of training additionally led to increased entry requirements for the courses, as the companies ordering the courses demanded higher educational levels of the participants. In 1999, only individuals having concluded the sixth level of primary education were able to register for the courses. The problem here is that about 60% of the students who enter primary education never manage to finish the sixth level and therefore never qualify for the SENAI courses. The new requirements barr the low skilled population from formalized professional education and contribute to a larger flow of newcomers into informality.

Next to the public SENAI and its branches (SENAI/SESI, SENAC/SESC, SENAT/SEST, SENAR and SEBRAE), there are additional vocational training programs offered, for example by the trade unions or by foundations. Private industry created several organizations catering the special qualification needs of some of the industrial sectors.

In 1996 the National Program for Professional Education (PLANFOR) was launched. This program aims at integrating, strengthening and/or restructuring national vocational training capacity by coordinating the activities of the public and private organizations involved in such programs. With the implementation of the PLANFOR, the focus groups were redefined, now including once again low qualified individuals with schooling levels below the first level of primary school. Women, especially when head-of-household, are another

[2] Salm (1998) gives a recent description of the performance of the SENAI.

focus group. Further groups are young adults with poor social background, Afro-Brazilians and indigenous people, and individuals with deficiencies, to name only some (ILO 2003). This program started in 1996, but coordination of the different interests of the industry and manufacturing services, and of the labor supply side on the other hand, is proving difficult. Until now, there has been no detailed evaluation of the performance of the integrated professional education strategy implemented by the PLANFOR.

6.2 Labor History and Transitions Between Segments

In 1999, about 25% of the urban occupied labor force was employed informally. About 45% held formal labor contracts and nearly all of the remaining economically active individuals fall in the category 'self employed'. This labor market structure is by no means rigid and there is mobility of workers between sectors in both directions. Table 6.1 shows absolute and relative numbers of the transitions between different labor market states.

About 12% of former informally employed individuals found a new job in the formal segment, while about 7% of former formally employees transited into informal employment, showing evidence that the formal sector is no closed segment for individuals coming from other segments.

Table 6.1 does not consider labor histories of the searching individuals. Table 6.2 shows transitions of unemployed workers split up by their former occupational state. Looking at the transitions of the unemployed, about 57% of those who entered formal employment already held a formal job before. Almost 30% had informal work experience and only 7.7% were of the newcomer's group.

Even using weights to compensate for different absolute numbers in the occupational groups yields that the rate of newcomers who were able to find formal employment in low-skill jobs was only about two thirds of that of former informally employed workers. Of all former informally employed, 2.6% found a formal job, but only 1.80% of the newcomers. Former formally employed workers had the highest transition rates back into formality, with 7.2% reentering this labor market segment. Another striking feature of the newcomer's group was the fact that 57.7% transited to inactivity, and only 30% remained searching in the next period. Within the other groups, the transition rate to inactivity was substantially lower, and a higher share of individuals preferred to remain searching to giving up. The transition numbers in both Table 6.1

Table 6.1: Cross tabulation of labor market transitions for all states

occupation in month one	occupation in month two formal	informal	self	inactive	searching	Total
formal	27906	2287	731	1366	590	32880
	84.87	6.96	2.22	4.15	1.79	100.00
	85.77	11.10	3.39	0.88	6.03	13.70
informal	2475	11971	2280	2720	986	20432
	12.11	58.59	11.16	13.31	4.83	100.00
	7.61	58.12	10.58	1.75	10.07	8.51
self	682	2340	13398	3930	1212	21562
	3.16	10.85	62.14	18.23	5.62	100.00
	2.10	11.36	62.17	2.53	12.38	8.98
inactive	1003	2745	3832	144515	2873	154968
	0.65	1.77	2.47	93.25	1.85	100.00
	3.08	13.33	17.78	92.89	29.34	64.56
searching	471	1254	1310	3040	4131	10206
	4.61	12.29	12.84	29.79	40.48	100.00
	1.45	6.09	6.08	1.95	42.19	4.25
Total	32537	20597	21551	155571	9792	240048
	13.55	8.58	8.98	64.81	4.08	100.00
	100.00	100.00	100.00	100.00	100.00	100.00

Source: Monthly Labor Survey (PME) (1999), own calculations
first row: absolute numbers
second row: row percentages
third row: column percentages

and Table 6.2 seem to support the neoclassical view of the labor market, where good and bad jobs do not result from segmentation of the labor market but only mirror the different levels of quality of workers.

Table 6.2: Cross tabulation of labor market transitions of unemployed workers

former occupation	**occupation in month two** formal	informal	self	inactive	searching	Total
formal	89	145	98	335	567	1234
	7.21	11.75	7.94	27.15	45.95	100.00
	57.05	28.66	30.82	23.31	38.73	31.80
informal	46	273	147	662	623	1751
	2.63	15.59	8.40	37.81	35.58	100.00
	29.49	53.95	46.23	46.07	42.55	45.12
newcomer	12	51	17	385	202	667
	1.80	7.65	2.55	57.72	30.28	100.00
	7.69	10.08	5.35	26.79	13.80	17.19
self	9	37	56	55	72	229
	3.93	16.16	24.45	24.02	31.44	100.00
	5.77	7.31	17.61	3.83	4.29	5.90
Total	156	506	318	1437	1464	3881
	4.02	13.04	8.19	37.03	37.72	100.00
	100.00	100.00	100.00	100.00	100.00	100.00

Source: Monthly Labor Survey (PME) (1999), own calculations
first row: absolute numbers
second row: row percentages
third row: column percentages

Chapter 7

Theoretical Aspects of Labor Allocation and Labor Market Transitions

7.1 The Human Capital Approach to Labor Market Transitions

In this chapter, the human capital approach and the dual labor markets approach are reviewed with the aim to identify factors determining labor market transitions. The identified factors and their direction of impact are then described in the following sections.

The flexibility of the labor market is important for the efficient allocation of labor. The degree of flexibility of the labor market determines the speed of adjustment of labor supply and of labor demand to changes in the demand for goods or in regulations. The labor market flexibility is determined by the flexibility of wages and by the mobility of workers with respect to locations and training.

As already introduced in Part 1, Section 2.2.2, neoclassical labor economists see the investment in training as fundamental for the wage a worker can obtain. Jobs with different characters in wages, working conditions and job security result from different characteristics of the worker. The level of education is seen as one of the most important characteristics determining the productivity and hence the wage that a worker can obtain on the labor market. In the human capital theory, the acquisition of knowledge is regarded as an investment leading to future income. The link is made by assuming that education increases productivity, and that wages are paid according to productivity. Job allocation is performed according to the human capital approach where employers consider productivity as a function of education and offer wages according to the amount of education obtained (Schultz 1961).

Becker (1962) was the first to incorporate firm specific and general training as two different types of human capital into his formal model. The general training increases the productivity of a worker within the firm where he is momentarily working, but also in every other firm offering a similar job. If the worker moves on to another company after taking the training, the training will also contribute to an increase in his future wage. Firm-specific training, on the other hand, increases the productivity of the worker in that specific firm providing the training, but is of no use to the worker if he decides to change to another company. So if the skills gained by firm-specific training do not have any market-value for the worker, there should be no incentive for the employer to increase the worker's wage after training. He already bears the cost of the training and would, in return, be rewarded by the increase in returns due to the rise in productivity of that worker. However, Becker (1962) argues that a worker's incentive to change his employer is independent of the amount of firm-specific training accumulated if wages are identical. But for the employer, it is a different story: he invested in that training, paid for courses and gave the worker time off to attend the training. If the worker decides to leave the company after concluding the training, and the employer paid for the training, the latter loses the future gains in productivity by that worker. In that case the employer is willing to increase the wage of the trained worker to diminish the probability that the worker will quit. If, on the other hand, the worker would have to pay for the training on the agreement of a wage increase thereafter, he would only take training if he considers the risk of being dismissed in the future, or of the employer's non-compliance to the wage-increase promise, to be reasonably low. Becker's solution to this complex optimizing problem involving risk is that both employer and employee will share training costs and future returns from the increased productivity. If this solution holds, then an increase in training will lead to a decrease in labor turnover, as both parties, employers and employees, have an interest in maintaining the labor relationship. This idea of training costs increasing the firing costs of certain workers has also been used to explain the existence of internal labor markets (Franz 2003) already discussed in 2.2.2.

7.2 Labor Transitions in the Dual Labor Market Theory

The Dual Labor Market Theory (Gordon 1972; Doeringer and Piore 1971) locates informal employment in a completely different labor market segment having no or little interaction with the formal sector. In the dualistic view the structure and requirements of the "primary segment" containing formal employment and the "secondary segment" containing informal occupation evolve in very different ways thereby almost excluding mobility between these segments. Wage determination and labor allocation follow mechanisms in which human capital factors play a less significant role. Within this theory frame employers screen potential new employees for several characteristics, one of the characteristics being education. The characteristics serve as proxies for the ability of the worker, but contrary to the human capital approach, the relationship between education and productivity is not regarded as a causal one.

Doeringer and Piore (1971) also use the concept of internal labor markets. They attribute the formation of internal labor markets within competitive labor markets to three factors which had not been previously considered: job training, firm-specific skills and the set of conventions and internal rules evolving in each firm. According to Piore and Doeringer, every worker gains specific skills while working in a company, even without attending specified training courses. Individuals learn about internal production processes simply by watching and imitating fellow workers, and develop an increasingly productive working routine over time. This informal learning increases the cost for employers if employees quit their job. Like in the human capital approach, the employers therefore have an incentive to reduce the rate of fluctuation amongst their employees.

The big difference to human capital theory that Piore and Doeringer introduce in their concept is the way employers try to minimize labor turnover cost. The claim that employers install a certain structure concerning social interactions, labor standards and work attitudes in their companies that itself is of a huge value to their workers. This structure may contain measures to increase job security, including seniority principles, where the time of service within a firm is a major factor for a worker's prospect of promotion. Further features may be good career options, including training possibilities or security systems like an additional health plan. This structure reduces labor rotation and creates an internal labor market functioning much more according to the internal structure than to the external labor market conditions. Of course, to create this structure a minimum firm size is required, and firms introducing such a structure will be likely to be the larger ones producing with advanced technology. This reasoning leads to the concept of a segmented labor market as already discussed in Part 1, section 2.3.2, with the large, capital-intensive and well organized firms operating in the formal segment of the economy and serving the stable demand, while the smaller secondary segment companies compete for the less stable demand, offering less attractive working conditions (Joll et al. 1983).

One of the main characteristics of segmented labor markets has been the lack of mobility between the segments. This rigidity has been explained by the above described extension of the concept of internal labor markets and their distinctive internal structures specific for each firm. The longer an individual works in one of the segments, the more he will absorb the internal rules valid within that segment. The assumption here is not only that the knowledge of the set of rules is specific knowledge without value on the job market of the other segment, but that it actually may cause harm. This has especially been pointed out for the structures prevailing in the informal segment, implying that the chances of a worker with a longer working experience in the informal segment to find a job in the formal segment are reduced to almost zero. Workers get scarred by their labor market histories, blocking them after a while from all chances to switch segments. This assumption of scarring by the labor history clearly contradicts the ideas of the human capital theory that any person, by choosing to invest into the accumulation of human capital may then be rewarded by a better paid job. This assumption could hold within the segments, but would not be valid for inter-segment transitions.

Even if in this theory framework education is not the principal criterion employers will use to make their decisions about whom to employ, nonetheless the level of skills will play a role, even in structures like internal labor markets. Employers will screen the possible candidates, and applicants will try to give positive signals. The main assumption of the screening hypothesis is an information disparity about the workers' skills and ability (beyond the basic level). Workers know their skills, employers cannot distinguish between workers with high and low productivity. Therefore, if wages are paid according to productivity, firms tend to pay lower wages as they don't know what they will get. On their side workers try to signal their skills to increase their wages. In most industrialized countries the publicly regulated professional education system helps to provide signals by issuing certificates and taking centralized examinations. Individuals are therefore interested to participate in vocational training and to obtain certificates they can use to signal their skills.

In Brazil, for most of the non-academic professions, there does not exist a publicly regulated system for professional education. Most training is on the job training. Still, some of the professions show mixed employment states, sometimes with equal proportions of formally and informally employed workers in certain professions. Furthermore, mobility between the sector of formal and informal employment exists in both directions (see Section 6.2 for numbers), contradicting the assumption of complete market fragmentation. This may be the case because of definition divergence: Within most of the literature, the informal sector is associated with small scale production and family-owned enterprises; activities are mainly in crafts, agriculture, and the provision of basic services. In Brazil, even larger companies sometimes employ informally, and the range of professions with informally employed workers is larger than in most other countries. In this study, I differentiate between self-employment and informal employment by an employer. Only informal employment will be considered in this thesis, as both states follow very different rules and a joint evaluation seems not make much sense.

7.3 Parameters and Hypotheses

7.3.1 Duration of Unemployment

I expect the probability of moving into formal work to decline as the 'duration of unemployment' increases: the longer a person keeps searching, the lower will be the probability to find formal work. One reason may be that employers use the 'duration of unemployment' as a screening device for a worker's quality. The underlying argumentation is that less qualified workers have longer search times as they have been rejected by more employers. The relation is less clear for individuals transiting into informality. I also assume that an increase in time of search reduces the probability of finding an informal employment, but I expect this effect to be weaker for two reasons: First, a substantial number of individuals might have been looking first for a formal employment for some months before starting to reconsider their expectations and also to consider an informal employment. The second reason is that a large share of informal employment opportunities requires a lower level of skills compared to formal jobs. There is therefore less concern for loss of human capital over time leading to less concern for the number of months out of work from the employers' side. The second argument holds less if I restrict the sample to individuals with primary schooling and only selected professions. Still, I expect the relation to be a monotonically declining one, but with a less steep decline than for formal employment.

The variable 'duration of unemployment' directly enters the term of the dependent variable in the transition data analysis, together with an indicator variable for the different occupational states and, conditioned on the fact that the person has been unemployed up to the start of observation. More details on the construction of the econometric model will be given in section 8.2.

7.3.2 Spell in the Last Job

In both theoretical approaches, the neoclassical one relying on the human capital theory, and the dual labor markets theory considering the screening approach, the ability of a worker plays a crucial role in the employer's selection process. Human capital theorists estimate ability and skills of a worker by taking schooling time and work experience as measures. The screening hypothesis also relies on education, but it does not incorporate a causal link between education and ability of a worker. It assumes that, on average, more able individuals on the average get more schooling, so that schooling and professional experience may serve as proxies for the ability of a worker. Workers with more work experience, both formal and informal, are therefore expected to find a formal job more easily. However, in segmented labor markets the effect of the work experience might be different and could depend on the sector in which the worker has been occupied. In the Brazilian case, the labor market for young workers up to about thirty years of age seems to conform to the neoclassical labor market theory, but with increasing age (and therefore experience) of the workers, the labor market seems to evolve more according to the dual labor markets theory. If this is really the case, it would also imply that prolonged work experience in the informal sector lowers the probability for workers to transit into formality, as they loose the abilities to work in formality. The effect of work experience in informality could then be an ambiguous one: some work experience in informal employment will increase the probability of a person to transit into formality. But after a certain, not identified time limit has been passed in informal employment, workers get scarred by the informal work and thereby become less interesting for formal employers.

7.3.3 Type of Last Job

According to the neoclassical labor market theory, the estimated future productivity of a worker is determined by his ability and knowledge. There are no explicit assumptions made concerning different knowledge requirements in different segments, as segmentation is not a central issue in this approach. The different job-specific knowledge acquired in a formal versus informal job is rather classified as knowledge specific to that particular firm the worker is working at and is not seen as "segment-specific". It is assumed that a worker acquires two types of knowledge while working. The first type includes skills that are also useful for work in other companies, at least of the same branch, and the second comprises skills that are only useful within that specific firm (Becker 1964). This view implies that the former type of employment should have no effect on the transitions of workers into the different labor market states.

In contrast to this, the dual labor market theory assumes that requirements in the different sectors are very different and that separation between the segments is so rigid because of these different skills and habits (Dickens and Lang 1988). As in the above section, scarring by the previous type of work plays an important role. From this view, the former occupational state of a worker should have a large, conservatory impact on future transitions: the former type of work determines all future types of work.

7.3.4 Education

Education plays a crucial role for labor allocation in both of the labor market theories I consider in my thesis. The only difference between them is whether or not the education of a worker is causal to future performance of a worker (Stiglitz 2002). Both theories here point in the same direction: the more education, the better the chances to find a good job. In neoclassic labor market theory a good job is a highly paid one; in dual labor market theory a good job is a formal one (associated with higher wages and more job security, a combination not necessarily met by the "good" neoclassical jobs).

Within the framework of the screening hypothesis, individuals looking for a job therefore have an incentive to signal their abilities. One of the possibilities is to provide certificates of completed education (Stiglitz 2002). These "proofs" of investment in education may create the so-called sheepskin effects, where not the years of education but only the possession of the diploma account for the difference between individuals earnings (Ferrer and Riddell 2002; Hungerford and Solon 1987).

Employers look out for characteristics of individuals that could serve as signals for productivity, and they use education as a proxy for productivity, screening the educational background of individuals for signals that might indicate the individuals personal ability endowment (Spence 1973).

7.3.5 Sex

I further on control for sex, as females tend to be employed in less favorable conditions than men and frequently their wages are below those paid to men (Berger and Buvinic 1989; Gallaway and Bernasek 2002). According to the discrimination theories discussed in section 2.2.2 in Part 1, women are more likely to be discriminated against on the labor market. Some jobs are male or female dominated; the female dominated ones usually pay worse. Sometimes male fellow workers do not like the company of women or have feelings of superiority and refuse to cooperate. Employers will then hire only male or only female workers to prevent the decrease in productivity. One reason given for the discrimination of women is that they will not work continuously due to birth and child-raising (Ehrenberg and Smith 1991).

A very large proportion of low educated women are classified as self employed, but this is a question of definition, as most of these work as household aid, but consider themselves self-employed. In a strict sense they are employed, and in most cases on an informal basis as most households do not sign labor cards and do not contribute to the social security for their household aid.

7.3.6 Age

Age, as well as the spell in the last job, may have an ambiguous effect on the transitions from unemployment to formality. Many countries, independent from their degree of development, experience high rates of youth unemployment (O'Higgins 2001). Usually, individuals tend to accumulate more skills with increasing age, both of general and firm-specific nature, and therefore tend to become more productive. But this learning curve is assumed to be a function that first increases and then decreases with advancing age. In many countries older persons have more difficulties to find a new job, although some of the highly industrialized countries like Sweden and Switzerland do not show evidence of this trend. According to the dual labor market theory, the segments each develop a very specific structure, and different requirements are made for workers. The longer a worker stays in one of the sectors, the lower is the probability that he is still able to meet the requirements of the other sector. Age, as well as the previous working spell, may be interpreted in this light and lead to a scarring of the workers.

The Brazilian data seem to support this thesis, as less workers above the age of thirty are transiting into formality. The way into informality seems less closed, but overall inter-sectoral transitions between dependent employment decline with increasing age. This, though, does not hold for transitions into self employment, as self employment requires much more self esteem and experience and, in most cases, also a very well developed working network. I therefore include "age" as an explanatory variable, expecting a declining relationship between the probability of transition into formal employment and age.

7.3.7 Position in the Household

The effect of a person's position in the household may also influence his or her transition behavior as heads of households usually have more responsibility for their dependent family members. Because of these responsibilities, it seems also reasonable to suppose that heads of households look for more job security and medical insurance. This would lead to the assumption that, all other variables being equal, heads of households hold proportionally more formal jobs than non-heads. On the other hand, unemployed heads in the lowest income segment will be under far greater pressure to gain money to support their dependent family members and therefore will take any job that comes first. About 40% of the heads of household in Brazil are females, and females have a higher probability of ending up in informal jobs, so the relationship is most probably not a monotonic one but a mix between the "heads -effect" and a "sex-effect". I therefore also included an interactive term 'head'-sex" in the model but the term did not show any significance.

7.3.8 Per Capita Household Income

The per capita household income is a measure of the financial resources of the worker. In Brazil the income of members of one household is still considered as a common good for the use of everybody in the household, much more so than in thoroughly industrialized countries. The higher the incomes of other household members, the lower will be the pressure of immediately finding a new job. I assume that less pressure and more financial resources therefore allow for a prolonged and more resource-intensive search and thereby lead to a better job, as this is a standard assumption in the literature (Ehrenberg and Smith 1991). A higher per capita household-income would therefore increase the probability of transiting into a formal job.

Furthermore, the per-capita household income captures part of the social background of an individual. The social background of an individual may determine the motivation to work in a specified segment of the labor market. If parents, present relatives and other persons in the social environment of a person are all self employed, then the chances will increase that that particular person ends up in the same work patterns. The same holds for individuals in highly educated environments, where the person's peer group tends to work in high wage formal sector jobs, here incentives will also lead to a similar job. Per-capita household income also determines the amount of money accessible for education and training. The public school system is free for all children, but is of poor quality. Pupils from public school are much less likely to continue onto university. Access to private schools, which are costly, is an important factor for a career in the formal sector. In the context of this thesis, the latter is of less importance, as I restrict my sample to persons with an educational level from zero to second level of primary school concluded (eight years of schooling). This second social indicator of the per-capita household income points in the same direction as the first one: with an increasing per-capita household income the chances to find a formal employment also increase.

7.4 Conclusion on the Theoretical Determinants of Labor Market Transitions

The effects of most of the variables considered point in the same direction concerning neoclassical or dualistic theory implications. Some are of an ambiguous nature, like the 'time in the previous job', the interaction between 'in previous job' and 'previous job informal', and 'age'. These covariates change their effect from positive to negative or vice versa with increasing values of the

Table 7.1: Expected impact of the covariates on the probabilities of transition into formality

Variable	positive effect	negative effect
duration of unemployment		X
time in previous job	X	X
time in previous job * previous job formal	X	
time in previous job * previous job informal	X	X
type of previous job	X	X
education	X	
male	X	
age	X	X
position in the household	X	
position in the household * male	X	
per-capital household income	X	

variable. Table 7.1 summarizes the expected effects of the explanatory variables. After having identified the factors influencing labor market transitions and their directions of impact, I now turn to the empirical analysis of workers' transitions. In Chapter 8, the empirical method used is described before estimation results are discussed in Chapter 9.

Chapter 8

Analysis of Inter-Segment-Transitions

8.1 Dependent and Explanatory Variables

The dependent variable of interest in the econometric estimation is the future labor market state of an individual who is now searching for a job. To obtain information about this variable, I observe the labor market state at month 2 of persons searching in month 1. The data allows me to distinguish between the following states: 'formally employed', 'informally employed', 'self-employed', 'searching' and 'inactive'.

Following the relations of this dependent variable with the characteristics of the individuals as discussed in Section 7.3, I include a vector of explanatory variables in the model, including 'time worked before', 'sex', 'age', 'age squared', 'head of household', 'family income per capita' and 'education'. I expect all of these covariates to influence the transition into different labor market states. I also include dummy variables for the different seasons of the year to control for economic conditions varying during the year.

The variable 'duration of unemployment' denotes the number of months since a person quit his last job. As this information is not available for the newcomers, I use a proxy generally applied in this case (see for example Ferreira and Barros (1999), p. 14): I calculate the time the specified person is out of school by subtracting the years of school performed plus six additional years (most children in Brazil start school at six) from the age at the time of observation. The found number of years are then transformed into months to show the same measuring unit as the months of unemployment. As I only have time in years (age and schooling) for the newcomers, there is a certain measurement error involved in the transformation into months. Aware of this problem, I still prefer to assign these values to the newcomers to applying a general mean, calculated by using the average duration of unemployment of the searching individuals. With increasing duration of unemployment, the values for 'duration of unemployment' anyhow tend to cumulate at the numbers of months of completed years (i.e. 36 months, 48 months).

The 'time in last job' can be measured directly for all individuals who have been working previously and are searching at the reference period of the survey. Newcomers to the labor market have a value of zero assigned for this variable. My database does not allow me to directly determine the 'time in last job' for individuals changing jobs without intermediate searching time. For the on-the-job searchers I therefore assign the mean value of former job spell of those persons searching. Next to the covariates 'time in last job' and 'age', I also entered a combination of both of these variables into my estimation. From the theoretical reflections follows that the impact of the previous work experience of former informally employed workers for a transition into formal employment may be first increasing but then decreasing with increasing time. To test for this, the covariate 'time in last job squared' has also been included in the model.

The variable 'type of last job' refers to the same occupational states as the dependent variable, except that the classifications 'searching' and 'inactive' are not considered as they are not jobs. Individuals who did not report a previous job are classified as 'newcomers'.

Education is measured both in years, a method supporting the human capital approach, and in ranges defining completion of a degree or similar according to the screening approach. The ranges used are 'no schooling', 'first part of primary school completed (four years)', 'second part of primary school completed (eight years)', 'high school completed (eleven years)' and 'superior education (university degree etc.)'.

Sex and 'position in the household' are coded as dummy variables, assigning all heads of the household a value of one and all other members a value of 0. 'Age' is measured in years. Additionally, the variable 'age squared' is entered into the estimation to cope with the possibly nonlinear relationship indicated by the theory.

The 'per-capita household-income' is measured both continuously and in ranges, the latter proceeding first in small and then increasing multiples of the minimum salary, starting with 'up to one minimum salary', to 'one minimum salary' etc. (refer to the annex for a complete overview of ranges). All income gained by household members is deflated by using deflators proposed for the use of data from the PME-Survey by Corseuil, Ribeiro, and Santos (2002). A variable 'log of per-capita household income' has also been included, but proved insignificant and was therefore removed again.

Regional differences have been accounted for by using either regional dummies or by stratifying for regions. The regions available in the data are the states of the metropolitan areas where the survey was conducted: Bahia, Minas Gerais, Paraná, Pernambuco, Rio de Janeiro, Rio Grande do Sul and Saõ Paulo.

The different seasons of the year may account for different propensities of employers to open vacancies or to dismiss employees. Variations in the rate of unemployment related to the seasons are controlled for by using dummies for the seasons, considering the usual seasons winter (June, July, August), spring (September, October, November), summer (December, January, February) and autumn (March, April, June). See Table A.1 in the appendix for a complete overview of these covariates.

8.2 The Econometric Modelling

8.2.1 Modelling Stepping Stone Transitions in the Literature

Most of the studies mentioned in Section 5.2 use transition data models[1] to estimate transition rates for the considered subgroups of individuals. Transition data models have the advantage that they also use the information of censored or truncated observations. An observation is called truncated either when no transition into a specific state occurred because the individual did not change his labor market state, or censored when the person transited into another state.[2] In the former case, only a lower bound for the time elapsed until the transition into the specified state occurred is known. In the latter case, the observation would be dropped from a model setting like a logistic regression. Some transition data methods can deal with censoring and the

[1] These models are known under a variety of names like survival analysis, duration analysis or transition data analysis. They all focus on transition from one state in the other, some emphasize the duration of an event and some on the destination that is entered at the end of an event (Lancaster 1992; Allison 1995). In the following text, I will use the above names as synonyms.

[2] Cleves, Gould, and Gutierrez (2002) give a more detailed description of the different types of censoring and truncation.

information contained in the censored observation still enters the estimation process. Other model types, like the logistic regression, do not allow one to deal with censoring or truncation, and estimates of these model types may therefore be biased (Allison 1995). A more detailed discussion of truncation and censoring occurring in the sample used here can be found in section 8.2.2.

Additionally, the odds-ratios obtained from (multinomial) logistic regression are comparative measures of the risk of a transition at the end of the observation time. In contrast, the hazard ratios obtained from transition data analysis are a comparative measure of the transition risk at any time during the observation time. Hosmer and Lemeshow (1991) conclude that odds-ratios and hazard ratios are two different measures and that the mere fact that both may show similar magnitudes in some settings is irrelevant.

The econometric model most commonly used in the analysis of transitions between different labor market states is the competing risks model using Cox regressions (see, for example, (Addison and Portugal 2003), (Van Den Berg, Heyma, and Zijl 2003)). A more detailed description of these models follows in section 8.2.2.

A constraint to the transition models is that estimators may be biased in the presence of left-censored data. The data from the PME unfortunately does not follow individuals over a period longer than 16 months, and even during the one-year-spell, the individual is only observed in the first and last four months of that spell; no information is available between these two periods. This means that all persons who found a job prior to entering the sample are excluded from the estimation process and therefore left-censoring is present (Cleves, Gould, and Gutierrez 2002).

8.2.2 Survival Data Analysis

The Competing Risks Framework

To test the hypotheses stated in Section 5.1 with duration models, I use a competing risks hazard model similar to the one used by Addison and Portugal (2003) except that I consider single spells according to the structure of the data. Competing risks hazard models allow one to examine the likelihood of transitions from one state to multiple other states, in this case the transition from the initial state "searching for a job" into "formal employment", "informal employment" etc. (Lancaster (1992), Chapter 5). Being in one of these states excludes the possibility of being in one of the other states at the same time, so states are mutually exclusive or "competing". Competing risks models also allow one to specify separate hazard functions for each of the different risk groups: newcomers to the labor market, former informally employed and former formally employed workers. The hazard rates estimated by the competing risks model measure the rate at which an individual transits from state A to state B at a specified moment, given that the individual has been in state A for t time units. Let $j = 1, 2, 3, 4, 5$ be the five occupational states "formally employed", "informally employed", "self-employed", "inactive" and "searching". T_i is a random variable denoting the time of change in an occupational state of individual i with characteristics x_i. The hazard h_{ij} for individual i to transit into state j at time t is specified as follows:

$$h_{ij}\left(t \mid x_i\right) = \lim_{\Delta t \to 0} \frac{Pr\{t \leq T_i < t + \Delta t, J_i = j \mid T_i \geq t\}}{\Delta t}, \quad j = 1, 2, 3, 4, 5. \tag{8.1}$$

This definition of a hazard function is the definition of a conditional probability density function (p.d.f.) which is defined as:[3]

$$f(t) = \frac{dF(t)}{dt} = -\frac{dS(t)}{dt}. \tag{8.2}$$

So equation 8.1, the p.d.f., is just the derivative of the cumulative density function (c.d.f.) $F(t)$, divided by $1 - F(t)$. By definition, $1 - F(t)$ is the survivor function $S(t)$, the cumulative density function of those individuals who did not experience the event until time t.

The hazard function also can be expressed as:

$$h(t) = \frac{f(t)}{S(t)}. \tag{8.3}$$

Together with equation 8.2, equation 8.3 yields

$$h(t) = -\frac{d}{d(t)} logS(t). \tag{8.4}$$

Integrating 8.4 gives a useful relationship between the survivor function $S(t)$ and the integrated hazard function $\Lambda(t)$:

[3] The p.d.f. is conditioned on $T_i \geq t$, for the sake of simplicity, I do not note the conditional term in the following equations.

$$S(t) = e^{-\Lambda(t)} \tag{8.5}$$

with $\Lambda(t) = \int_0^t h(u)du$. Within the multiple exit framework with five possible exits, the aggregate hazard function is denoted as

$$h(t) = \sum_{j=1}^{5} h_j(t), \tag{8.6}$$

and the survival function is

$$S(t) = \prod_{j=1}^{5} S^j(t), \tag{8.7}$$

with $S(t) = e^{-\Lambda(t)}$.

The vector x_i containing the individual characteristics or covariates includes the former occupational states of the individual: 'formerly formally employed', 'formerly informally employed' and 'newcomer', 'time worked before', 'time worked before (squared)', 'sex', 'age', 'age squared', 'head of household', 'family income per capita' and 'education'. The relation for 'time worked before' is assumed to be increasing with higher values: workers with more work experience are expected to find a formal job more easily. To check if the time of former employment enters the estimation in a quadratic function I also add the covariate 'time worked before (squared)'. Refer to Table A in the annex for a complete list of covariates used in the estimations and their statistics.

The proportional hazards specification

Within the competing risks hazard model, I calculate hazard rates using the Cox proportional hazards regression model (Cox 1972). This type of model is a semi-parametric model, where the hazard rate for the ith individual in the data is composed of a non-specified (non-parameterized) baseline hazard $h_0(t)$ and a subject-specific hazard $exp(x_i\beta_x)$ assumed to be multiplicatively related to the baseline hazard:

$$h_{ij}(t \mid x_i) = h_0(t)\, e^{x_i\beta_x}. \tag{8.8}$$

The baseline hazard $h_0(t)$ specifies how the hazard function changes as a function of survival time in the original state. The other function, the subject-specific hazard $exp(x_i\beta_x)$, determines how the hazard function changes as a function of the individual covariates. The baseline hazard is assumed to be the same for all individuals in the sample, but no assumptions about its shape over time are made. In technical terms this means that the distribution of the survival time does not have to be explicitly specified. This special feature of the Cox-regression has the advantage that misspecifications of the baseline hazard can be avoided. The price to be paid for this is a loss in efficiency in estimating the parameters β_x, as the full maximum likelihood function cannot be estimated because of the lack of the error term. Cox (1972) developed a partial likelihood function depending only on the parameters of interest without relying on the baseline hazard function. Equation 8.9 below shows such a partial likelihood function. With the help of these partial likelihood functions, estimates for the β_x can be obtained, and Efron (1977) showed that the loss of efficiency resulting from discarding the information contained in the baseline hazard is quite small in most cases. When estimating the hazard rates, the baseline hazard is left unestimated; actually it drops out from the calculation. This implies that comparing individual i's hazard to that of any other individual k:

$$\frac{h\,(t \mid x_i)}{h\,(t \mid x_k)} = \frac{e^{\,x_i\beta_x}}{e^{\,x_k\beta_x}}, \tag{8.9}$$

the model yields a constant value for the hazard ratio, assuming that the covariates x_i and x_k are not time-dependent (Allison 1995; Cleves, Gould, and Gutierrez 2002).

As the individuals in the sample are observed once per month, the event time of the transitions can only be determined on a monthly basis, event time is not measured continuously but discretely. So the probability of a worker transiting in a given month m into a job in segment j is

$$f_m^j\,(t \mid x_i) = \frac{S_{m-1}^j\,(t \mid x_i) - S_m^j\,(t \mid x_i)}{S_{m-1}^j\,(t \mid x_i)} S_{m-1}\,(t \mid x_i) = h_m^j(t) S_{m-1}\,(t \mid x_i), \tag{8.10}$$

with m being the realization of a discrete random unemployment duration variable, $m = 1, ..., M$.

Interval censoring

Cox regressions maximize the conditional probability of failure (the risk of transiting into formality). To calculate this probability, the risk pool (here the group of individuals at risk of transiting into formal employment) at each failure time is considered. The time a transition takes place is not relevant, but the ordering of the individuals events is fundamental for calculating the Cox likelihood function:

$$L\left(\beta_x\right) = \prod_{i=1}^{n} \left(\frac{e^{\,x_i \beta_x}}{\sum_{m \in R_i} e^{\,x_m \beta_x}} \right). \tag{8.11}$$

As the time out of work of an individual in the PME data set is recorded in months, the precise time of transition cannot be measured. Therefore, the exact ordering of the subjects failure can not be determined, the event-time recordings are so-called interval-censored. Consequently, many workers appear to transit into other labor market states at the same time; because of the imprecise time measurement they are seemingly tied. Still, I do not assume that transitions take place at exactly the same point of time. One possible solution to this problem of tied failures is to calculate the conditional probability of one transition occurring before the other for all tied transitions and use the sum of these probabilities to calculate the likelihood. This method is called the exact-marginal calculation. Unfortunately, it needs a lot of computational time, especially when there are many tied data in relatively few intervals of time. To handle this problem, several approximation techniques have been developed. I use the Efron approximation (Efron 1977), a method to approximate the exact-marginal calculations suitable for risk groups with relatively few transition events compared to the number of individuals in that risk group, as it is the case for the PME data.

Next to interval-censoring, other types of censoring and truncation may appear in the data. Truncation occurs when the recordings of the time at risk are incomplete due to the setting of the study. If the starting point of the time an individual has been at risk is unknown, the data is left-side truncated, if the individual did not experience the event by the end of the study the data is right-side truncated. Censoring may occur because of random factors for each person. If an individual has already experienced the relevant event before entering a study, the observation is left-censored. An individual leaving the risk group because of a transition into another than the state the researchers are interested in, or just dropping out of the sample because he moved or died, leads to a right-censored observation. As already mentioned in section 8.2, Cox regressions can deal with right-censored and truncated data, and information of such observations can be included into the model to improve estimates.

The PME-survey records the time out of work for all individuals searching for a job at the time of the survey, and only individuals actually searching for a job enter the sample that I use for estimation of the hazard rates. So if I define 'being at risk' as being unemployed, the starting point for being at risk for transiting into formality is always known in my sample, there is no left-side truncation or left censoring. This would of course not be the case if I would consider all economically active individuals at risk for on-the-job transitions without intermediate unemployment. The Monthly Labor Survey does not record on-the-job transitions within one segment, so I decided to consider only transitions from unemployment. As I match observations of the same individuals for two consecutive months, there are no early exits. Observing only two months in the labor history of a worker, some individuals transit out of the searching state in the second month, but not into formal employment (the state that is of major interest to my research), but into other labor market states or inactivity. These observations are also right censored. Most of the searching individuals though remain searching during these two months. I do not have any information on when, if ever, they experience a transition into formal employment. These observations are right-side truncated. Within the competing risks framework, right censoring and truncation are dealt with by classifying all event-times of individuals who do not transit into the specified state as censored. Having different states into which individuals may transit, different hazard functions are specified, classifying all transitions into other states or no-events as right censoring. As I am particularly interested in transitions into formal employment, I consider all transitions into states other than formal employment as right censoring.

Unobserved heterogeneity

The economic activity of individuals in the labor market and their personal careers in that area depend not only on characteristics like sex, age or education, but also on characteristics that remain unobserved, like motivation or social background. Such unobserved heterogeneity in these areas may lead to a bias in the estimates.

To test and correct for unobserved heterogeneity, I introduce a multiplicative error term v_{ij} into the subject-specific hazard term of the hazard function:

$$h\left(t \mid x_i, v_{ij}\right) = h_{0j}\left(t\right) e^{\,x_i\beta_x}\ v_{ij}. \qquad (8.12)$$

The $v_{k,j}$ are subject- and state-specific, but are assumed to be constant for a given individual.

As distribution of the errors v_{kj}, I follow Cocks (1997) and Addison and Portugal (2003) and assume a gamma distribution with mean 1 and variance σ_j^2 to insure that the probability values remain always positive. I further assume that these terms are uncorrelated. Using the specific survivor function for gamma mixtures (Lancaster 1992), p.66,

$$\bar{S}_m^j = (1 + \sigma_j^2 \Lambda_m^j)^{-\frac{1}{\sigma_j^2}}. \tag{8.13}$$

The partial likelihood contribution for an individual can be derived:

$$\begin{aligned} L(\theta, \sigma^2 | t, j, x) \quad = \quad & \left\{ \prod_{m=1}^{M-1} \prod_{j=1}^{5} \left[\frac{1 + \sigma_j^2 \Lambda_{m-1}^{j}{}^{-\frac{1}{\sigma_j^2}} - (1 + \sigma_j^2 \Lambda_m^j)^{-\frac{1}{\sigma_j^2}}}{(1 + \sigma_j^2 \Lambda_{m-1}^j)^{-\frac{1}{\sigma_j^2}}} \right]^{\delta_{mj}} \right\} \times \\ & \left\{ \prod_{m=2}^{M} \prod_{j=1}^{5} \left[\frac{1 + \sigma_j^2 \Lambda_m^j{}^{-\frac{1}{\sigma_j^2}}}{(1 + \sigma_j^2 \Lambda_{m-1}^j)^{-\frac{1}{\sigma_j^2}}} \right] \right\}^{1-\delta_m} . \end{aligned} \tag{8.14}$$

The vector θ contains the regression coefficients. The likelihood comprises two terms, the first term giving the probability that the individual exits to state j, with switch δ_{mj} assuming the value of one if the individual transits into another state within month m and zero if no transition takes place during that interval. The expression $\delta_m = \sum_j^5 \delta_{mj}$ takes on the value zero, so that $1 - \delta_m$ is one if the individual did not transit during the observed interval, and is therefore censored. Equation 8.14 is the partial likelihood function used to estimate the impact of the individual characteristics x_{ij}. The estimation method used is maximum likelihood. The data was prepared with SAS-software, the maximum likelihood iteration was performed with Stata-software. The estimation controlling for unobserved heterogeneity was carried out using the software package R.

Chapter 9

Interpretation of the Estimation Results

9.1 Inter-Segment Transitions of Employed Workers

Within the competing risks framework, I estimated several proportional hazard models for exits into different labor market states. First, I obtain hazard rates for changes between labor market segments for workers employed in one of the segments in the first month and in another segment in the next month as well as for individuals registered as searching in the first month. The data do not allow one to observe transitions within one segment because the time in the last occupation is not registered, and the questionnaire does not contain a question about on-the-job transitions without a searching interval. Table 9.1 reports Cox-regression estimation results for on-the-job transitions; the only exit state considered here is formal employment. The four columns show the hazard ratios for individuals departing from one of the following occupational states: formal employment, informal employment, self employment and searching, respectively. The estimates shown in the first column, valid for transitions from formal employment to formal employment, are to be interpreted as estimates for the persistence in this labor market state, for reasons explained above. Recall Table 6.1 in chapter 6, showing that almost 86% of the formally employed workers stay in that segment in the next month. This is also reflected by the fact that all hazard ratios for the formally employed group are greater than one (see Table 9.1). There are no estimation results displayed for the group of inactive individuals as this group is far too heterogeneous and no information is available on the former labor history of inactive individuals.

Note that not all of the covariates discussed in Chapter 8.1 are included in the final, fitted models. Criteria for including covariates have been economic considerations derived from the theoretical implications presented in Chapter 7 as well as from econometric model fitting considerations. The main model fitting procedure has been re-estimation as described in Cleves, Gould, and Gutierrez (2002) where some of the above discussed covariates were used to asses the robustness of the model.

The hazard ratios indicate that the sex of a worker has no significant impact on the persistence of formally employed workers and self-employed individuals transitions, but is significant at the 5%-level for informally employed workers and significant at the 1%-level for individuals searching for a new job. The pattern is a quite interesting one as male workers currently employed informally are about 11% less likely to transit into formality than their female colleagues. Contrary to this, unemployed males searching for a job have hazard ratios more than 82% higher than those of female job-searchers. The estimates for the last of the states, searching, do not take into consideration the labor history of the workers. I will include dummies for the former occupational state in a later analysis.

The position of an individual in his household is the only characteristic showing a significant impact for all observed groups of workers. Being the head of the household increases the transition rates for individuals in all labor market states, with the weakest impact, about 4%, for formally employed workers. Informally employed heads of household are about 30% more likely to transit into formal employment than dependent family members. For searching individuals, the impact increases to 61%. As already mentioned above, this group is composed of individuals with different work experiences and will be considered in detail later in this chapter. Apart from age, being the head of household is the only significant characteristic for self-employed: it increases the likeliness to take up formal employment by around 60%.

Age also shows a significant effect albeit a quite small one, and only for informally employed workers and the self-employed. For each additional year, the probability of transition into formality increases around 0.7% for those currently informally employed. Here it should be remembered that the age in the sample is restricted from 15 to 29 years. Age is also significant for the group of self-employed, but here it shows a negative effect of about 2% per additional year on the entry into formality. The covariate 'age squared' showed no significance and has therefore been left out in the final estimation.

The educational level shows no significant impact on transitions of formally occupied workers. For informally employed workers, having completed the first level of primary school increases the transition probability by about 12%,

Table 9.1: Hazard ratios for on-the-job transitions into formality

Covariate	(1)	(2)	(3)	(4)
male	1.019	0.893	0.874	1.821
	(0.015)	(0.046)*	(0.110)	(0.129)**
head of household	1.042	1.303	1.601	1.610
	(0.015)**	(0.050)**	(0.117)**	(0.146)**
age	1.000	1.007	0.979	0.989
	(0.00063)	(0.0018)**	(0.0043)**	(0.0066)
first primary	1.016	1.123	0.930	1.108
	(0.017)	(0.054)*	(0.110)	(0.173)
second primary	1.031	1.264	1.006	1.230
	(0.020)	(0.068)**	(0.146)	(0.1981)
per capita househ.	1.000	1.000	0.999	1.000
income	(0.000047)**	(0.00016)	(0.00035)	(0.00068)
Observations	27179	17473	15481	5545

Standard errors in parentheses
* significant at 5%; ** significant at 1%
(1) occupational state: formal
(2) occupational state: informal
(3) occupational state: self employed
(4) occupational state: searching

having completed all eight years of primary school increases the transition probability up to 26%. These estimates can be interpreted as a sign, that formal work experience itself is a value employers consider when contracting new employees, while for informally employed workers, the educational level plays a role. Having primary school completed is naturally valued higher than having just completed the basic four years, but both effects are positive and increase transition rates substantially.

The last covariate tested for is the per capita household income. The per capita household income is highly significant only for formal workers, but the hazard ratio is close to 1.00 and has therefore no substantive effect. So the income available in the household of a person does not have an influence on transitions into formality, at least not for the groups of individuals considered in this sample. I also included this covariate squared, and in higher exponentials, and took its log, but it remained insignificant.

Concluding from these numbers, women and heads of household with primary school level completed are more likely to transit into formality if they had a job before. This may be explained by the stronger wish of female heads of household to increase security for themselves and their family members than in the case of male heads of household (Berger and Buvinic 1989).

9.2 Transitions From Unemployment Considering the Labor History

To test my hypothesis about informal employment being a stepping stone for workers who would not be able to directly find employment in the formal segment, I now include labor history variables in my estimation to differentiate between workers with different work experience. I calculate hazard rates for newcomers to the labor market and for individuals being unemployed and searching for a job. As I am interested in the transition into formal employment, I only report hazard rates for this transition. Results from this estimation are shown in Table 9.2.

All hazard ratios for the covariates for labor market history are smaller than one when 'self-employed' is the comparison group. From the hazard ratios it can be seen that an unemployed individual has a substantially higher likeliness of finding a formal job if he was previously formally rather than informally employed, but the effect is not significant. Formerly informal employment though has a significant effect, reducing the hazard rate to enter formality to 43%. Certainly, informal work experience is less valuable than formal one for an employer who wants to contract a new worker formally, this explains the reduction in the hazard ratio. However, compared to the newcomers hazard ratio the hazard rate for formerly informally employed workers is quite high: being a newcomer significantly reduces the hazard rate of a transition into formality: the hazard rate for newcomers is only 4.5% of that of self-employed individuals, showing that this group is facing enormous difficulties to find formal employment.

The other covariates behave like those for searching individuals in Table 9.1: being male increases the likelihood of entering formality by about 79%, and the position as a head of household increases the hazard of transition up to 56%. The latter covariate though is now significant only at the 5%-level. This is due to the reduction of the sample size from 5545 to 3881 observations. Again, educational levels do not seem to play a significant role for obtaining a formal job when being unemployed and searching. The per capita household income is still not significant with a hazard rate contribution

Table 9.2: Hazard rate contributions for transitions from unemployment to formal employment

Covariate	Hazard Ratio
last job formal	0.921 (0.23)
last job informal	0.437 (2.22)*
newcomer	0.045 (5.84)**
male	1.786 (3.42)**
head of household	1.562 (2.18)*
age	0.991 (0.39)
first primary	1.377 (1.07)
second primary	1.415 (1.07)
per capita household income	1.000 (0.07)
winter	0.968 (0.14)
spring	0.859 (0.80)
summer	0.528 (2.12)*

Observations: 3881. Left-out category: self-employed.
Absolute value of z statistics in parentheses
* significant at 5%; ** significant at 1%

close to one. When taking a closer look at this covariate, a high skewness could be observed. Transforming the covariate did not lead to any change in the estimates; nor did removing the covariate. As this is one of the few covariates controlling for the social background of a person, I still report the estimates. Another explanation for the insignificance and the values of this covariate may be that the effect is already captured by the variable 'duration of unemployment'. Additionally, I included the dummies for the seasons in the Table, and it can be noticed that the summer season significantly reduces the likelihood of unemployed individuals to find a formal job. The unfavorable climatical conditions during the summer months, summer holidays, and not least, carnival may reduce employment during this season.

I also included an error term into the partial likelihood estimation function (see section 8.2.2) to control for unobservable heterogeneity of the workers. The estimation results for this factor did not show any significance. It can therefore be assumed, that unobserved characteristics like motivation do not have an important impact on the outcome of the transition process.

When testing for proportionality of the different subgroups, the results for the group of newcomers indicate that the baseline hazard for this particular group cannot be assumed to be identical to the baseline hazard for the other groups, the former informally and formally employed workers. I therefore specify a separate hazard function for each group according to their labor market history to allow the baseline hazards to vary more freely.

9.3 Estimations for Each Occupational Subgroup

To obtain estimates for each subgroup of individuals searching for a job, I performed a transition analysis for each of these groups. The results are shown in Table 9.3. Hazard ratio values are displayed in columns for the following groups: former formally employed workers, former informally employed workers and newcomers, respectively. The two last columns show values for the groups former formally employed and former informally employed, respectively, including an additional variable about the time worked before. This results from the fact that one of my hypothesis is that informal employment serves as an indicator for employers for the experience of a worker. As learning takes place on-the-job and no official certificates about skills and quality of a worker are issued in informal employment, the new employer may rely on two possible indicators of productivity of the worker: the mere fact that the individual has been employed, and the time he worked in that job. To test for the latter, I included the covariate "time worked before" in the estimations considering only one former occupational state at a time.

I assumed the relationship between this covariate and the hazard ratio to be either a linear or a quadratic one and tested this by also including "time worked before (squared)", but neither of both covariates showed any significance. The estimation for the category of newcomers is lacking results for these covariates as they did not work before and all values of the variable are zero. These

Table 9.3: Hazard rate contributions for different former occupational states

Covariate	(1)	(2)	(3)	(4)	(5)
male	1.397	3.108	1.805	1.403	3.100
	(1.48)	(3.46)**	(0.93)	(1.50)	(3.46)**
head of household	1.706	1.004	4.186	1.725	0.999
	(1.97)*	(0.01)	(1.71)	(2.02)*	(0.00)
age	0.943	1.055	0.489	0.937	1.057
	(1.81)	(1.34)	(2.86)**	(1.95)	(1.36)
first primary	1.307	1.360	16.461	1.325	1.369
	(0.61)	(0.62)	(1.98)*	(0.64)	(0.64)
second primary	1.415	1.559	113.573	1.448	1.573
	(0.75)	(0.83)	(2.45)*	(0.80)	(0.85)
per cap. househ. income	0.999	1.001	1.004	0.999	1.001
	(0.32)	(0.46)	(1.23)	(0.35)	(0.49)
winter	1.127	0.807	0.308	1.108	0.811
	(0.41)	(0.47)	(0.90)	(0.36)	(0.46)
spring	0.765	1.192	0.968	0.768	1.191
	(1.02)	(0.50)	(0.05)	(1.01)	(0.50)
summer	0.547	0.531	0.474	0.548	0.528
	(1.51)	(1.12)	(0.61)	(1.51)	(1.13)
time worked before				1.008	0.996
				(0.89)	(0.29)
Observations	1234	1751	667	1234	1751

Absolute value of z statistics in parentheses
* significant at 5%; ** significant at 1%
(1) former occupational state: formal
(2) former occupational state: informal
(3) former occupational state: newcomer
(4) former occupational state: formal, additional covariate "time worked before"
(5) former occupational state: informal, additional covariate "time worked before"

results indicate that employers do not seem to use the time worked before as an indicator for productivity or skillfulness of the worker, contradicting one of my hypotheses stated above. Another interesting observation in this context is that the educational levels are only significant within the group of newcomers, but do not show any impact either in the group of former formally employed or in that of the informally employed workers. The fact of having been employed before seems to be a stronger signal for employers than the levels of schooling concluded, at least at the low educational levels. Contrary to this, a completed first or second level of primary schooling substantially increases the transition rate to formality of workers currently informally employed (see Table 9.1). These findings indicate that the idea about the function of education as a signal from the worker and as a screening device for the employer does not apply for the selection process for low-skilled formal workers with previous working experience.

Contrary to the informally employed males, being a former informally employed male increases the hazard ratio to enter formal employment by more than three times compared to the hazard rate of former informally employed women. For the other occupational states, the sex of a worker does not play a significant role.

As for the estimation reported in Section 9.2, I controlled for unobserved heterogeneity, but again, no significant effect could be observed.

To obtain more information on how the different former occupational states influence transitions into formality, I calculated transition rates into formality. Figure 9.1 shows the cumulative hazard functions for the four different occupational states, clearly indicating the differences. The hazard to enter formal employment for former formally employed and former informally employed workers increases sharply, while the slope for the newcomers is quite shallow at the beginning. The function for the group of newcomers constantly lies below the hazard functions of the other groups.

For values above 50 months, observations are only available for the group of newcomers, therefore no evidence can be obtained about the hazard curves for the other occupational states. Note that the hazard functions in this figure are not all proportional to each other. This follows naturally as I specified different hazard functions for each subgroup of workers, according to their work history. The proportionality-assumption therefore is only valid within each of these subgroups: individuals of one group, for example the newcomers, are assumed to have the same baseline hazard. Individuals of different groups are allowed to have differing hazard functions including different baseline hazards. Therefore, the hazard functions may appear not to be proportional within the competing risks framework.

Transition rates for formerly informally employed workers are substantially higher than those for newcomers. These results allow me to assume that informal employment may be considered as a stepping stone to formality for young unemployed male workers who would not have the chance to enter formality

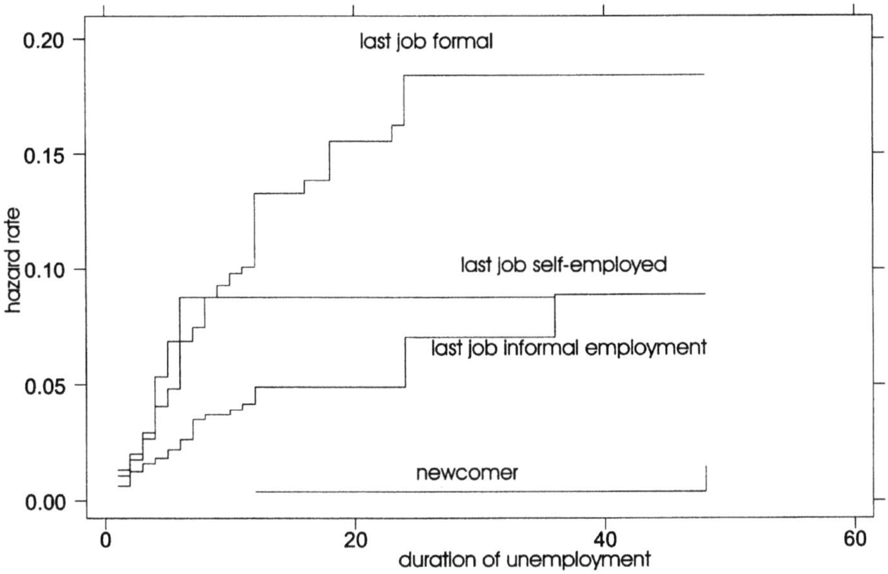

Source: "Monthly Labor Survey (PME) (1999), own calculations"

Figure 9.1: Transition rates into formal employment.

in a direct way. Informality also serves as a stepping stone for young female workers, if they are currently employed and searching for a new job.[1]

[1]The hazard rate of 0.893 for informally employed men in Table 9.1 indicates that these men are about 11% less likely than women to transit into formality.

Chapter 10

Conclusion

In this part of the thesis, I have investigated the rigidity of the labor market segmentation, the stepping stone hypothesis for informal employment and its determinants, like the 'time worked before'.

The dual labor market theory assumes that the structures concerning work attitudes and required skills develop differently in both labor market segments. Workers adapt their attitudes to these different structures and are therefore less likely to transit into the other segment as their work spell in one segment increases. Following from this approach, segmentation should be rigid for the majority of the economically active population. Still, the term "rigid" remains blurred as there is no transition rate level defined as a criterion for rigid segmentation anywhere in the literature. The cross tabulations of labor market transitions show that for the selected non-academic professions transitions can be observed from formal to informal employment and vice versa. As the transitions are observed from one month to the next, the reported transition rates are high, considering the short period of observation. This supports my hypothesis that the "first" and "second labor market segment" in Brazil do not show the almost complete separation assumed by the dual market theorists, at least when only non-academic professions are considered.

My second hypothesis states that informal employment can be considered as signal for potential employers and therefore a stepping stone to formality. This hypothesis is investigated by estimating hazard rates using semi-parametric Cox regression models in a competing risks framework. Three different estimations are performed. First, hazard rates for a sample containing working as well as searching individuals are estimated. Although the data does not allow me to identify on-the-job transitions within the same segment, hazard rates for transitions into different segments can be obtained. The estimation results show that 'head of household' is the only covariate significant for all groups of occupational states considered, and the impact is always positive. An interesting result is that being male reduces the probability of transiting from informal to formal employment by almost 11% compared to the transition hazard for women, a result until now not reported in the literature. In contrast to this result, within the group of unemployed, men are 82% more likely to transit into formality than women. The results for the impact of education on the transition into formal employment indicate a significant and positive effect for informally employed workers, as supported by both theory approaches presented above. Again in contrast, education has no significant impact on the transition out of unemployment.

The second estimation considers only job seekers and calculates the hazard rates for transition into formal employment simultaneously for all groups of unemployed so that the impact of the individual labor history can be obtained. The hazard rates show that newcomers are very unlikely (around 5%) to enter formal employment compared to all other groups of former occupational states, reflecting for example the difficulties of young adults to find a first job. Compared to this group of first-entrants, the hazard rate for former informally employed individuals is around 44%, supporting my stepping stone hypothesis for informal employment.

In the third estimation, hazard rates have been calculated separately for the different groups of job searchers according to their former occupational state. This is done to see whether the impact of the covariates differ between groups with different labor history. It can be seen that 'head of household' is now only significant for individuals that have been formally employed before. The sex of a person shows only a significant impact on the transitions of formerly informally employed. This time men are even more than three times more likely to find formal employment than women. This result again contrasts the one obtained for the on-the-job transitions from informal employment. Another interesting finding is that education only plays a role for the newcomers, with more education leading to higher transition rates. So unlike for informally employed individuals, education does not seem to be a signal for those with former informal employment experience.

Additionally, the covariate 'time worked before' was included in the regressions for the groups of former formally and informally employed to test my third hypothesis that the 'time worked before' is a signal for the experience of the worker. In this case, no evidence could be found that the time worked before has any impact on the transition rates into formality, thus this finding provides no support for my hypothesis.

The results of the estimations and the graphed hazard rates allow me to confirm that informal employment can be considered as a stepping stone for young unemployed male workers, who would not have had the chance to enter formal employment directly, as indicated by the extremely low hazard rates for the newcomers. Women show higher hazard ratios for a transition into formality when they manage to do an on-the-job transition without being intermediately unemployed. So this part of the thesis explores the different effects of informal employment on the allocation of males and females into formal employment that have not been studied in the literature before.

In this part of the thesis, I investigated the workers' mobility between formal and informal employment in the segmented Brazilian labor market. The focus was especially on transitions into formal employment and on the role informal employment played in this process. In the last part to come, I will pay more attention to the search process itself that has been neglected until now in this thesis. In particular, the impact of a worker's labor history on the choice of search methods and the impact of different search methods on the result of job search are studied.

Part III

Job Search in a Segmented Labor Market

Chapter 11

Introduction

11.1 Motivation and Aim of Part III

Theoretical models of job search like the search approach tend to treat the process of job search as a uniform activity. It is only recently that differentiation between search channels is being more regularly included in the theoretical modelling of job search, reflecting empirical findings that the choice of search methods matters at least as much as time devoted to searching does (Böheim and Taylor 2002). In countries with labor markets where employment is heavily segmented into formal and informal working relationships the choice of the search channel may be even more important. In these labor markets the use of a specific search channel does not only have an impact on the duration of unemployment and the subsequent wage, but additionally may influence the labor market state in which an unemployed person finally ends up. As soon as there are more forms of dependent employment relationships, the use of some of the search channels may increase the probability of getting, for example, a formal employment, while other channels are more likely to lead to informal employment, or even increase the probability of remaining searching, or becoming inactive. There exists a range of theoretical and empirical papers explicitly considering the impact of different search channels on the outcome of the search process. All the empirical studies focus on labor markets in industrialized countries, which may be the reason that none of the studies differentiates between exits into formal and informal employment.

In this part of the thesis I therefore investigate the impact of the choice of search methods on the outcome of job search in the segmented labor market of Brazil. Expanding on a search theory approach that already allows for several different search channels, I additionally consider four different exit states next to remaining unemployed. I argue that increasing segmentation, even in industrialized countries, and the already fairly segmented labor markets of developing countries, call for a more differentiated treatment of the available search channels.

Empirically I follow two different lines of investigation concerning the search channels. First I examine the impact of the labor history of an individual on the choice of the search method. In a second approach I examine the effects of various job search methods on the transitions of unemployed Brazilian workers into the different occupational states.

The reasoning for the first line of investigation is as follows. In Brazil, employers use different channels to search for new employees. Jobs requiring special skills, academic training or other superior education are often advertised in the newspapers. Public employers like the police and public administration, but also universities and the public research institutes usually recruit new employees via tests or examinations; I will refer to this channel simply as 'test'. The public sector also provides assistance in job search via the National System for Employment (SINE). SINE agencies organize qualification and training programs, provide assistance in job placement and job matching for the unemployed, and administrate parts of the unemployment insurance like the payments of benefits. Recently SINE has returned into the focus of political interest, as evaluations of the program show poor performance in all activities (Ramos and de Freitas 1998; Ministério de Trabalho e Emprego (MTE) 1999).

I argue that vacancies in different labor market segments (formal/informal) are promoted via different channels and that part of the labor market segmentation originates from lack of information on vacancies in the formal sector. Some search methods are more effective for finding a job in the formal sector, other channels tend to lead to informal employment. This assumption implies that labor market policies can model labor market transitions up to a certain degree by designing customized job-matching programs. Job placement or job matching could improve labor search processes by facilitating access to labor market information that otherwise may be hard to obtain for unemployed workers. To design an efficient job-placement service, a careful analysis of potential focus groups is essential to maximize efficiency. The design of public job placement assistance might improve individual utility by promoting search methods shifting more workers into formal employment.

To evaluate the different search methods in my second line of investigation, I estimate their impact on exit rates of unemployed Brazilian workers by using multinomial logit models. "Exit rates" here designate the probability of transition from one labor market state to another. To obtain more information about the search process, I first test the influence of the former labor market state on the choice of search methods. I assume that most individuals will consider a job in the formal sector as a better option than informal work. I therefore expect to find a search pattern for the group of formerly formally employed workers, as they already have the experience of finding a job in this sector. However, for the formerly informally employed, no specific and determined search pattern is expected. Second, the effect of different search methods on exit rates in general and exit rates into the different occupational states 'formally employed', 'informally employed', 'self-employed', 'searching' and 'inactive' is investigated. My hypothesis here is that there are specific search channels for the different sectors. Although the fact of holding a formal or an informal job does not allow one to deduce the educational background, Soares, Carvalho, and Kipnis (2003) show evidence that individuals with higher educational levels are more likely to hold formal jobs. So I assume that search channels that use print media or involve studying and writing, like examinations, are more likely to be chosen by higher educated individuals and therefore more likely to lead to formal jobs.

This part of the thesis is structured as follows: in the remainder of this chapter, I first review the studies on the effects of different search channels on exit rates. The purpose of this review is to check for repeating patterns of the impacts of search methods on transition rates of unemployed workers. A description of the used sample is also part of this chapter. An overview concerning job search in Brazil, the public employment service and the unemployment insurance follows in Chapter 12. In Chapter 13.1, a basic search model with endogenous search intensities is presented. This is followed by some model extensions allowing for different search channels and exits into different labor market segments. In the last section of the chapter, I formulate a theoretical model adapted to segmented labor markets, considering both different search channels and also transition possibilities into more than two occupational exit states. The econometric model used for the estimation, a multinomial logistic regression model, is explained in Chapter 14. In Chapter 15, the estimation results for both lines of investigation are discussed in detail and conclusions are drawn in Chapter 16.

11.2 Search Methods in the Literature

The process of job search has been quite heavily investigated during the last three decades, both theoretically and empirically. A major focus has been laid on the impact of unemployment benefits on the duration as well as the outcome of job search. Reservation wages have been subject to another line of research. Atkinson and Micklewright (1991) as well as Devine and Kiefer (1991) provide comprehensive surveys on the research activities in this field. However, only relatively few studies though focus on the impact of search methods on the outcome of the search process; see Devine and Kiefer (1991) for an early overview.

In one of the early works, Holzer (1988) differentiates between the effects of various job search channels used by unemployed young U.S. workers by analyzing data from the Youth Cohort of the National Longitudinal Survey in 1979. He assumes an endogenous arrival rate of job offers that depends on the search channel chosen, namely 'friends and relatives', 'newspapers', 'state employment agencies', 'direct employer contact' and 'other'. The choice of search method by the workers depends on the costs and expected productivity related to the different channels. The decision to accept an offer is determined by the reservation wage. Concerning the impact of search methods on the outcome of the search process, Holzer estimates two probit regressions. The first one models the number of methods used, and the second the type of search channel. The results show a positive and significant coefficient for the total number of methods for the first regression and positive and significant coefficients for 'friends and relatives' and, although weaker, 'newspapers', for the second regression.

Blau and Robins (1990) analyze the use of search methods using data from the Employment Opportunity Pilot Projects of 1980 (EOPP). They estimate the job offer and job acceptance rates of U.S. workers conditioned on the use of various search channels. Both unemployed and employed workers enter their sample. Like Holzer, they find positive, significant impacts for the 'friends and family' channel.

Using British labor market data, Gregg and Wadsworth (1996) evaluate the public employment service. They report high rates for the use of this search channel (around 70 %), being, together with 'media' (advertisements) the most popular search method. Other methods considered are: 'friends and relatives', 'direct applications', 'private employment agencies' and 'other'. Probit regression is used to estimate exit rates out of unemployment. The analysis shows positive and significant coefficients for 'direct applications', 'advertisements' and 'jobcenter', the latter showing highest impact for long-term unemployed workers. Gregg and Wadsworth also estimate the probability of using a certain search channel conditional on finding a job. Interestingly, the reception of unemployment insurance benefits has a negative and significant impact on the use of the public employment service, indicating a lower probability of workers receiving benefits to find a job by the help of the 'jobcentre'. The category 'jobcentre' is also the only one seemingly suited for low-skilled workers and on which the unemployment spell duration has a positive effect.

Besides Holzer (1988), Koning, van den Berg, and Ridder (1997) and Van Den Berg and Klaauw (2001) present two of the few papers providing a theoretical background for their empirical studies. Koning, van den Berg, and Ridder (1997) investigate the impact of individual characteristics on the choice of search methods and on the impact of the different search channels on unemployment duration, duration of the subsequent job and subsequent wages. Their theoretical innovation is the introduction of search channel-specific wage distributions. They consider two search channels: a formal one where the search is conducted by sending application letters, and an informal one where job offers arrive by referral by a third individual, usually one already employed in that specific firm. Their results indicate that both search channels do not generate significantly different wage offers, and that unemployment spells are not different for these channels. They therefore conclude for their Netherlands labor market data that the distinction between formal and informal search channels is irrelevant. Van Den Berg and Klaauw (2001) investigate the impact of counselling and monitoring on the duration of unemployment and the choice of search channels of Netherlands unemployed workers participating in a social experiment. In their theoretical model they also allow for two search channels, a formal and an informal one. The formal search channel comprises of three different search channels: the public employment service, commercial employment agencies and personnel advertisements. The informal channel includes open application letters and search through friends and family. Individuals may use both channels simultaneously. They consider only two states into which the unemployed may exit: either an individual transits to work or he stays unemployed. Van Den Berg and Klaauw (2001) find that the use of counselling and monitoring stimulates the use of formal search channels, reducing the use of the informal ones at the same time. They do not estimate the impact of the use of either formal or informal search methods. Still, in a theoretical expansion of their model, they predict that workers with lower exit chances from unemployment rely to a relatively larger extent on the use of formal search channels.

Addison and Portugal (2002) analyze the impact of search channels on exit rates from unemployment and on future earnings using Portuguese labor market data. The search methods investigated are 'direct approach', 'friends/relatives', 'advertisement', 'public employment agency', 'self employment' 'examinations' and 'other'. The categories 'self-employment' and 'examination' are treated like job-finding methods, considered as search channels from the employer's side. Although observing these seven categories of channels, Addison and Portugal focus especially on the effectiveness of the public employment service; they find low hit rates and job offers that are more likely to be low-paid and of short-term nature. Various factors complicating the analysis of this search channel are reported that leave the results ambiguous.

Apart from the exit out of unemployment, Böheim and Taylor (2002) also study the impact of search channels on the re-employment wage. They allow for the simultaneous use of different search channels and consider the two occupational states 'employed' and 'unemployed'. Using British data, they find that the most successful channel for re-entry into the labor market is to apply directly to a potential employer, especially when combined with answering advertisements and asking friends and family. Concerning subsequent wages, answering advertisements seems to be the best strategy. As a further result, Böheim and Taylor find that the choice of search methods affects the outcome of the search process more than search intensity, measured here in the number of search methods used.

The results of the studies presented above are summarized in Table 11.1, the table only includes those studies testing for the impact of different search channels and is by no means comprehensive. All of the above studies were based on labor market data from industrialized countries. Still, no distinctive pattern of impact of search methods on labor market transitions can be discerned. This is certainly due to the small number of studies. Also, the structure of the labor markets and design of labor market policies differ for the different countries. Additionally, the samples used for the U.S. studies are not representative for overall U.S. labor market.

The Youth Cohort data used by Holzer (1988) only comprises young workers aged 16 to 23, and the data used by Blau and Robins (1990) stems from the EOPP, an experimental program specially designed to assist low income workers, oversampling low and middle income families. The data used by Van Den Berg and Klaauw (2001) is taken from a social experiment with full randomization. But all studies report that the public employment service has a low efficiency, showing relatively low hit rates compared to other search methods. Especially in the case of Portugal, job offers reported by firms are of bad quality, and numbers of reported vacancies are low. The poor performance of the public employment service seems to be common public opinion held by both employers and job searchers, thus leading to a self enforcing mechanism. The role of the public employment service will be discussed in more detail in Section 12.2.1.

As none of the studies considers the use of different search channels simultaneously with exits into different labor market segments, my aim is now to investigate the effect of different search channels on exit rates into employment split up into various occupational states providing different utilities to workers.

Table 11.1: Empirical studies on the effects of job search Methods

Author	Holzer (1988)	Blau and Robins (1990)	Gregg and Wadsworth (1996)	Koning, van den Berg and Ridder (1997)	van den Berg and van der Klaauw (2001)	Addison and Portugal (2002)	Böheim and Taylor (2002)
Data	U.S. labor market data	U.S. labor market data	British labor market data	Netherlands market data	Netherlands market data	Portug. labor market data	British labor market data
Dependent variable	job offers received	offer rates, acceptance rates	exiting unemploym.	exiting unemploym. and wages	exiting unemploym.	exiting unemploym.	exiting unemploym. and wages
Search channels							
friends and relatives	positive effect	positive effect		none			positive effect
advertise-ments	positive effect (weak)		positive effect	none			positive effect
asked employer			positive effect				positive effect
public employ-ment service			positive effect				
efficiency of the public employment service	low	low	low		none	low	

My hypothesis is that different search channels lead to different occupational states and that part of the labor force exiting into informal employment or self employment could find formal jobs if they had better access to labor market information and assistance with the application procedure. The study of segmented labor markets like the Brazilian one might be interesting for the analysis of labor search processes in industrialized countries, too. The segments of the Brazilian labor market reflect the grouping of jobs with similar qualities that, in industrialized countries, are all collected under the one labor market state of formal employment.

11.3 The Data

The sample used here is again taken from the Monthly Employment Surveys (PME) collected in 1999. For more general information on the PME please refer to Chapter 4. As estimating exit rates requires data of two consecutive months, three blocks of data have been constructed each combining two months of PME survey data. Blocks are composed as follows: January-February, June-July and November-December. This has been done to avoid the same individual entering the sample twice while investigating the probability of labor market reentry when being unemployed or inactive in the month before. Every block of data is treated as an independent one.

The PME distinguishes between the following occupational states: employed, self-employed, employer, searching and inactive. For my analysis, I further divide the employed into formally and informally employed by controlling for the possession of a labor card. The PME questionnaire additionally collects information about the search method used by individuals who reported searching in the week of reference. The search methods and the set-up of the questionnaire are discussed in more detail in Section 12.1.

The sample used for the estimation contains data on 8899 individuals. Of these, 3891 workers (43.72%) had held formal jobs before unemployment, 3118 (35.04%) were informally employed, 996 (11.19%) were newcomers and 894 (10.05%) were self-employed. Additional information about the covariates used for estimation is provided in Table B.2 in the appendix. The sample size is not the same for all estimations computed. For example when estimating the impact of unemployment insurance benefits, only former formally employed individuals enter the sample, as they are the only ones who can achieve entitlement to benefits.

Many studies (Böheim and Taylor 2002; Gregg and Wadsworth 1996; Holzer 1988) focus on male job searchers, as the share of female searchers in their samples was very low. This is not the case for Brazil; in the sample used here, 4064 (45.67%) of the 8899 individuals observed are female. The proportions of male and female employment in the formal segment are almost equal: 45.92% versus 41.12%, respectively. In informal employment, women dominate slightly with a proportion of 38.31% versus the male proportion of 32.29%. About 15% of the women report that they are newcomers, versus 8.8% of the males. The year 1999 showed a slight upswing in the overall economic situation, a fact that may have encouraged more women to enter the labor force. Table B.1 reports the whole cross tabulation of sex and former occupational state.

Chapter 12

Job Search and Labor Market Policies in Brazil

12.1 Search Channels

Brazilians face the same decision problem when choosing a search method as do unemployed workers from industrialized countries. They have to choose the type of search channel or channels to be used and the search intensity to be invested in each channel. They also have to consider in which segment they want to work: formal or informal employment or self-employment.

All individuals who reported searching for a job in the week of reference were asked about the method they chose for their job search. Search conducted on-the-job is therefore not recorded in the questionnaire. The questionnaire differentiates between the following search channels: (1) asked employer, (2) took an ability test, (3) consulted the public employment service or the union, (4) answered to or posted an advertizement, (5) asked friends and family, and (6) other. Unfortunately, the design of the questionnaire does not allow the interviewed to report more than one search channel. Furthermore, there is no question capturing the search channel that led to a successful wage offer, e.g. one that the individual accepted. Most interestingly, many employment survey questionnaires lack this latter question. The option to report more than one search channel may lead to difficulties of the treatment of this information, as the individuals would also have to report the proportion of time devoted to each search channel (Addison and Portugal 2002). Without this additional information about the weight of each specific channel, and without any information about the successful channel, the gained insight on the search process would still be small. Some authors take the number of channels used as a proxy for search intensity (see for example Böheim and Taylor (2002)). In my analysis I assume that the search channel reported by an individual is the one the individual either used most intensively or believes to be the most successful one. Table 12.1 reports the search channels used by individuals with different labor market histories. The numbers show that in Brazil the channel used by far the most is 'asked employer', with 60 to 70% of individuals of all different labor market groups reporting this channel. 'Asking friends and family' is the next popular one, with an average of 14% of the individuals in the sample giving this option. For this channel there is a larger spread, with only 11% of former formally employed using this channel but 22% of the former self-employed. Former informally employed take a middle position between these both extreme groups.

In the literature, the channel 'asked employer' is classified as an 'informal' one as the process of job search is not formalized by a special procedure like a test, or advertisements posted in a journal or the internet, or an intermediate like an agency. The worker simply directly contacts the employer for whom he would like to work, or sends an unsolicited application.

Some authors studying the impact of search channels generally find that the informal search channels like 'asking employer' or 'asking friends and family' yield more and higher-wage offers (Montgomery 1991). Contrary to this, Koning, van den Berg, and Ridder (1997) find that informal search methods like the channel 'asked friends and family' do not lead to higher wages or an increased job acceptance rate. For Brazil, the story is different. Asking an employer directly or asking friends and family may be quite effective in generating job offers, especially in some of the low-skill professions. But it may also lead to a relatively larger share of job offers without a labor card, as negotiations are lead directly between employer and aspiring employee and no offers are posted in printed media or at the public employment service. So the probability of being controlled for informally contracting employees is substantively lower for the employer and informal labor contracts are more likely. Asking friends and family also may serve as the channel of last resort: if an individual cannot find a job on the labor market, social bonds within the family may still make one of the relatives offer a job at the gas station or in the fruit stall. Most of these jobs leave the individual underemployed and do not provide much in terms of human capital accumulation, but are still accepted to sustain a living.

The group of formal search channels includes the methods 'test', 'advertisement' and 'agency or union'. These search methods are considered as formal in the literature as they involve formalized processes like testing or an intermediary like a newspaper or an agency. Table 12.1 shows that the formal channels are less frequently reported by the interviewed individuals. Altogether they account for only 16% of the used channels, with 'test' being the least reported

Table 12.1: Cross tabulation of former labor market state and search method chosen

former occupation	search method chosen test	agency or union	advertisement	friends and family	other	asked employer	Total
formal	19	412	329	425	51	2655	3891
	0.49	10.59	8.46	10.92	1.31	68.23	100.00
	36.54	51.12	49.62	32.42	51.00	44.49	43.72
informal	18	249	201	536	32	2082	3118
	0.58	7.99	6.45	17.19	1.03	66.77	100.00
	34.62	30.89	30.32	40.88	32.00	34.89	35.04
newcomer	10	90	72	153	7	664	996
	1.00	9.04	7.23	15.36	0.70	66.67	100.00
	19.23	11.17	10.86	11.67	7.00	11.13	11.19
self employed	5	55	61	197	10	566	894
	0.56	6.15	6.82	22.04	1.12	63.31	100.00
	9.62	6.82	9.20	15.03	10.00	9.49	10.05
Total	52	806	663	1311	100	5967	8899
	0.58	9.06	7.45	14.73	1.12	67.05	100.00
	100.00	100.00	100.00	100.00	100.00	100.00	100.00

Source: Monthly Labor Survey (PME) (1999), own calculations
first row: absolute numbers
second row: row percentages
third row: column percentages

channel, with only up to 1% in each group. The search method 'test' is especially common in the public sector in Brazil, but the overall number of promoted jobs is rather low. This channel involves reading and writing skills and the will to study for the test. Besides the prerequisite that an individual must access to the information about the existence of the channel, the required skills are additional limiters for certain groups of job searchers. Similar conditions apply to the channel 'advertisement', where access to newspapers, reading and writing skills and the will to produce letters and application material are necessary. Additionally, there are costs for the sources and the material. To participate in the tests, sometimes a registration fee has to be paid, but in most cases this will be refunded when the individual shows up for testing. Of the formal channels, the 'agency or union' is the one involving the least skills and resources. Still, people have to go there, probably wait for a considerable time and discuss their personal situation with an unknown person, especially if they cannot read and need aid to scan the posted offers. Interestingly, former formally employed individuals show largest percentages in using 'agency or union' and 'advertizement' of all occupational groups, but the lowest percentages for 'test'. The low proportion of former formally employed workers choosing 'test' is due to the kind of jobs in the public sector where tests serve as selection criterion: Although scientific staff like researchers are also recruited via tests, most people taking the test try to get a job in the police or in low-skill jobs in the public administration. In the latter professions, comparatively more jobs are offered and more people take the tests. Of the three 'formal' search channels, the public employment service has been studied most as it is part of the active labor market policy instruments and therefore under direct control of the policy decision makers. More detailed information on the Brazilian public employment service is given in the following section.

12.2 Labor Market Policies

12.2.1 Active Labor Market Policies

In Brazil, the National Employment Service (SINE) has been providing job-placement services since it's foundation in 1975.[1] By the end of the year 1998, 941 SINE agencies had been established throughout Brazil, most of them in the densely populated south-east region containing the metropoles of Rio de Janeiro and São Paulo. The agencies collect vacancies and offer counselling to all Brazilians searching for a job, including former informally or self-employed persons and newcomers to the labor market. Despite almost 30 years of existence, a more recent evaluation of the system's performance is quite scarce. Cardoso (2000) finds that only 5% of all hired persons found their job via SINE; the true percentage is even lower considering the high and increasing rates of informally and self-employed workers. An earlier study by Ramos and de Freitas (1998) tries to compare the performance of SINE with results obtained by public employment services in OECD countries. The authors encounter difficulties to find suitable indicators for the comparison of performance as the public employment systems within the OECD countries are already very diverse. When evaluating the Brazilian system, they find that the interest of workers in the services provided by SINE, measured by the ratio of registered individuals versus the overall number of hired and fired workers in that period,

[1] See Section 3.7.1 for general information on SINE.

is low. In 1998 only 13.5% of the entitled individuals in the south-east region registered with SINE. The highest registration rate was in the southern region where about 62.5% of the entitled individuals are registered. Performance was no better on the employers' side: on Brazilian average, only 6.51% of all vacancies available were posted at the SINE agencies. Low registration of job searchers and low vacancy posting are connected to each other and lead to a downward spiral explaining the low importance of the service provided by SINE concerning the intermediation of the overall labor force. Many other empirical studies come to the same conclusions regarding the performance of public employment services, see Table 11.1 in Section 11.2. Kröger and van Suntum (1999) provide a theoretical analysis of the public employment service concluding that this service has a positive impact on reducing frictional unemployment duration and increasing the employment ratio and the absolute number of employed. The effect on the magnitude of the future wages is uncertain. They review empirical studies on the performance of the public employment service in various European countries[2] and find the positive impact confirmed. Fougère, Pradel, and Roger (2002) come to the same results, both theoretically and empirically, for French labor market data.

The Ministry of Labor and Employment itself provides annual data on the performance of the different areas of activity of SINE and computes indicators used to evaluate the system. Table 12.2 reports these numbers and indicators for the year 2000. In a detailed evaluation of SINE covering the years 1991 to 1998, the Ministry defines various concepts to assess the performance of the different areas of activity of SINE Ministério de Trabalho e Emprego (MTE) (1999):

- Productivity: quantity of rendered service per employee of SINE or per agency, per unit of time.
- Efficiency (eficiência): quantity of financial resources used per unit of service and time.
- Effectiveness of services (eficácia): adequacy of the rendered services concerning the attainment of the goal (or similarly: attainment of the intermediate goals necessary to reach the final goal), in a determined period of time.
- Capacity of covering: capacity of service to the public as a function of the number of service points, the number of staff employed or the volume of financial resources spent.

[2]They present results for Denmark, Germany, Great Britain and Sweden.

- Covering: individuals using the services offered by the SINE agencies compared to the group entitled to these services (effective and potential).
- Overall effectiveness (efetividade): relationship between the realized result and the original goal.

The indicators listed in Table 12.2 are used to measure the **effectiveness** of the service of SINE, that is the adequacy of the rendered services concerning the goal of matching job searchers and vacancies. The first indicator listed, the ratio of individuals sent to an employer versus number of registered individuals (S/R), suggests that about 50% of the persons registered at SINE agencies received a job offer via SINE. This proportion does not indicate if half of the registered individuals received job offers or if a certain group of individuals received more than one offer per person because of their special characteristics. Although the proportion of distributed offers is highest in the economically strongest south-east region[3], the share of individuals matched via SINE is lowest in this region. Ramos and de Freitas (1998) conclude that especially in the metropolitan area of São Paulo there may be other, more effective or at least more attractive search channels than the public employment service. Unfortunately, there are no data on the number of job offers received by individuals not registered at SINE agencies, so no comparison can be made in this case. The next indicator, 'matched/registered', shows an average of 12%, with a rate for the south-east region of only 9%. Even considering that all these indicators are based on flow numbers and not on stocks, this is quite a low rate. The indicator 'vacancies per registered' gives the maximum percentage of workers that can be matched, low percentages indicate that the number of vacancies is very low. Percentages vary around 30% for all regions, the south being lowest and the north highest. On average, 2 persons were sent per vacancy (indicator S/V), only in the north the ratio was substantially lower (1.5 persons per vacancy). Of the vacancies posted at SINE agencies, the north scored highest in matching them with unemployed registered at the agency, with 72% of the vacancies matched. This was twice the percentage of matches performed in the south-east region, where only 34% of the posted vacancies were actually filled by individuals sent by SINE agencies. The Brazilian average was at 45% of the posted offers. Considering the percentage of people finding a job versus those sent out, the ratio was substantially lower than that of the filled vacancies. Again, the northern region scored best with 47% of those sent accepting the work or being accepted by the employer, versus 16% in the south-east region. The nation-wide average was 23%.

[3]This region comprises the states Rio de Janeiro and São Paulo with their metropoles.

Table 12.2: Numbers and performance indicators of SINE activities for the year 2000

Region	registered	vacancies	sent	matched	S/R	M/R	V/R	S/V	M/V	M/S
North	163,440	51,841	80,125	37,507	49	23	32	1.5	72	47
North-East	717,506	184,186	354,416	104,479	49	15	26	1.9	57	29
Central-West	300,729	90,640	169,592	49,330	56	16	30	1.9	54	29
South-East	2,253,764	623,841	1,306,019	209,479	58	9	28	2.1	34	16
South	1,370,307	330,976	649,726	180,913	47	13	24	2.0	55	28
Brazil	4,805,746	1,281,484	2,559,878	581,708	53	12	27	2.0	45	23

Source: Ministério de Trabalho e Emprego (MTE) (2003c)
registered: all workers contacting SINE agencies
vacancies: all jobs posted at the SINE agencies
sent: all registered individuals receiving an offer via SINE
matched: all registered workers transiting into a formal employment intermediated by SINE
S/R: Sent/Registered in %
M/R: Matched/Registered in %
V/R: Vacancies/Registered in %
S/V: Sent/Vacancies in %
M/V: Matched/Vacancies in %
M/S: Matched/Sent in %

The productivity of SINE is measured by the indicator 'matched workers per SINE agent'. This is only a rough proxy, as the productivity of the agencies may depend on many other factors like technical equipment, spatial distribution of the agencies, to name only some. As it is difficult to assess the maximal productivity of a SINE agent, only the improvement versus the productivity of the previous years is reported. From 1997 to 1998, with the exception of the central-east region, the number of matched workers per agent increased in all regions. Most increases were small, ranging around 10%, with the number of individuals matched per agent varying between 20 and 40 in the different regions. Only in the southern region, the ratio increased by 20%, from 77 matched workers to 98 workers, and in the North an increase of more than 100%, but from a far lower level of 17 to 35 workers, could be observed.[4]

To determine the efficiency in the definition presented by the Ministério de Trabalho e Emprego (MTE) (1999), the financial resources allocated to the public employment service would have to be exactly determined. As this is not possible due to the current structure of the SINE, the variable costs are used as a proxy. For 1998 the MTE reports an average cost of R$ 111.60[5] per matched worker and regard this value as a benchmark for efficiency. Agencies needing more resources to match an individual are considered less efficient, those needing fewer, more efficient. Only the northern and the southern region report costs below the benchmark, and costs in the south-east region are twice as high as the benchmark value.

The effectiveness of SINE is evaluated via the indicators 'registered/ dismissed', 'vacancies posted at SINE agencies/hirings in the formal segment', and 'matched/ hirings in the formal segment'.[6] The higher the ratios of these three indicators, the better the performance of SINE in the formal labor market. As the latter two indicators have already been discussed earlier in this section, I only report values for the first one as evaluated in Ministério de Trabalho e Emprego (MTE) (1999). In 1998, the national average of 'registered/dismissed' was 28.74%. This percentage, which is already quite low, and even lower if one considers that part of the registered may have held informal employment before, or are newcomers, thereby reducing the percentage even more. The observed values of this indicator follow the pattern of the other indicators with the regions North and South performing at around 60%, and the others between 29 and 39%, with the exception of the south-east region, where only 13.5% of the formally dismissed are registered with SINE.

[4]For exact numbers, please refer to Ministério de Trabalho e Emprego (MTE) (1999).

[5]About US$ 55 in values of 1998.

[6]The term 'dismissed' includes all individuals loosing formal employment in the period, 'matched' are those obtaining employment via intermediation of SINE.

12.2.2 Passive Labor Market Policies

In the standard search theory approaches, unemployment insurance benefits play a role in reducing search costs. It is therefore usually assumed that higher benefits and longer payment periods lead to a certain persistence in the state of unemployment (Belzil 2001; Bover, Arellano, and Bentolila 2002; Røed and Zhang 2003). In the basic search model, neither the previous work situation nor the duration of unemployment affect the probability of reentering the labor market. It may though be assumed that the length of the unemployment spell will have a negative effect on the reemployment probability, as employers will assume that the higher qualified workers will be hired first. Loss of skills and diminishing work experience are further factors lowering rehiring probability. Furthermore, Narendranathan and Nickell (1985) point out that individuals collect information during the search process which will result in adjustment of the reservation wage and sectors searched for jobs. There is a trade-off between unemployment insurance benefits leading to higher-wage jobs and time spent unemployed leading to a lower reservation wage.

In this section, I present more details about the performance of the Brazilian unemployment insurance concerning the coverage of workers. For a general description of the structure of the unemployment insurance system in Brazil see Section 3.7.2 in the first part of this thesis.

As the proportion of formally employed workers in Brazil is quite small in relation to the overall labor force, the proportion of the unemployed entitled to unemployment benefits is even smaller. A larger proportion of workers leave formal employment before completing the minimum six months of employment spell required to qualify for benefits. Of the 3883 formerly formally employed individuals of my sample, 1047 (27%) are not entitled to benefits, 595 (15%) receive three months of benefits, 789 (20%) four months and 1452 (37%) five months of benefits. The Ministry of Labor and Employment provides data on the number of former formally employed individuals requesting and receiving benefits (Ministério de Trabalho e Emprego (MTE) 2003b) and on the total numbers of dismissed workers who held a formal job prior to dismissal. Table 12.3 reports some indicators on the ratios of workers requesting and receiving benefits for the years 1998 through 2002.

Over the whole period, the rate of individuals receiving benefits first fell from slightly over 50% to 46%, but then recovered until 2002 to 53%. The rate of those requesting benefits followed the same course, roughly cycling around 50% of all those who lost or quit their formal employment, but constantly lying about one percentage point higher than the rate of benefit receivers.

Table 12.3: Brazilian unemployment insurance benefits: requests and coverage for the years 1998 –2002

Year	received benefit/ dismissed	requested benefit/ dismissed	received benefit/ requested	av. benefit in units of minimum wage
1998	52.02	52.50	99.07	1.56
1999	49.90	51.06	97.72	1.55
2000	46.35	47.29	98.01	1.51
2001	48.02	48.90	98.20	1.48
2002	53.02	53.93	98.31	1.43

Source: Ministério de Trabalho e Emprego (MTE) (2003b), Ministério de Trabalho e Emprego (MTE) (2003a), own calculations
received/dismissed: individuals who received benefits versus dismissed formal workers
requested/dismissed: individuals who requested benefits versus dismissed formal workers
received/requested: individuals who received benefits versus those who requested benefits

Using Brazilian labor market data, Cunningham (1997) investigates the relation between unemployment insurance benefit payments and re-employment wage levels for Brazil and finds no evidence of a wage increase. She concludes that this is a sign of a well integrated labor market. Chahad and Fernandez (2000) test for the impact of unemployment benefit payments on the rate and duration of unemployment in Brazil. They find that the effect of the unemployment insurance is negative for both rate and duration, not because workers entitled to benefits find work in less time, but because they transit into inactivity. The reported effect is especially valid for non-head-of-households. The authors explain this phenomenon by the usually lower income of non-heads, leading to less pressure to find a new job and to reduced search activities which make them more likely to be classified as inactive. Paes De Barros, Corseuil, and Foguel (1999) also report a delayed re-entry into the labor market for Brazilian benefit recipients and an overall higher rate of unemployment. On the other hand, they point out that benefit payments improve matching, leading to better jobs and longer subsequent job duration.

Chapter 13

Theoretical Aspects

13.1 Search Theory – a Basic Model

Individuals looking for a job find themselves confronted with a set of decisions regarding how to perform their job search. Costs and benefits of search have to be balanced while facing uncertainty regarding future income and the quality of the offered jobs. The costs involved in job search are of direct and indirect nature. Direct costs include travel expenses for interviews and the cost of buying information about the labor market via journals and other media. Indirect costs may consist of foregone leisure time and foregone earnings during the time of search. A worker will weigh up these costs against the benefits he expects from the search process: The more an individual searches the more likely he is to discover a good job-match. The problem is that the outcome of search processes is always uncertain and its returns lie in the future. A better-paid job may appear by searching for one more unit, but maybe the best offer already appeared in the first unit of search performed. This is even more important if a good match is not only determined by the magnitude of the wage: A high wage may be combined with a high uncertainty regarding job-stability, so future returns would have to be adjusted according to these additional features, too.

As income from labor is the main source of financial resources for most households, the decision regarding which job to accept, and thereby the related wage, is an important one. To be able to determine the end of the search process, the criterion 'acceptable wage' has to be determined. In early search theory approaches, the formulation of the search process was regarded as an optimal sample size problem (Stigler 1961; Stigler 1962).[1] In this approach, workers collect a random wage sample of size n at a cost c per observation. The job providing the highest wage will be accepted. Under the assumption of perfect information, the cost of sampling wages is zero. A worker will therefore search the entire population of available jobs and then select the one that suits him best. If time limits are introduced, for example, that only one offer can be observed at a point of time, then the size of the sample needs to be taken into account. Remaining unemployed for an additional unit of search imposes additional cost on the worker. A rational worker will only continue searching as long as the marginal benefit of search exceeds its marginal cost. To balance benefits and costs of search, individuals may rely on different search principles. If workers are acting according to the fixed sample size rule, they determine a fixed number n of wage offers they will research before accepting the best wage offer out of this sample. Chow, Robbins, and Siegmund (1971) developed another search principle known as the sequential decision rule, incorporating a process using the sequential 'stopping' approach originating in statistical decision theory (De Groot 1970). Following this search principle, a worker defines a minimum reservation wage below which he will reject job offers. He will therefore search until he finds a job offering a wage equal to or higher than his set reservation wage. Usually, this search strategy leads to "better" results than the fixed sample procedure as its maximal expected present value of future income is higher.

In the following sections, I will first present a standard search model with sequential stopping rule and endogenous search intensities originally developed by Mortensen (Mortensen 1977; Mortensen 1986). In the subsequent sections, the model will be extended to include labor market segmentation, and to allow for different search channels.

In his search model, Mortensen considers an unemployed worker looking for a job. Wage offers w arrive with probability q at random intervals denoted by h, according to a Poisson process with parameter δ. The offers are drawn from a wage offer distribution which remains constant over time and is known to the worker, with $F(w)$ being the cumulative distribution function. The wage offers are assumed to be independent and identically distributed (i.i.d.). This implies that the chance of finding a good job does not depend on the time the worker is already unemployed. Each job has just one observable property: the wage w. Mortensen allows for job-availability by assuming that the number n of wage offers arriving during a period h is an independent random draw with probability function $q(n, h)$, $n = 0, 1, \ldots$ The assumed Poisson distribution for $q(\cdot)$ reflects the time-consuming and sequential search

[1] For an overview on the early developments in search theory, see the surveys by Lippmann and McCall (1976a) and Lippmann and McCall (1976b)

process and the independence of the length of time between the arrivals of wage offers. The wage w is defined as the maximum wage received during one period of length h; and $G(w,n)$ represents the probability that the best of n received offers is less than or equal to w, conditioned on $n \geq 1$.

If an individual accepts a wage offer, the job is assumed to last forever. Devine and Kiefer (1991) point out that this condition may be dropped without crucial changes of results by, for example, introducing layoffs occurring according to a Poisson process. Given these assumptions, the worker optimizes the present discounted value of a job by discounting the future income with discount factor $\beta(h)$. The present discounted value of a permanent job paying wage w is denoted $W(w)$. $W(w)$ is assumed to be continuous and strictly increasing, with $W(0) = 0$. To make a decision to accept a current offer, the worker compares this expected present value of future income, $W(w)$, with the value of continuing to search during the next period, $V(\cdot)$, given the worker's information Ω on the wage offer distribution. A worker will only accept a wage offer if

$$W(w) > V(\Omega). \tag{13.1}$$

Further consider that job search involves costs c in form of time and money, but that the worker has access to unemployment insurance benefits, b, which are paid as a constant amount while the worker is unemployed. Note that Mortensen (1986) does not consider unemployment insurance benefits but leisure time. The benefits b could also be annuity income or the family member's share of the household income, although continuous access to those kinds of income would have an impact on the future stream of income when working (Devine and Kiefer 1991). As the acceptance rule 13.1 also applies to the next period, the value of search for one more period, $V(\Omega)$, can be described by the following function:

$$V(\Omega) = (b-c)h + \beta(h)E\{\max[V(\Omega(t+h)), W(w_{t+h})] | \Omega(t) = \Omega\}, \tag{13.2}$$

with w_{t+h} being the best wage offer received during the next period of length h, and $\Omega(t+h)$ is the information available to the worker in the next period. As benefit payments are assumed to be constant over time, the first term on the right side denotes the value of net unemployment income in period h. The second term represents the discounted expected present value of following the optimal strategy once next period's best wage offer w_{t+h} is received and $\Omega(t+h)$ is known, conditional on the information available in the current period.

As net-income flow during unemployment is a constant, wage offers are i.i.d. and their distribution and arrival rate for each period are known, the value of continued search while being unemployed, V, is a constant over time. V can be described by the following function(Mortensen 1986):

$$V = (b-c)h + \beta(h)\left[\sum_{n=1}^{\infty} q(n,h)\int_{0}^{\infty} \max[V, W(w_{t+h})]dG(w_{t+h}, n) + q(0,h)V\right]. \tag{13.3}$$

Rearranging terms yields

$$(1-\beta(h))V = (b-c)h + \beta(h)\left[\sum_{n=1}^{\infty} q(n,h)\int_{0}^{\infty} \max[0, W(w_{t+h}) - V]dG(w_{t+h}, n)\right]. \tag{13.4}$$

By applying Bellman's principle of dynamic optimality (Bellman 1957), a unique solution to equation 13.4 can be obtained for the optimal value of one additional period of job search, V.[2] At the optimum, the expected present value of accepting an offer, $W(w)$, will be the present value of expected lifetime income at that wage:

$$W(w^*) = \frac{w^*}{r} = V, \tag{13.5}$$

with w^* representing the reservation wage of the worker and r the interest rate. Recall here, that for the continuous case,

$$\beta(h) = e^{-rh}, \text{ so that } \lim_{h\to 0}[1-\beta(h)]/h = r. \tag{13.6}$$

[2]The theory of dynamic programming is the mathematical decision framework for resolving the wage search and optimal stopping problems posed within the search theory approaches. A standard technique for this kind of optimization problem is the Bellman's principle of dynamic optimality. According to this principle, "an optimal policy has the property that, whatever the initial state and control are, the remaining decisions must constitute an optimal policy with regard to the state resulting from the first decision" (Bellman (1957), p.83) For the case of job search this implies that the present decision to accept or reject a job in the sequence of decision maximizes the current net value plus the discounted expected future stream of wages, if future decisions are equally made optimally on the expectation conditional on current information (Mortensen (1986), p.856). For a detailed formal treatment of Bellman's principle and it's uses in economics refer for example to Malliaris and Brock (1981).

Recall also that $q(\cdot)$ is assumed to be Poisson distributed

$$q(n,h) = e^{-\delta h}(\delta h)^n/n!, \tag{13.7}$$

and so

$$\lim_{h\to 0} q(1,h)/h = \delta \quad \text{and} \quad \lim_{h\to 0} q(n,h)/h = 0, \quad \text{for } n > 1. \tag{13.8}$$

$W(w)$ is continuous and strictly increasing in w. V does not depend on w. The optimal strategy for an unemployed, job-searching worker is to set a reservation wage w^* at which he will accept a job offer w: $w \geq w^*$. Following from the optimality condition 13.5, the worker will accept any offer fulfilling the following condition:

$$w^* = rW(w^*) = rV \tag{13.9}$$

This result is quite interesting, as it implies that the reservation wage, w^*, is a constant and therefore time-invariant. This time invariance results from the stationarity of the worker's environment, as benefit payments are constant and and paid indefinitely, and job offer arrivals are neither dependent on past labor market history nor on the time already spent unemployed.

Substituting equations 13.5 and 13.9 for $W(w^*)$ and V, equation 13.3 yields:

$$(\delta/r)\int_{w^*}^{\infty}[w_{t+h} - w^*]dF(w_{t+h}) = c + w^* - b. \tag{13.10}$$

From this equation, the value for the reservation wage may be obtained:

$$w^* = (b-c) + (\delta/r)\int_{w^*}^{\infty}[w_{t+h} - w^*]dF(w_{t+h}), \tag{13.11}$$

which can be rewritten as

$$(w^* - (b-c))r = \delta\int_{w^*}^{\infty}[w - w^*]dF(w_{t+h}). \tag{13.12}$$

The left side of this equation represents the marginal cost of rejecting an offer equal to w^* and continuing to search, with $(b - c)$ designating net-unemployment-income: the imputed interest difference between the income of the employed versus the unemployed state. The right hand-side of the equation shows the marginal expected return to continued optimal search provided that offers will only be accepted if they exceed the reservation wage, multiplied with the probability that an acceptable offer will be received. In other words, the optimum reservation wage of a worker is the one equating the marginal cost and marginal return of search activity.

13.2 Extensions of the Model

13.2.1 The Choice of Different Search Channels

Job search may be performed in many different ways and with many different instruments. Checking the job-section in the newspaper or posting an advertizement, informing friends and looking for a job within family-owned business, but also using the government-provided job-assistance programs are all possible job search instruments. These instruments are associated with different job search intensities and may show different efficiency, depending on the characteristics of each worker and the sector he is searching in.

Several authors have worked on including search intensity and the choice of job search methods in the theoretical search models. Burdett (1979) adopts the classical stationary job search model by allowing workers to make decisions on allocating their work and leisure time, conditioned on the reservation wage and current job offer. By doing so, workers also make decisions on the intensity of their job search. The arrival rate of job offers in Burdett's model depends on the search intensity devoted to search, measured in time units. Holzer (1988) further extends this model by allowing job searchers to choose from a set of search channels. The cost and profitability of each search channel varies for every individual. For example, individuals with a well established social network may profit more by using the 'friends and family' channel, and costs of using this channel may generally be assumed to be lower than for other channels, and to be especially low for people with good networks. Living in a bigger city may increase the productivity of the channel 'asked employer', and so on.

Van Den Berg and Klaauw (2001) generalize a model with endogenous search intensity like the one presented by Mortensen (1986) and in Section 13.1 by allowing for two search channels. Workers may use both formal and informal search methods, grouped together in a formal or an informal search channel, respectively. The search channels s differ concerning their "own associated structural parameters", for example they assume that the wage offer distributions F_s from which the offers are randomly drawn are channel-specific. Offers provided by channel s arrive according to a Poisson process with rate $\delta_s e_s$, with e_s denoting the search effort or search intensity. The worker optimizes his search process by choosing the search intensity devoted to the search via each channel. In their model, Van Den Berg and Klaauw (2001) do not allow workers to reconsider earlier job offers; individuals have to decide in each period whether to accept or to reject the current offer and continue searching. Furthermore, workers are not assumed to perform on-the-job search.

The search costs are assumed to be proportional to the search intensity, e_s, following the literature on search models with endogenous search efforts (refer to Mortensen and Pissarides (1999). The cost function for job search, $c(e_1, e_2)$,[3] is specified to be increasing and convex in its arguments. They propose the function:

$$c(e_2, e_2) = a_0(a_1 e_1^\gamma + a_2 e_2^\gamma)^{2/\gamma} \tag{13.13}$$

with $a_s > 0$ and $1 < \gamma < 2$. In the case that only one channel is used, or that channels are identical, this cost function reduces to a quadratic specification like the ones specified for search models with only a single search channel (refer to Mortensen and Pissarides (1999)). Using this cost function, Van Den Berg and Klaauw (2001) obtain the following equation for the unique reservation wage rV:

$$rV = \max_{e_1, e_2 \geq 0} b - a_0(a_1 e_1^\gamma + a_2 e_2^\gamma)^{2/\gamma} + \sum_{s=1}^{2} \delta_s e_s E_s \max\{\frac{w}{r} - V, 0\}. \tag{13.14}$$

Here $E_s(w)$ denotes the expected wage of a job offer arriving through search channel s. Equation 13.14 is solved by applying Bellman's principle of dynamic optimality. Mortensen (1986) and Albrecht, Holmlund, and Lang (1991) show that the optimal, and in this case unique, solution is V. The optimal search intensities are given by the values of e_1 and e_2 which maximize the right-hand side of equation 13.14. The optimal search strategy is to accept a job only when the job value ω associated with that job exceeds rV, the unique reservation wage.

[3]The subscripts denote the formal and the informal channel, respectively.

13.2.2 Exit Into Different Labor Market Segments

As most studies use data from countries without a large segment of informal employment, usually no importance is given to the incorporation of different exit possibilities. Working with Brazilian data, Cunningham (1997) differentiates between sectors to allow one to distinguish between various potential states of employment: formal, informal or self employment. In her optimization, she uses the 'job value' ω instead of the wage, defining it as a function of the wage w and a term z_i. The term z_i captures an individual's non-wage components of the job value: $\omega = \omega(w, z_i)$. A state $z_i \leq 0$ would be equivalent to no job offer existent with minimal requirements on non-wage qualities. Some authors (refer to Devine and Kiefer (1991) for a survey) prefer the job value to the wage for the following reason: Search theory models like the one presented here may evoke the idea that unemployment is always voluntary, as individuals are "deliberately" choosing to accept or to decline arriving wage offers. This results from the fact that an acceptable job is defined via the reservation wage only. In reality non-wage qualities may play an important role in a worker's decision to accept a job offer. A good job may be characterized by various criteria including the magnitude of the wage, the risk of being laid off in the future, but also work satisfaction and other features which may differ substantially from worker to worker, depending on personal preferences. As a worker's utility of a job is therefore hard to observe, in most standard search models a good match is defined via the present value of discounted future expected wage payments. In the case of Brazil, advantages linked to self-employment or to the access to social security linked to a job in the formal sector may be regarded as such non-wage qualities. The value of these qualities depends on the preferences of each worker. Cunningham (1997) defines a job value $\omega_{ij} = w_j + z_{ij}$ for Brazilian workers where $z_{ij} \geq 0$ is individual i's segment-specific non-pecuniary value of working in segment j. Both wage offer distributions, $F - j(w)$, and distributions for the job-value, $H - j(\omega)$, are segment-specific and assumed to be known by job searchers.

Individuals are assumed to search in these different sectors for jobs. Furthermore it is assumed that each sector j requires different search methods and therefore will generate different search costs, c_j. The total search cost is $c = \sum_{j=1}^{3} c_j$. Contacting possible employers or placing a job advertisement may be appropriate search instruments for jobs in the formal sector, but not for becoming active in the self-employed sector.

Considering these reflections in a discrete setting, the value of search is:

$$V = \frac{1}{1+r}(b - \sum_{j=1}^{3} c_j) + \frac{\delta}{1+r}\sum_{j=1}^{3} c_j \int_{\omega^*}^{\infty} [\omega - \omega^*]\, dG_j(\omega). \qquad (13.15)$$

The optimal level of search, c_j, now has to be found for each sector by maximizing 13.15 for all sectors j subject to

$$\sum_{j=1}^{J} c_j \leq b. \qquad (13.16)$$

At the optimum, search resources are distributed over search activities across all sectors searched in a manner equalizing the ratio of marginal benefit to marginal cost of search.

13.3 A Model for Brazil

In this section I formulate a model for Brazil including both the possibility of using different search channels and the possibility of exiting into different labor market states. I use the basic search model presented in Section 13.1 and modify the presented extensions for a continuous setting.

The changes introduced by Van Den Berg and Klaauw (2001) concerning the search channels are twofold: they modify the cost function assigning search channel-specific costs due to channel-specific search costs and they introduce search channel-specific wage offer distribution functions. Implementing the specified cost function (Equation 13.13) into Equation 13.3 yields

$$V = (b - c(e_2, e_2))h$$
$$+\beta(h)\left[\sum_{n=1}^{\infty} q(n,h) \int_{0}^{\infty} \max[V, W(\omega_{t+h})]dG(\omega_{t+h}, n) + q(0,h)V\right], \qquad (13.17)$$

using the short form of c for the sake of simplicity. The assumption of channel-specific wage offer distributions leads to modified probability parameters. Mortensen (1986) allows for job-availability by specifying that the number of wage offers arriving during one period is drawn with probability $q(n,h)$, and $q(\cdot)$ is Poisson distributed with parameter λ. In the search channel specific case, wage offers arrive with channel-specific probabilities. Additionally, workers may influence these probabilities by increasing their search efficiency e_s:

$$V = (b - c(e_2, e_2))h$$
$$+\beta(h)\left[\sum_{n=1}^{\infty} q_s(n,h)e_s \int_0^{\infty} \max[V, W(\omega_{t+h})]dG_s(\omega_{t+h}, n) + q_s(0,h)V\right], \quad (13.18)$$

Considering now the additionally possibility of exiting unemployment into different labor market states, and following Cunningham (1997), I specify a cost function with segment-specific search costs. This is justified, because, for example, the search channel 'test' will only lead to formal employment, while preparing for self-employment would require one to spend time and money on loan applications and market research, activities that certainly do not leading to formal or informal employment. Since job-value distributions for the different segments may overlap, the individual is therefore assumed to search all potential segments containing his reservation wage value rather than to search only in a specific segment. The decision to accept a job is then based on the job value rather than only on the segment where the job is located. Inserting the segment-specific cost function, Equation 13.18 modifies:

$$V = (b - \sum_{j=1}^{3} c_j(e_1, e_2))h + \beta(h)\Bigg[\sum_{1}^{\infty}\sum_{j=1}^{3} q_{s,j}(n,h)e_s$$
$$\int_0^{\infty} \max[V, W(\omega_{t+h})]dG_{s,j}(\omega_{t+h}, n) + q_{s,j}(0,h)V\Bigg], \quad (13.19)$$

where j is the index for segment, designating formal employment, informal employment or self-employment.

Like the model presented in Section 13.1, unemployment insurance benefits are assumed constant and paid infinitely. The term $(b - c)$ is therefore a constant that shifts up the value of searching V and increases the reservation wage, w^*. Since the accepted wage w depends on w^*, w increases with b, too. This implies that unemployment insurance benefits lead to higher-wage jobs, as the provision of unemployment insurance benefits will increase the lower bound of the potential job value range resulting in a search in better sectors, or among higher paying jobs. On the other hand, a higher reservation wage may lead to increased duration of unemployment because fewer job offers with a sufficiently high wage arrive. In their model, Van Den Berg and Klaauw (2001) treat unemployment benefits as constant and indefinitely paid, see the model extension discussed in Section 13.2.1. Berg shows in an earlier paper (Van Den Berg 1990) that for high exit rates and distant decreases in benefits the anticipation of the decrease is very low and Netherlands workers behave approximately as if b is constant. The situation for Brazil though is a different one. Unemployment insurance benefits are constant over the time they are paid, but they are only paid for a short interval ranging from three to five months, rendering the future loss of income an important consideration. During the time of entitlement, the magnitude of the benefits does not change. In the following econometric estimation, I will therefore also include the duration of unemployment to capture the effect of the ending payments.

The model presented above in this Section still implies a constant reservation wage due to the stationarity of the environment of the worker. Not only unemployment insurance benefits are constant and paid indefinitely, it is also assumed that wage distributions are unchanging and independent of the previous labor market state or the duration of unemployment. Burdett, Kiefer, and Sharma (1985) assume a semi-Markov process to introduce impacts of the length of the unemployment spell on the probability of reentering the labor market. This requires one to compute an optimal strategy for each period k, $k = 1, ..., T$, in which the value of unemployment insurance benefits, b_k, the remaining periods of entitlement to unemployment insurance, t_k, the probability of a job offer, δ_k, the potential job value range, ω_k^*, and the search costs, c_k, are all period specific. The time interval k is a constant and equal to the duration of one period of unemployment insurance benefit collection. This specification allows ω_k^* to vary with b_k, yielding a period specific reservation wage. In a discrete setting, the value of search can be formally described as

$$V = \frac{1}{1+r}(b_k - c)h$$
$$+\delta_k \int_0^\infty \left\{ \sum_{k=1}^{T} \left(\int_{\omega^*}^\infty \max[\omega - \omega_k^*]\, dG_j(\omega) \right) \right\} d\Phi(\tau). \qquad (13.20)$$

The lifetime expected utility of search is now obtained by summing over all periods in the unemployment spell and integrating over all possible triples $\tau = \{..., (b_k, t_k, \delta_k), ...\}$ for $k = 1, ..., T$, where $\Phi(\tau, X_i)$ represents the probability measure for all possible futures of individual i, with X_i being the vector of personal characteristics. Solving this equation yields a sequence of reservation wages and search intensities for each possible set of triples. The level of benefits may change as well as the optimal reservation wage thereby allowing the search process to be effected by the expiration of unemployment insurance benefits. For the sake of simplicity, and following Van Den Berg and Klaauw (2001), I do not attempt to fuse these ideas into the above constructed model here.

Having expanded the theoretical setting, the availability of the necessary data to test the model empirically needs to be considered. This is a problem encountered by many authors using the search approach as a theoretical basis for their empirical analysis. Even authors using data from social experiments, like Van Den Berg and Klaauw (2001), lack some of the necessary data and they limit their analysis to selected aspects within the search approach. Concerning the Brazilian case, the Monthly Employment Survey does not collect data on pre-unemployment wages, individual reservation wages or on the wage offer distributions. For this reason, some of the terms of the model developed above cannot be econometrically identified, especially the parts including reservation wages. The theoretical model will therefore serve as background for the interpretation of the estimation results presented in Section 15. Apart from the already largely discussed search channels and the unemployment insurance benefits, I will also include the usual personal characteristics into the econometric analysis because these characteristics at least partly determine the preferences of an individual and hence the individual's job value.

Chapter 14

Econometric Analysis of Job Search Processes

14.1 A Multinomial Logistic Regression Model

To measure the impact of the individual labor history on the choice of search methods and the impact of search methods on the exit from unemployment, I apply multinomial logistic regression. This type of regression is designed to model multinomial categorical response variables so that estimates concerning the different labor market exit states can be obtained.

The multinomial logit model is a generalized form of the logit model for binary response variables (Christensen 1997). The standard form of the binary logit model is:

$$log\left[\frac{Pr(y=1|x_i)}{1-Pr(y=1|x_i)}\right] = \beta_k x_{ik}, \tag{14.1}$$

where x_{ik} represents the kth explanatory variable for individual i,($i = 1,\ldots,n$; $k = 1,\ldots,K$), and β_k is the parameter associated with the kth explanatory variable. The probability of an event occurring, $Pr(y = 1|x_{ik})$, is nonlinear as a function of x_{ik}, and also as a function of β_k, as can be shown by solving equation 14.1 for $Pr(y = 1|x_{ik})$:

$$Pr(y=1|x_{ik}) = \frac{e^{(\beta_k x_{ik})}}{1+e^{(\beta_k x_{ik})}} = \frac{1}{1+e^{-(\beta_k x_{ik})}}, \tag{14.2}$$

Logit models are called "generalized linear models", the (logit-)transformed probabilities are assumed to be linear functions of the covariates. For a multinomial response, the model is formulated as:

$$log\left[\frac{Pr(y=m|x_{ik})}{Pr(y=r|x_{ik})}\right]=\beta_{kj}x_{ik}. \tag{14.3}$$

where β_{kj} is the regression coefficient for covariate k in category j, $j = 1,\ldots,J$. $Pr(y = m|x_{ik})$ denotes the probability that individual i ends up in outcome category m. Like binary logit models, multinomial logit models do not calculate direct probabilities of a worker moving into a certain occupational state but the 'odds of probabilities'. Unlike in the standard binary logit model, the multinomial logit model yields odds that compare the probability of falling in a certain category m with the probability of falling in a reference category r: $Pr(y = r|x_{ik})$, $m, r \in \{1,\ldots,J\}$. In the following analysis, for example, these odds compare the probability of being in a certain labor market state to the probability of being in the reference labor market state. To simplify explanations, in the analysis of the results I will use the expression of 'odds of being in a certain occupational state' to express the odds mentioned above. Solving equation 14.3 for $Pr(y = m|x_{ik})$ yields

$$Pr(y=m|x_{ik})=\frac{e^{(\beta_{km}x_{ik})}}{1+\sum_{j=1}^{J-1}e^{(\beta_{kj}x_{ik})}}=\frac{1}{1+\sum_{j=1}^{J-1}e^{(\beta_{kj}x_{ik})}}, \tag{14.4}$$

To estimate the impact of former occupational states on the choice of search methods, equation 14.3 would read as the odds of the probability (Allison 1999, p.11) that individual i (with characteristics given in the vector x_i) chooses job search method j to the probability of choosing search method r (the reference category, in this case category 'other').

The effect of the choice of a search method on the exit rates to different occupational states is measured in a similar way. The dependent variable is the new occupational state with its five categories 'informally employed', 'self-employed', 'searching' and 'inactive'. The explanatory variables are the search channel chosen, sex, position in the household and education.

14.2 Interpretation: Odds Ratios and Discrete Changes

Models for categorical variables are nonlinear, leading to the fact that the interpretation of the results is not as straightforward as for those of linear regression models. In general, the parameter coefficients estimated in the multinomial logistic regression do not provide information directly useful to understand the relationship between the covariates and the outcome. For this reason, odds ratios and predicted probabilities and functions thereof (marginal effects or discrete changes) are usually used for substantively meaningful interpretation instead of the coefficient estimates. As I will extensively rely on values of discrete change or marginal effects to interpret the relationship between the covariates and the outcomes, I will introduce the concept of marginal effects and discrete changes in this section.[1]

For linear regression models like

$$y = \alpha + \beta x + \gamma d, \tag{14.5}$$

with x being a continuous independent variable and d being a binary independent variable, the effect of x on the dependent variable y can be computed as the partial derivative, holding d constant:

$$\frac{\partial y}{\partial x} = \frac{\partial(\alpha + \beta x + \gamma d)}{\partial x} = \beta. \tag{14.6}$$

The calculated effect, often called the marginal change or marginal effect, is the same for all values of x and d in a linear model. The effect of d cannot be obtained by partial differentiation because d is discrete. A discrete change has to be computed for d changing from 1 to 0, holding x constant:

$$\frac{\Delta y}{\Delta d} = (\alpha + \beta x + \gamma 1) - (\alpha + \beta x + \gamma 0) = \gamma. \tag{14.7}$$

For linear models, the marginal change equals the discrete change because of the linearity.

[1]For a detailed discussion of the interpretation methods for nonlinear regression models like the binary and multinomial logistic regression models see for example Long (1997) and Kaufman (1996).

The above results do not hold for nonlinear models like the multinomial logistic regression used here. In a nonlinear model, the impact of a change in a variable depends on the values of the other variables in the model and is not given by the partial derivative of the respective variable. For a multinomial logistic regression model with J nominal outcomes, m denoting an outcome category and r being the reference outcome category, $m, r \in \{1, \ldots, J\}$, the predicted probability that $y = m$ given x_{ik} is:[2]

$$Pr(y = m|x_{ik}) = \frac{e^{(\beta_{km} x_{ik})}}{\sum_{j=1}^{J} e^{(\beta_{kj} x_{ik})}}. \tag{14.8}$$

The marginal effect is defined as (Long 1997):

$$\frac{\partial Pr(y = m|x_{ik})}{\partial x_k} = Pr(y = m|x_{ik}) \left[\beta_{km} - \sum_{j=1}^{J} \beta_{kj} Pr(y = j|x_{ik}) \right]. \tag{14.9}$$

This equation includes all of the $\beta_{k,j}$'s, so the value of the marginal effect depends on the value of all covariates considered in the model. The marginal effect may also change it's sign in the course of the x_k changing. So a covariate may first have a positive impact on the probability of being in occupational state j, but as the x_k's change, this impact may change to a negative one or, vice versa.

Since the value of the marginal effect depends on the level of all the covariates entering the estimation, a decision has to be made regarding which values of the covariates are to be used to compute the effect. It is possible to compute an average effect over all observations, or to hold all other covariates at their mean. The latter method is a popular summary measure in many papers using logistic regression. Long (1997) though argues that the method of marginal effects is difficult to apply in cases where only discrete changes in the covariates can be observed. This holds especially for binary covariates (dummy variables) which are not continuous by definition. Long therefore proposes the use of discrete changes for a change in the predicted probabilities for a discrete change in the covariates.

[2] To identify the model, a constraint on the β's must be imposed. Here it is assumed that $\beta_1 = 0$. For a more detailed discussion on the identification of multinomial logistic regression models and the choice of the constraint see Long (1997).

The discrete change in the probability for a change of δ in x_k is defined as

$$\frac{\Delta Pr(y=m|x_{ik})}{\Delta x_k} = Pr(y=m|x_{ik}, x_k+\delta) - Pr(y=m|x_{ik}, x_k), \qquad (14.10)$$

with $Pr(y = m|x_{ik}, x_k)$ denoting the probability that $y = m$ given the matrix x_{ik} and the specific value of x_k. The marginal change is represented by $x_k + \delta$. It is important to note that, unlike in the linear regression case, the marginal effect and the discrete change for a given change in a covariate, holding all other covariates at the same values, are not the same for $\lim_{\delta \to 0}$. As for the marginal effect shown in equation 14.9, the levels of all of the covariates entering the model have an impact on the size of the discrete change. Therefore, equally, a decision has to be made at which values to hold the covariates. In the following analysis, I will hold all the covariates at their mean. Additionally, for the discrete change case, the magnitude of change has to be chosen. There are several common options for the choice of the amount of the discrete change of the covariate in question: a unit change, $\delta = 1$, or changes in standard deviation units are widely used. Kaufman (1996) suggests to use changes centered around the mean to produce the same effect for an increase as for a decrease of the covariate's value. For dummy variables, the change option is from 0 to 1 to avoid that the change in the variable results in a value exceeding the variable's range:

$$\frac{\Delta Pr(y=m|\bar{x}_{ik})}{\Delta x_k} = Pr(y=m|\bar{x}_{ik}, x_k=1) - Pr(y=m|\bar{x}_{ik}, x_k=0), \quad (14.11)$$

Of those papers that report statistics apart from the odds ratios for interpretation, most report marginal effects. However, I follow Long (1997) and Kaufman (1996) in their argumentation in favor of discrete changes as a more appropriate method and I will report the discrete changes of selected covariates, in addition to the odds ratios.

A possibility to make the effects of the different covariates visible is to draw plots of discrete change and odds ratios (Long 2001). Plotting discrete change coefficients shows how a unit increase in the covariate affects the probability of each of the outcome categories. In the plot, there is one line for each of the covariates. The horizontal axis measures the change in the predicted probability for the dependent variable categories (in the following analysis first the different search channels and then the different post-unemployment labor market states). If the outcome category is plotted to the left/right of the zero-mark, this category is less/more likely to be observed in case the magnitude of the covariate increases. The distance between a pair of the plotted categories is a measure of the magnitude of the effect, the larger the distance the larger the effect. Interpreting the plot it should be remembered that that, contrary to the odds ratios, different values for discrete changes are obtained at different levels of the variables.

An odds ratio plot allows one to observe the pattern among the different outcome categories. Again there is one line for each of the covariates in the plot. The horizontal axis indicates the magnitude of the β coefficients associated with the outcome category. The upper scale of the horizontal axis measures changes in the odds ratios, the lower scale measures changes to the log coefficients. Both scales use the indicated base category (in the following analysis first 'asked employer', then 'remaining searching') as reference category. If another category is plotted to the left of the base category, an increase in the covariate decreases the probability of this category to be chosen. If the category is plotted to the right of the reference category, this category is more likely to be observed in case the magnitude of the covariate increases. Again the distance between a pair of the plotted categories is a measure of the magnitude of the effect; the larger the distance the larger the effect, always with reference to the base category. The choice of the base category is arbitrary and does not alter the observed patterns. Additionally, the plots reflect the statistical significance of compared groups of outcome categories by drawing lines between those groups for which the coefficients are **not** significant. As the discrete change may increase or decrease with changing values of the variables, numbers in the plot can be presented in different sizes proportional to the magnitude of the change. The larger the discrete change, the bigger the number is drawn.[3]

[3] As some of the numbers turn out to be minuscule and therefore hard to read, I do not include the discrete change in the figures reported in this and the following section. Instead, I report the odds ratio plots including the discrete change in the appendix; see Figures C.1, C.2, C.3 and C.4.

Chapter 15

Estimation results

15.1 Labor History and Search Methods

15.1.1 Former Occupational State

In this and the following three sections, I will first present and discuss the results of the regressions concerning the influence of an individual's labor history on the choice of the search channel. I will start with the discussion of the covariates describing the former occupational state of searching individuals in this section. The impact of unemployment insurance benefits on the group of former formally employed workers follows in the second section. Results for covariates describing personal characteristics like sex, age or position in the household are discussed in the third section, and the results for the educational covariates are presented in the fourth section. In the second part of this chapter, in Section 15.2, the estimation results for the impact of the different search channels on the outcome of the search process are discussed. A first section deals with the impact of the search channels, and the remaining sections present results analogous to the first part of this chapter.

Table 15.1 reports the odds ratios for the estimation of the impact of the individuals labor history and other covariates on the choice of search methods.

The first three covariates listed describe the former occupational state of a searching person. The category 'self-employed' is omitted. Having been 'formally employed' shows a significant odds ratio for the probabilities to have asked 'agency or union' and 'asked friends and family'. Individuals who held a formal job before are about 40% more likely to use the 'agency or union' channel compared to asking employers directly. This may seem a strange

Table 15.1: Odds ratios for the choice of search methods

Covariate	(1)	(2)	(3)	(4)	(5)
last job formal	0.7338 (0.600)	1.3921 (2.165)*	1.0369 (0.241)	0.5022 (6.911)**	0.8492 (0.458)
last job informal	1.0934 (0.170)	1.0699 (0.421)	0.8840 (0.773)	0.7933 (2.312)*	0.7296 (0.831)
newcomer	1.9904 (1.136)	1.0394 (0.202)	0.9323 (0.357)	0.7661 (2.015)*	0.3982 (1.759)
male	1.2409 (0.729)	0.8384 (2.235)*	1.0069 (0.079)	0.9451 (0.873)	0.9770 (0.109)
head of household	0.6266 (1.154)	0.9167 (0.867)	0.8334 (1.652)	0.8926 (1.430)	0.8290 (0.669)
age	1.0260 (1.479)	0.9959 (0.898)	1.0098 (1.986)*	1.0055 (1.571)	0.9909 (0.694)
first primary	0.6760 (0.319)	1.1850 (1.020)	1.2662 (1.201)	0.9224 (0.815)	1.7402 (0.722)
second primary	3.3117 (1.117)	1.5232 (2.507)*	1.5849 (2.311)*	0.5886 (4.771)**	3.4897 (1.668)
high school	9.9317 (2.229)*	1.8215 (3.637)**	2.8780 (5.558)**	0.6061 (4.542)**	7.7616 (2.809)**
superior education	3.6114 (3.563)**	0.6536 (2.013)*	1.3008 (1.605)	0.9023 (0.543)	2.2148 (2.577)**
per capita household income	1.0002 (0.612)	1.0004 (2.480)*	1.0003 (2.071)*	0.9997 (1.428)	1.0006 (2.061)*

Base category: (6) asked employer. Absolute value of z statistics in parentheses.
* significant at 5%; ** significant at 1%
(1) search method: participated in test versus asked employer, (2) search method: contacted agency or union versus asked employer, (3) search method: answered to an advertisement versus asked employer, (4) search method: asked friends and family versus asked employer, (5) search method: other versus asked employer

result, remembering the values of the cross tabulation presented in Table 12.1 in section 12, which indicate that about 10.5% of the the former formally employed recur to an agency or union for job search, but 68% try 'asked employer'. The odds ratios presented here show the odds of a former formally employed person choosing one search instrument and not the reference search instrument, compared with the odds of the omitted group of workers, in this table the self-employed. And examining the values of Table 12.1 again it can be observed that of the former self employed only about 6% do recur to 'agency or union' versus 63% reporting 'asked employer'. On the other hand, workers with a formal working background are by 50% less likely to ask friends and family than asking possible employers, again compared to the odds of the former self employed. The same holds for former informally employed workers, they show a 20% reduced inclination to ask 'friends and family' versus 'asked employer'. Being a newcomer also decreases the probability of asking friends and family. The decrease in the odds for the outcome category 'asked friends and family' indicates that in the omitted fourth occupational category 'self employed' there is a higher propensity of using this search channel. Those who have been self employed before seem to rely even less on employee-related institutions like the public employment service or employment agencies set up by the unions. All other estimates of the category 'former occupational state' are not significant in this model.

Recalling my hypothesis that formal employment is a preferred occupational state, I assumed that individuals who have previously held a formal job will try the same channel that led to the previous formal job. Furthermore, if I assume that more formal search channels like 'answering and posting advertisements' or 'participating in tests' predominantly lead to formal jobs, I would expect the formerly formally employed to use mainly these channels. But the impact of both these search channels is far from significant, and in the case of test participation even indicates a negative relationship (odds ratio smaller than one). The channel 'asked employer' comprises for both formal and informal ways of searching for a new job, by either submitting a formal application, or 'just' passing by and literally asking for a job. From the data, it cannot be observed which kind of application within this category has been applied. But all groups of job searchers seem to prefer this search channel, with roughly two thirds of each group reporting it as the used method. 'Asking friends and family' is also significant throughout all occupational groups, not shedding any light on the choice mechanism of search channels. What is not apparent from Table 15.1 is that former formally and former informally employed use clearly distinct search patterns. In fact, with the exception of the significant positive propensity of former formal workers to contact a job placement agency, the pattern of all three groups in this model, even including the newcomers, is very similar.

Figure 15.1[1] shows the odds ratio plot for the occupational variables. Looking at the plot for the former formally employed workers (uwork1), the outcome category 4 ('asked friend and family') lies quite far to the left, with an odds ratio of about 0.50. This indicates that a former formally employed person is

[1]As already mentioned, I do not include the discrete change in the figures reported in this and the following section. Instead, I report odds ratio plots, including discrete changes in the appendix (Figures C.1, C.2, C.3 and C.4).

less likely to choose this search channel. The more to the right an outcome number lies, the more likely it is that a former formally employed individual chooses this search method. Switching the dummy variable 'uwork1' from zero to one makes it more likely that the person resorts to a job placement agency.

The pattern for the former informally employed (uwork2) is less spread, showing no big differences in the choice of the different search channels. This figure supports my hypothesis that the search pattern of this group is less differentiated.

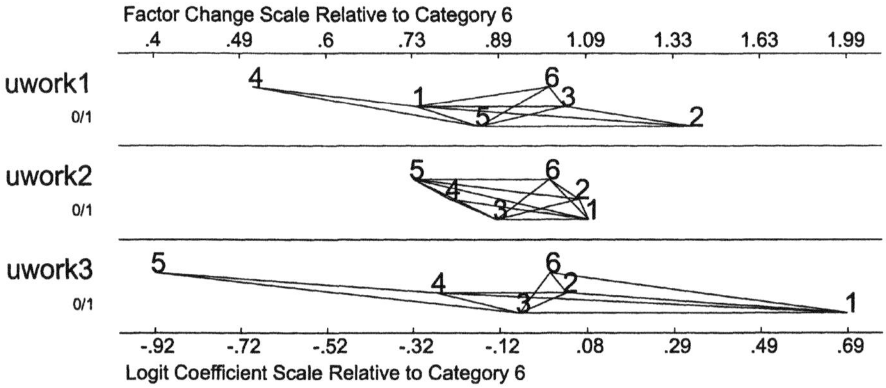

Source: "Monthly Labor Survey (PME) (1999), own calculations"
Covariates: uwork1: former formally employed, uwork2: former informally employed, uwork3: newcomer
Outcome categories: (1) search method: participated in test, (2) search method: contacted agency, (3) search method: answered to an advertisement, (4) search method: asked friends and family, (5) search method: other, (6) search method: asked employer

Figure 15.1: Odds ratio plots for the type of previous job.

The most outstretched is the pattern for the group of newcomers. Being a member of this group increases the likeliness of participating in a test by a factor two, and decreases the odds for asking 'friends and family', or of using 'other methods' compared to 'asking an employer'.

As the odds ratio values always depend on the categories of a covariate entering the estimation, I re-estimated the odds ratios, now dropping the group of former formally employed and entering the group of self employed. So all odds within the group of the former occupational state ('former formally employed', 'former informally employed', 'newcomer', 'self employed') are now made in comparison to the group 'former formally employed'. Table 15.2 reports these odds ratios for the former occupational state covariates. The

Table 15.2: Estimation results for the choice of search methods – only former occupational states with the group of former formally employed as a base category

Covariate	(1)	(2)	(3)	(4)	(5)
last job informal	1.4901	0.7686	0.8526	1.5795	0.8591
	(1.185)	(2.993)**	(1.644)	(6.233)**	(0.652)
newcomer	2.7124	0.7466	0.8992	1.5254	0.4689
	(2.315)*	(2.214)*	(0.729)	(3.823)**	(1.800)
last self employed	1.36285	0.7183	0.9644	1.9911	1.1775
	(0.600)	(2.165)*	(0.241)	(6.911)**	(0.458)

Base category: (6) asked employer. Absolute value of z statistics in parentheses
significant at 5%; ** significant at 1%
(1) search method: participated in test versus asked employer, (2) search method: contacted agency or union versus asked employer, (3) search method: answered to an advertisement versus asked employer, (4) search method: asked friends and family versus asked employer, (5) search method: other versus asked employer

values for the other covariates match those from Table 15.1 up to the second digit and are therefore not reported again.

Values from Table 15.2 show that, compared to the group of former formally employed workers, the former informally employed are 24% less likely to use the channel 'agency or union'. This may be partly explained by the fact that informally employed individuals usually do not have an affiliation with the unions and do not seek their help. But this interesting feature may also indicate that former informally employed either are less informed about the existence of employment services, or believe that they are not entitled to use them. Alternatively, they may consider them as less effective than other search channels preferred by this group. In Section 15.2, I therefore investigate the impact of the choice of different search channels on the outcome of the search process.

Job searchers who have held an informal job before are about 58% more likely to ask friends and family than former formally employed ones. The reason could be that friends and family are the source most readily available, and mostly at no or very low cost. Additionally, part of the popularity of this channel may stem from the fact that, unlike participating in a test, answering advertisements or submitting written application forms, this channel does neither require any reading and writing skills, nor access to newspapers and typewriters. Information about public job placement agencies or service offered by the unions may simply be lacking, thereby reducing the demand from the side of the former informally employed. On the other hand, the lower likeliness of the former formally employed individuals of using this channel could support my hypothesis that this group of individuals is more likely to use more formal search channels to secure a formal job again.

Once again, the pattern of the odds ratios gets clearer when they are plotted, see Figure 15.2.

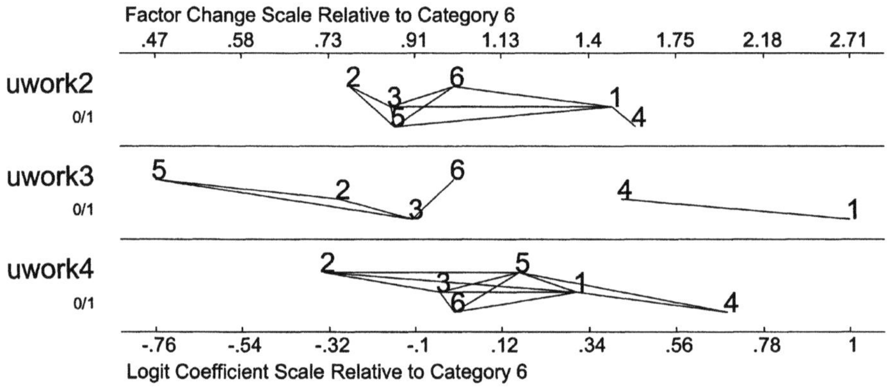

Source: "Monthly Labor Survey (PME) (1999), own calculations"
(1) search method: participated in test, (2) search method: contacted agency, (3) search method: answered to an advertisement, (4) search method: asked friends and family, (5) search method: other, (6) search method: asked employer

Figure 15.2: Odds ratio plots for the type of previous job former informally employed (uwork2), newcomer (uwork3), self employed (uwork4).

The estimates indicate that newcomers are much more likely to participate in tests than the former formally employed, and also less likely to contact an agency than are the former informally employed. Plausible reasons for the low use of the job placement agencies may be ignorance of their existence, but also a reputation of low efficiency in allocating people. As in the previous model, the channel 'asked friends and family' shows highly significant odds ratios, indicating that all the listed occupational groups are more likely to use this channel than the former formally employed.

To obtain additional insight into the behavior of the searching individuals, I also computed discrete changes for each covariate, holding all other covariates

Table 15.3: Discrete changes for the choice of search methods

Covariate	(1)	(2)	(3)	(4)	(5)	(6)
last job formal†	-0.0007	0.0360	0.0070	-0.0858	-0.0008	0.0442
	(0.48)	(2.82)**	(0.73)	(7.61)**	(0.28)	(2.53)*
last job informal†	0.0004	0.0094	-0.0060	-0.0269	-0.0022	0.0253
	(0.24)	(0.71)	(0.60)	(2.36)*	(0.77)	(1.4)
newcomer†	0.0027	0.0071	-0.0022	-0.0296	-0.0053	0.0272
	(0.9)	(0.44)	(0.17)	(2.17)*	(2.34)*	(1.23)
male†	0.0007	-0.0137	0.0021	-0.0048	-2.86e-06	0.0158
	(0.81)	(2.16)*	(0.37)	(0.61)	(0.00)	(1.54)
head of household†	-0.0011	-0.0043	-0.0098	-0.0105	-0.0012	0.02687
	(1.11)	(0.54)	(1.45)	(1.12)	(0.55)	(2.15)*
age	0.0001	-0.0005	0.0006	0.0006	-0.0001	-0.0007
	(1.38)	(1.26)	(1.93)*	(1.49)	(0.79)	(1.30)
first primary†	-0.0011	0.0132	0.0153	-0.0148	0.0049	-0.0175
	(0.37)	(0.94)	(1.12)	(1.28)	(0.63)	(0.87)
second primary†	0.0046	0.0382	0.0335	-0.0695	0.0144	-0.0212
	(0.80)	(2.38)*	(2.13)*	(6.52)**	(1.21)	(0.93)
high school†	0.0102	0.0455	0.0776	-0.0790	0.0258	-0.0791
	(1.31)*	(3.00)**	(4.65)**	(7.03)**	(1.82)	(3.45)**
superior education†	0.0069	-0.0309	0.0215	-0.0129	0.0098	0.0055
	(1.90)	(2.60)**	(1.65)	(0.61)	(1.86)	(0.22)
household income per capita	5.93e-07	0.0000	0.0000	-0.0000	4.42e-06	-0.0000
	(0.55)	(2.60)**	(2.11)*	(1.85)	(1.97)*	(0.69)

† dy/dx is for discrete changes of the dummy variable from 0 to one. Values without † are for continuous variables. Absolute value of z statistics in parentheses
* significant at 5%; ** significant at 1%
(1) search method: participated in test, (2) search method: contacted agency, (3) search method: answered to an advertisement, (4) search method: asked friends and family, (5) search method: other, (6) search method: asked employer

at their means[2]. While the odds ratios give information about the direction of an effect and the relation of odds of different outcome and variable categories, the discrete effects reveal information about the magnitude of the change in

[2]See Section 14.2 for a formal description of these effects.

the probability when changing the value of a covariate while holding all others constant. Table 15.3 reports these effects.

Looking at the values of discrete change of the occupational variables, it can be seen that most effects are quite small. Having been formally employed is the largest one, reducing the probability of choosing 'asked friends and family' by 8%. This result is in line with my assumption that former formally employed individuals are more likely to use formal search channels. The discrete changes for the rest of the covariates follow the same significance pattern found in the odds ratios presented above.

The pattern of the discrete changes can be observed better using plots. Figure 15.3 reveals that the discrete change for the use of the channel 'asked friends and family' is negative for all categories of former occupational state, but the effect is largest for those former formally employed. This pattern again shows that this method seems to be used mostly by the former self-employed. Asking an employer though is positive for all labor-history-categories shown, and is once again highest for the former formally employed. As the results mainly confirm the findings from the analysis of the odds ratios, they are not further discussed in detail.

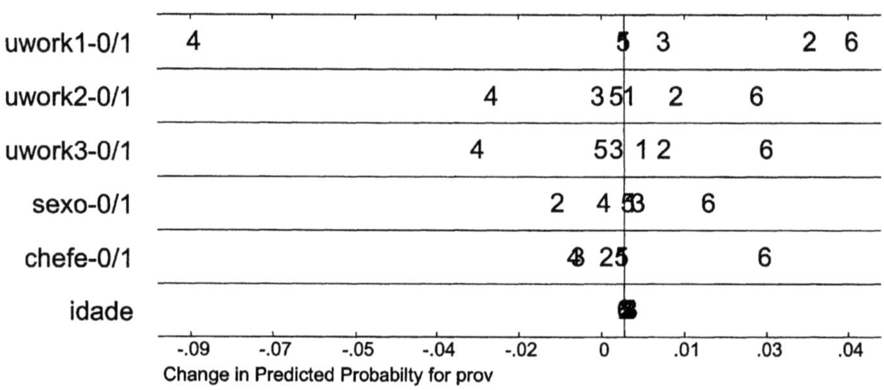

Source: "Monthly Labor Survey (PME) (1999), own calculations"
Covariates: (uwork1): former formally employed, (uwork2): former informally employed, (uwork3): newcomer, sexo: sex, chefe: head of household, idade: age.
Outcome categories: (1) search method: participated in test, (2) search method: contacted agency, (3) search method: answered to an advertisement, (4) search method: asked friends and family, (5) search method: other, (6) search method: asked employer.

Figure 15.3: Discrete change plots for former occupational states and other selected covariates.

15.1.2 Unemployment Insurance Benefits

The payment of unemployment insurance benefits is assumed to have a large impact on the search process both in theoretical and empirical studies (see Section 12.2.2). Concerning the choice of search methods though, no indication of a significant association of the payment of unemployment insurance benefits is found. As there is no compulsory counselling in Brazil for those job searchers receiving unemployment benefits, there should be found no significant effect for the use of the public employment service. Results for the benefit covariates for the group of former formally employed workers are reported in Table 15.4; for the results for all covariates refer to Table C.1 in the appendix. The odds ratios show that, as expected, benefit payments have no significant impact on the choice of search methods.

Table 15.4: Odds ratios of the impact of benefit payments on the choice of search methods

Covariate	(1)	(2)	(3)	(4)	(5)
3 months benefits	1.1320	0.9217	0.8720	0.9869	1.1943
	(0.171)	(0.483)	(0.685)	(0.080)	(0.388)
4 months benefits	0.6917	0.8407	0.9060	0.8686	0.4937
	(0.513)	(1.107)	(0.563)	(0.910)	(1.325)
5 months benefits	0.6369	0.9547	0.9172	0.8605	1.4716
	(0.779)	(0.340)	(0.573)	(1.106)	(1.082)

Base category: (6) asked employer. Absolute value of z statistics in parentheses
significant at 5%; ** significant at 1%

(1) search method: participated in test versus asked employer, (2) search method: contacted agency or union versus asked employer, (3) search method: answered to an advertisement versus asked employer, (4) search method: asked friends and family versus asked employer, (5) search method: other versus asked employer

The same result holds for the discrete changes displayed in Table C.2 in the appendix.

15.1.3 Sex, Age, Position in the Household and Per Capita Household Income

Looking again at the remaining covariates in Table 15.1, it can be observed that almost none of the odds ratios for 'male', 'head of household' or 'age' show any significance. One exception is that women are more likely to use 'agency or union' versus 'asked employer'. This relatively stronger attachment to labor market institutions is an interesting fact because proportionally less females hold formal jobs than males (refer to Table B.1) and so it could be expected that more males request the services. The second exception is that the odds of answering advertisements increase very slightly, by almost 1%, with increasing age. The odds ratio plot, Figure 15.4, shows that males are more likely to participate in tests and less likely to go to a job placement agency. Being a head of household decreases the use of all search channels compared to the option to directly 'ask an employer'. An increase in age makes search channels like 'tests', 'answering ads' or 'asking friends and family' more likely than 'asking an employer'.

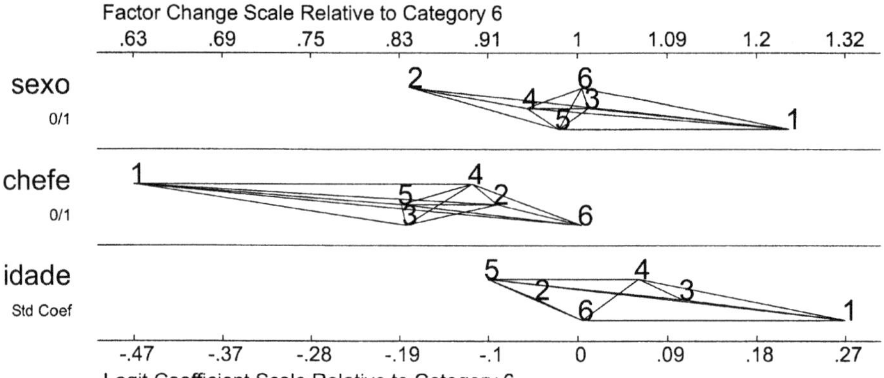

Source: "Monthly Labor Survey (PME) (1999), own calculations"
(1) search method: participated in test, (2) search method: contacted agency, (3) search method: answered to an advertisement, (4) search method: asked friends and family, (5) search method: other, (6) search method: asked employer

Figure 15.4: Odds ratio plots for sex (sexo), head of household (chefe) and age (idade).

The last variable reported in Table 15.1, the household income per capita, was entered into the model to investigate the hypothesis that financial resources influence the choice of search channels. The assumption is that the more resources an individual has at his disposal, the more likely it is that he will search for a formal job. An increase in the per capita household income increases the likeliness of using 'agency' or 'answering to an advertisement' as well as that of using 'other channels'. The values of the odds ratios are quite close to one due to the fact that a one unit increase of income, measured in units of one Real, will not have a large effect. Additionally, some of the effect of the increased income is captured in the educational variables, as it can be assumed that individuals with a higher schooling level tend to come from households where other members also obtained more education,[3] and individuals with higher levels of education tend to have better paid jobs. However, excluding the educational covariates from the estimation though does not change the magnitude of the odds ratios for the 'per capita household income'. As the effects of this covariate on the odds ratios are very small, they overlap in the odds ratio plot and I therefore do not show the plot here.

15.1.4 Education

The four covariates in Table 15.1 are used as dummies for the different levels of education. Unlike the previous covariates, many of the odds ratios are now highly significant, except for the first one reported: completed first four years of primary school. The reference group within the category education is the group of individuals without schooling. Having completed all eight years of primary school ('second primary') increases odds ratios for choosing 'contacted agency' and 'answered to an advertisement' by more than 50% and decreases the likeliness of 'asking friends and family' by more than 40% compared to individuals with no schooling when all other variables are held constant. Schooling seems to increase the choice of more formal search channels versus informal ones. A natural explanation for this is simply that individuals have acquired reading and writing skills. 'Having completed high school' shows about the same effect on the pattern of search method choice as 'having completed the second level of primary school', and additionally increases the odds of taking tests, and of using other, not further specified search channels (category No. 5, 'other'). The odds ratios are large in magnitude, originating from the fact that the reference group is the group without schooling. The decrease in the odds ratio for 'asked friends and family' remains about the same as that for the 'second primary' group. Having acquired a high school degree leads to a higher likeliness of participating in tests to about the same extent as for the 'second primary' group, showing that academics are not as much a target group for those tests as individuals graduating from high school. Superior education also leads to a decreased likeliness of contacting an agency. Possible explanations for this are that only few jobs are posted for academics at the

[3]See for example the survey from Behrmann (1999).

public employment service, and that individuals with superior education do not tend to be members of a union.

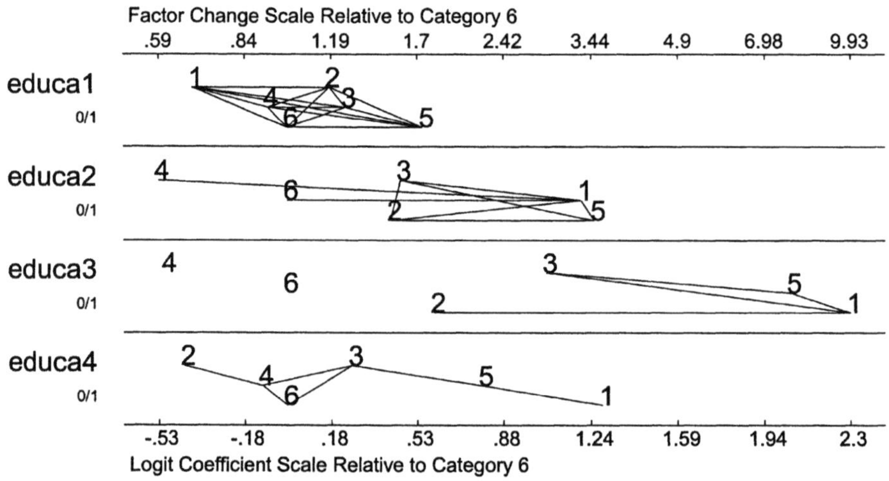

Source: "Monthly Labor Survey (PME) (1999), own calculations"
Covariates: educa1: first part primary school completed, educa2: second part primary school completed, educa3: high school completed, educa4: superior education completed
Outcome categories: (1) search method: participated in test, (2) search method: contacted agency, (3) search method: answered to an advertisement, (4) search method: asked friends and family, (5) search method: other, (6) search method: asked employer

Figure 15.5: Odds ratio plots for different levels of education.

The odds ratio plot (Figure 15.5) clearly shows how the channel 'asked friends and family' becomes less important with an increasing level of education. The largest effects on the choice of search channels are to be observed for the variable 'high school completed'. This result is confirmed by the discrete change plot shown in Figure 15.6, which shows that the changes for the informal channels 'friends and family' and 'employer' are largest and negative. Formal channels like 'test' or 'answering to an advertisement' gain most in the group 'completed high school'. Interestingly, the use of the public employment service also increases with rising educational levels, but is negative for individuals with completed superior education. This is contrary to the assumption that the image of the public employment service is connected with low-skill job-offers of poor quality.

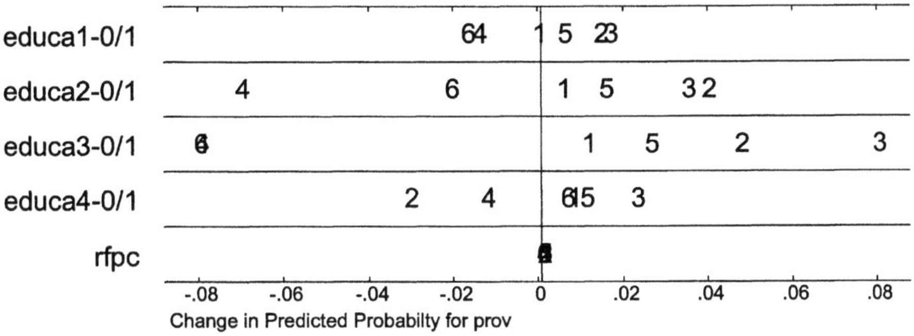

Source: "Monthly Labor Survey (PME) (1999), own calculations"
Covariates: educa1: first part primary school completed, educa2: second part primary school completed, educa3: high school completed, educa4: superior education completed, rfpc: household income per capita
Outcome categories: (1) search method: participated in test, (2) search method: contacted agency, (3) search method: answered to an advertisement, (4) search method: asked friends and family, (5) search method: other, (6) search method: asked employer

Figure 15.6: Discrete change plots for educational levels and per capita household income.

15.2 The Impact of the Choice of Search Methods

15.2.1 Search Methods

Table 15.5 presents estimation results for the impact of the search channels on the transition into different labor market states. The variables listed in the first column are observed in period t, the different categories of the response listed in the first row are observed in period $t + 1$. The values reported are odds ratios comparing the odds of exiting into a certain new occupational state compared to the reference state 'remaining searching'.

The upper section of the table shows the odds ratios for the different search channels. Participating in a test is not significantly associated with a transition out of unemployment. As already shown in Table 12.1, only a very small proportion of individuals, 0.58%, reported having used this search channel. This may be explained by various facts: first, in Brazil, this channel is often used to recruit employees for the public sector, but these tests take place rather seldom and there are only few openings; 2000 applicants for five places is a common ratio. Second, the decision process takes some time and it seems natural that people will stay inactive while waiting for the results.

Table 15.5: Odds ratios for the labor market transitions depending on the choice of search methods

Covariate	(1)	(2)	(3)	(4)
search channels				
test	0.4236	0.2549	1.4311	1.3816
	(0.836)	(1.332)	(0.693)	(0.973)
agency	0.8171	0.9217	0.8066	0.7232
	(1.087)	(0.643)	(1.427)	(3.415)**
advertisement	1.1945	0.6985	1.1463	1.1225
	(0.956)	(2.136)*	(0.893)	(1.151)
friends and family	0.7530	1.0856	1.3112	1.4439
	(1.588)	(0.771)	(2.554)**	(4.916)**
other channels	0.3333	0.5421	0.9916	0.9937
	(1.515)	(1.404)	(0.021)	(0.027)
personal characteristics				
duration of	0.9864	0.9885	0.9971	1.0183
unemployment	(3.205)**	(4.019)**	(0.943)	(11.285)**
male	1.1260	1.1361	1.9530	0.5800
	(1.067)	(1.638)	(7.399)**	(10.038)**
head of household	1.2326	1.3075	1.3853	0.6438
	(1.584)	(2.919)**	(3.404)**	(6.200)**
age	0.9951	0.9844	1.0193	0.9961
	(0.801)	(3.688)**	(4.794)**	(1.279)
per capita	0.9997	0.9999	0.9991	1.0002
household income	(0.949)	(0.536)	(3.252)**	(1.390)
education				
first primary	1.5727	0.7630	0.5790	0.8992
	(1.751)	(2.113)*	(4.691)**	(1.046)
second primary	2.2154	0.6678	0.4093	0.7994
	(3.060)**	(2.965)**	(6.699)**	(2.122)*
high school	1.8621	0.5466	0.3396	0.5575
	(2.403)*	(4.449)**	(8.165)**	(5.595)**
superior education	1.0512	0.6694	1.0892	0.6895
	(0.204)	(1.737)	(0.416)	(2.551)**

Base category: (5) 'searching'. Absolute value of z statistics in parentheses
significant at 5%; ** significant at 1%
(1) new state: formal employment, (2) new state: informal employment, (3) new state: self-employed, (4) new state: inactive

The next category, 'agency or union', is of special interest for the evaluation of active labor market policies as it also concerns the public employment service. As already mentioned, the public employment service in Brazil is performed by the SINE agencies. The principal aim of these agencies is the (re-) allocation of workers in the labor market. The unions provide a similar service on a smaller scale in terms of numbers of service posts and staff. The main goal is to increase the number of formally employed workers, and thereby to extend access to unemployment insurance and to the social security system. Informal and self-employed workers may make contributions to the latter voluntarily, but their share of contributions is very small. To accomplish their goal, the task of the SINE agencies is to collect information about vacancies and to help workers to apply for these positions. However, the odds for moving into formal work versus searching are not significant for this type of search channel. A factor to be considered is the number and quality of jobs posted at the agencies. Most of them are low paid, therefore attracting more unskilled workers to use the agencies. Although there are reported increases in job offers posted, the level of offers posted is rarely higher than the 5%-level of overall job vacancies. This may lead to a vicious cycle: Bad performance of the SINE leads to adverse selection and attracts more 'hopeless' cases and proportionally more low skilled workers. This leads to more low quality and hard-to-fill job offers from the employers' side. The low significance for both formal and informal work are in line with the sparse evaluations of the SINE agencies which all state low efficiency (Cardoso 2000; Ministério de Trabalho e Emprego (MTE) 1999). On the other hand, the odds ratio of becoming inactive versus remaining searching in period two when using 'agency or union' is 0.72% and significant, indicating that individuals using this channel are more likely to continue the job search than to transit into inactivity.

The category 'advertisements' is a search channel apt to lead to formal employment. Advertised job offers are certainly addressed to individuals who are able to read and likely to buy and read newspapers or have access to the internet. Nevertheless, the odds ratio for transiting into formal employment versus remaining searching is not significant with the use of this search channel. But the use of this method significantly reduces the likelihood of transiting into informal employment versus remaining searching by about 30%, indicating that advertisements are not used for finding informal employment. About half of the economically active population in Brazil holds informal jobs and firms are rarely prosecuted for not providing labor cards as it is difficult to control them. Although a large part of informal jobs are located in the low-wage and low-skill levels, there still remains a considerable number of better-paid informal positions requiring higher educational levels. There seems to be no plausible reason why firms looking for higher-level informal employees should not look for them using the media.

The category 'friends and family' is also a widely used one (14.88%). This may result mainly from the fact that it needs little effort in terms of time and resources. On the other hand, this informal search channel is poorly specified. It is interesting that this channel shows only highly significant estimates for the odds of exiting into self-employment (1.31) and inactivity (1.44), both with respect to staying 'searching'. These results indicate that the search activities covered by this label in Brazil do not lead to employment relationships. Asking friends and family is a channel most likely to lead to jobs in the social environment of the searching worker. In industrialized countries, this informal search channel is often used by highly skilled individuals and, for example, Montgomery (1991) reports that this channel is highly effective for this group of job searchers. The results for Brazil do not support this findings. Like the category 'agency or union', this search method may rather be one of the last resort: likely to be performed when all other channels failed, when work has to be found immediately or when there are no financial resources to use other channels. The reasons why it is used by far more than the free service of the agencies may be the even lower level of time and mobility required, the lack of an agency at the location of the individual, and the rather bad reputation of the efficiency of the agencies. Another fact to be considered is the social bond that still exists to a high degree within families: if members of a family become unemployed and can not find a job, the probability of being employed in the business of a relative is quite high. These jobs are often very low-paid or even unpaid. But if the individuals report 'working', they will not appear in the 'unemployed' or 'searching' categories of the PME surveys. The Statistical Institute of the Unions (DIEESE 1999) calculates unemployment and underemployment rates for six metropolitan areas taking into account the circumstances described above and reports a rate of about 20 % of underemployment, which mainly occurs in informal occupational states.

The odds ratio plot for different search channels (Figure 15.7) shows a large spread for search outcomes when using 'test' or 'other methods'. But neither of these channels is significantly associated with transitions out of employment. The remaining channels are less spread. It can be seen that advertisement has a quite different effect on the transition into informal employment (compared to remaining searching) than it has on all the other transition possibilities. While the remaining exit states are clustered quite closely together and the impacts are not significant, individuals responding to advertisements are significantly less likely to transit into informal employment.

As in the previous section, I calculate discrete changes for the covariates used in the estimation to get an idea about the direction of the effects of the covariates. The discrete changes computed are displayed in Table 15.6. Concerning the choice of search methods, the discrete changes follow the pattern

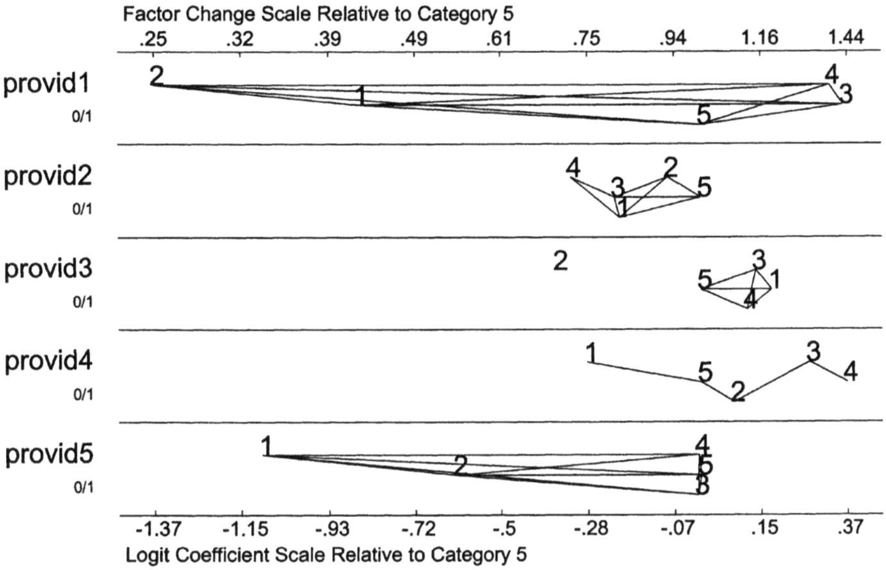

Source: "Monthly Labor Survey (PME) (1999), own calculations"
Covariates: provid1: test, provid2: agency, provid3: advertisement, provid4: friends and family, provid5: other channels
Outcome categories: (1) new state: formal employment, (2) new state: informal employment, (3) new state: self-employed, (4) new state: inactive, (5) new state: searching

Figure 15.7: Odds ratio plots for different search channels.

described by the odds ratios. Holding all other covariates at their mean, and changing the value for the dummy 'test' from zero to one significantly decreases the likelihood of transiting into informal employment, the same holds for the use of the channel 'advertisement'.

The transition probability to formal employment is negatively influenced when using 'friends and family' or 'other channels'. The effect of 'agency' to reduce the odds of transiting into inactivity versus remaining searching indicated by the odds ratios are confirmed by the discrete changes reported here.

Again, the pattern of changes are easier to discern by examining the plot of discrete changes. The most obvious pattern is that almost all search methods show a smooth spread without clusters for the different outcome groups. The channel 'test' has the largest spread, and 'advertisement' is least spread. The outcome category 'self-employed' is least affected by discrete changes and is the most consistently positive. Transitions into 'inactivity' or 'remaining

Table 15.6: Discrete changes for the labor market transitions depending on the choice of search methods

Covariate	(1)	(2)	(3)	(4)	(5)
search channels					
test†	-0.0270	-0.0831	0.3113	0.0975	-0.0186
	(1.45)	(3.10)**	(0.61)	(1.28)	(0.25)
agency†	-0.0034	0.0048	-0.0072	-0.0550	0.0608
	(0.46)	(0.40)	(0.69)	(3.21)**	(3.15)**
advertisement†	0.0075	-0.0356	0.0099	0.0288	-0.0106
	(0.85)	(3.03)**	(0.81)	(1.40)	(0.50)
friends and family†	-0.0166	-0.0063	0.0113	0.0735	-0.0619
	(2.94)**	(0.67)	(1.37)	(4.74)**	(3.93)**
other channels†	-0.0291	-0.0449	0.0068	0.0252	0.0420
	(2.42)*	(1.72)	(0.22)	(0.50)	(0.81)
personal characteristics					
duration of unemployment	-0.0008	-0.0016	-0.0005	0.0044	-0.0015
	(4.39)**	(6.21)**	(2.31)*	(14.17)**	(4.09)**
male†	0.0094	0.0236	0.0620	-0.1373	0.0424
	(2.07)*	(3.38)**	(9.97)**	(12.96)**	(3.71)**
head of household†	0.0124	0.0371	0.0338	-0.1082	0.0250
	(2.05)*	(3.99)**	(4.30)**	(8.55)**	(1.75)
age	-0.0002	-0.0016	0.0017	-0.0007	0.0007
	(0.60)	(3.96)**	(5.97)**	(1.20)	(1.11)
per capita	-9.18e-06	-6.09e-06	-0.0001	0.0001	0.0000
household income	(0.81)	(0.33)	(3.45)**	(2.68)**	(0.88)
education					
first primary†	0.0267	-0.0201	-0.0360	-0.0079	0.0372
	(2.01)*	(1.84)	(5.01)**	(0.40)	(1.73)
second primary†	0.0536	-0.0284	-0.0538	-0.0293	0.0580
	(3.09)**	(2.60)**	(7.67)**	(1.47)	(2.52)*
high school†	0.0478	-0.0335	-0.0593	-0.0865	0.1315
	(3.20)**	(2.99)**	(7.60)**	(4.57)**	(5.88)**
superior education†	0.0088	-0.0264	0.0198	-0.0653	0.0631
	(0.72)	(1.50)	(1.08)	(2.54)**	(2.20)*

† dy/dx is for discrete changes of the dummy variable from 0 to one. Values without † are for continuous variables. Absolute value of z statistics in parentheses

significant at 5%; ** significant at 1%

(1) new state: formal employment, (2) new state: informal employment, (3) new state: self-employed, (4) new state: inactive, (5) new state: searching

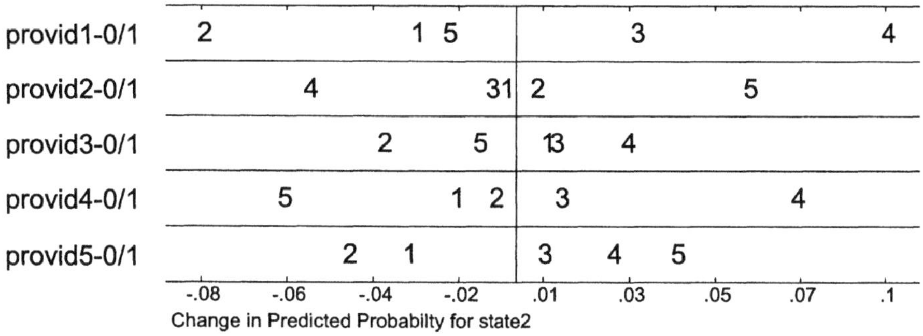

Source: "Monthly Labor Survey (PME) (1999), own calculations"
Covariates: providl: test, provid2: agency, provid3: advertisement, provid4: friends and family, provid5: other channels
Outcome categories: (1) new state: formal employment, (2) new state: informal employment, (3) new state: self-employed, (4) new state: inactive, (5) new state: searching

Figure 15.8: Discrete change plots for different search channels.

searching' are more affected, in both directions. Transition into informality, on the other hand, is mostly negatively affected by discrete changes in the search method chosen.

15.2.2 Unemployment Insurance Benefits

Paes De Barros, Corseuil, and Foguel (1999) find empirical evidence that unemployment insurance benefits lead to better matching of the job searchers. In their study, the quality of matching is measured in the relation of pre- and post-unemployment wages, but not in terms of formal or informal employment. I estimate the impact of unemployment insurance benefits on the exit into the different occupational states. Results for the benefit covariates are displayed in Table 15.7; the complete table can be found in the appendix (Table C.3).

Interestingly, there are only two significant odd ratios in Table 15.7: individuals who receive three months of unemployment insurance benefits tend to be 9% less likely to transit into inactivity than to stay searching. This is a result that contradicts Chahad and Fernandez (2000), who found that unemployment insurance benefits lead to an increased transition into inactivity. Individuals receiving four months of benefits are 13% more likely to take up informal work than to stay searching. The latter result is counter-productive in the sense that the unemployment insurance should lead to more formal jobs and not to an increase of the probability of taking up informal employment.

Table 15.7: Odds ratios of the impact of benefit payments on the transition into employment

Covariate	(1)	(2)	(3)	(4)
search channels				
three months	0.9012	0.9980	0.9767	0.9073
benefits	(1.250)	(0.031)	(0.353)	(2.072)*
four months	0.9288	1.1327	0.9405	0.9802
benefits	(0.870)	(1.916)*	(0.851)	(0.424)
five months	1.0804	1.0254	0.8922	0.9422
benefits	(0.925)	(0.342)	(1.509)	(1.202)

Base category: (5) 'searching'. Absolute value of z statistics in parentheses
significant at 5%; ** significant at 1%
(1) new state: formal employment, (2) new state: informal employment, (3) new state: self-employed, (4) new state: inactive

But it can partly be explained by the fact that the benefits are very low and therefore people may tend to take up additional informal employment to gain complementary income while queuing for formal employment. Another explanation is in line with those authors claim is that workers ask to get dismissed in order to claim their FGTS savings and continue informally in the same job, or with a different company.[4]

The estimated discrete changes reveal no further information as none of the estimates shows any significance. The values for the discrete change are reported in Table C.4 in the appendix.

Concluding from the results obtained here, it can be said that no significant impact of unemployment benefits on the outcome of the search process is evident in this sample.

15.2.3 Personal Characteristics and Duration of Unemployment

In the estimation, personal explanatory variables like sex, age and the position in the household, the per capita household income and the duration of unemployment have been considered. Apart from the odds ratios in Table 15.5,

[4]For a discussion about the effect of the FGTS and references refer to Section 3.2.

both the odds ratio plot (Figure 15.9) and the plot of discrete changes (Figure 15.10) also provide information on the impact of these covariates.

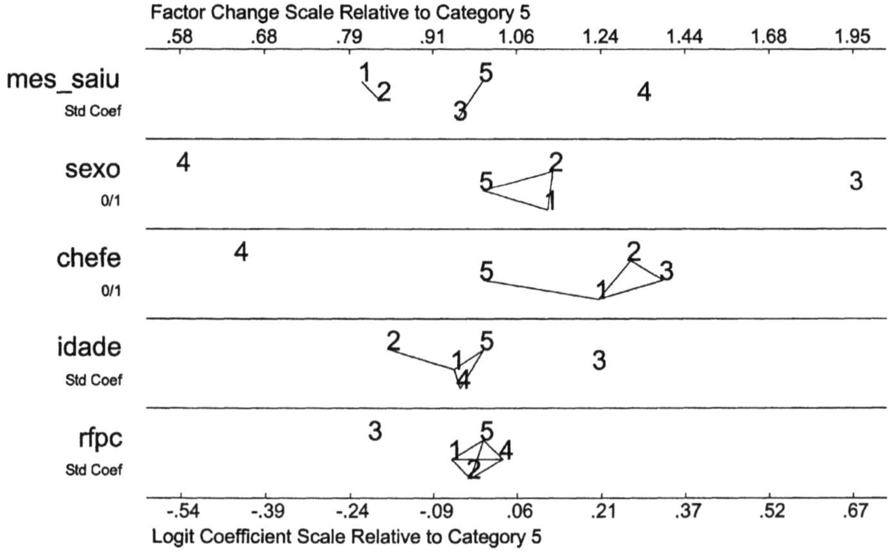

Source: "Monthly Labor Survey (PME) (1999), own calculations"
Covariates: mes_saiu: duration of unemployment, sexo: sex, chefe: head of household, idade: age, rfpc: per capita household income
Outcome categories: (1) new state: formal employment, (2) new state: informal employment, (3) new state: self-employed, (4) new state: inactive, (5) new state: searching

Figure 15.9: Odds ratio plots for the duration of unemployment and personal characteristics.

The odds ratios for the 'duration of unemployment' are highly significant for the transitions into formal and informal employment. In both cases, they reduce the likelihood of transition versus remaining searching. The transition into self-employment is not significantly associated with an increase in the unemployment spell. Not surprisingly, increasing unemployment spells lead to higher odds ratios to transit into inactivity versus remaining searching. The odds ratio plot (Figure 15.9) reflects these findings, as does the plot of discrete changes (Figure 15.10). An increase of one standard deviation in the unemployment spell slightly decreases the probability of transiting into formal or informal employment and increases the probability of transiting into inactivity. The phenomenon that transition probabilities into work decrease with increasing unemployment duration is a result found by many other studies working on the duration of unemployment.[5]

[5]Compare for example (OECD 1994).

Sex has no significant impact on the transitions into formal or informal employment, but both the odds ratio for transition into self-employment and that for transition into inactivity are highly significant. The odds of becoming inactive relative to remaining searching are 42% lower for men than for women. Men are almost twice as likely to take up self-employment than women. These results, which are also reflected in the odds ratio plot and the discrete change plot, are observable within most countries.

A less obvious result is that being a head of household versus a dependent household member increases the likeliness of exiting into informal employment by 30% and the likeliness of self-employment by almost 40% compared to 'remaining searching', but has no significant impact on taking up formal employment. Heads of households are under greater pressure to earn income to sustain their household members, so the fact that they take up informal or self-employment instead of remaining searching is a plausible one. On the other hand, it would also be plausible to assume that heads try to obtain stable employment offering protection against unjust dismissal, a feature that only formal employment offers. Recalling the results in Part II, heads though show a higher likeliness of making on-the-job transitions from informal employment to formal employment than non-heads, an observation that also holds for women (see Table 9.1). For these groups, informal employment seems to be a stepping stone into formality when performing on-the-job search.

Age increases the likelihood of transiting into self-employment and decreases the likelihood for transitions into informal employment, when compared to 'remaining searching'. This behavior confirms the assumed pattern formulated in the theoretical section in this part. For transitions into formal employment or inactivity, age shows no significant impact. The discrete change plot shows no large spread in the impact of age on the transition in any of the outcome categories.

Table 15.5 shows a highly significant negative impact of the per capita household income on the transition into self-employment, but the odds ratio value is very close to one (0.999). This may be the case because at least a part of the information contained in this covariate, the social background and the financial resources available for search and living, are already captured by the covariate 'duration of unemployment'. The odds ratio plot shows a cluster at the reference category 'remaining searching', with the exception for the outcome category 'self-employed', and the overall spread is low. The same holds for the plotted discrete changes; the spread is low. Although the numbers lie close together it is interesting that the positive discrete change for a transition into inactivity has the same absolute magnitude as the negative discrete change for a transition into self-employment.

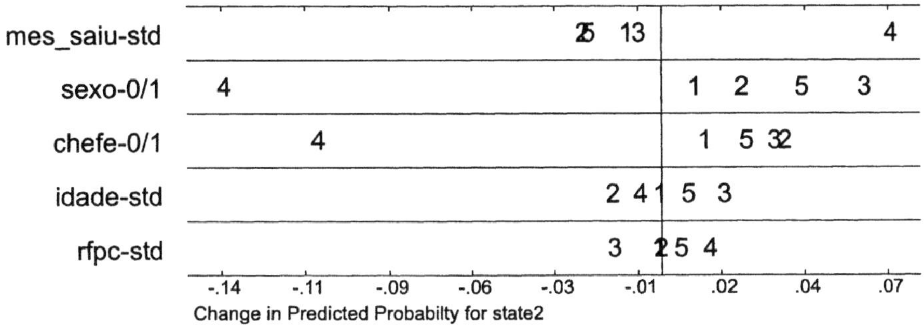

Source: "Monthly Labor Survey (PME) (1999), own calculations"
Covariates: mes_saiu: duration of unemployment, sexo: sex, chefe: head of household, idade: age, rfpc: per capita household income
Outcome categories: (1) new state: formal employment, (2) new state: informal employment, (3) new state: self-employed, (4) new state: inactive, (5) new state: searching

Figure 15.10: Discrete change plots for the duration of unemployment and personal characteristics.

15.2.4 Education

The educational variables show many significant impacts on labor market transitions. Most results follow the expected patterns: low educational levels like 'first part of primary school concluded' lead to lower odds to transit into informal employment or self employed, compared to remaining searching.

'First primary' has no impact on the transition into formal employment or inactivity. 'Second primary' concluded increases the odds for transiting into formality by a factor larger than two compared to remaining searching.

A high school diploma makes an individual about 85% more likely to take up formal employment while both a completed primary school education and a high school diploma decrease the likelihood of a person to become informally or self-employed.

Interestingly, a university degree or other superior education does not have any significant impact on the transition into employment; the only significant association is the substantial decrease in the odds for becoming inactive. This reaction concerning inactivity is also observable for the other educational levels with the exception of 'first primary' which does not show a significant effect.

The odds ratio plot reveals that with increasing schooling level, the probability of transiting into self-employment declines rapidly compared to the odds

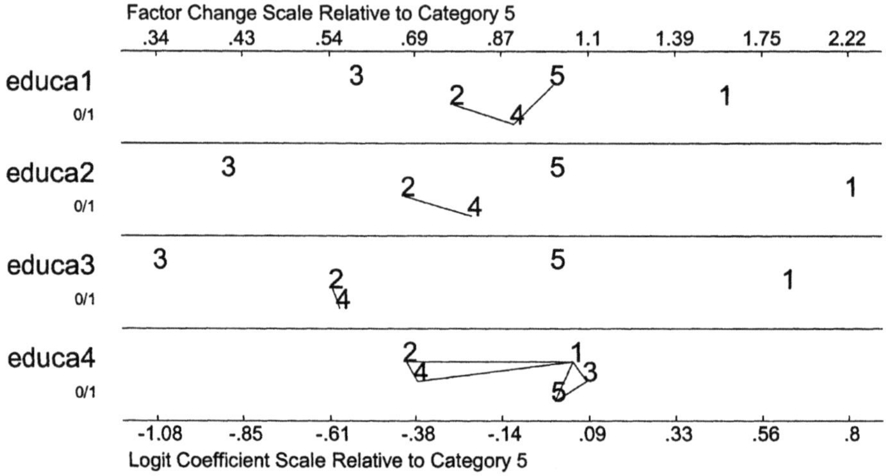

Source: "Monthly Labor Survey (PME) (1999), own calculations"
Covariates: educa1: first part primary school completed, educa2: second part primary school completed, educa3: high school completed, educa4: superior education completed
Outcome categories: (1) new state: formal employment, (2) new state: informal employment, (3) new state: self-employed, (4) new state: inactive, (5) new state: searching

Figure 15.11: Odds ratio plots for different educational levels.

ratios for the other outcome categories. For individuals with superior education completed, the picture changes substantially. Here, the odds ratio for a transition into self-employment at once gets positive.

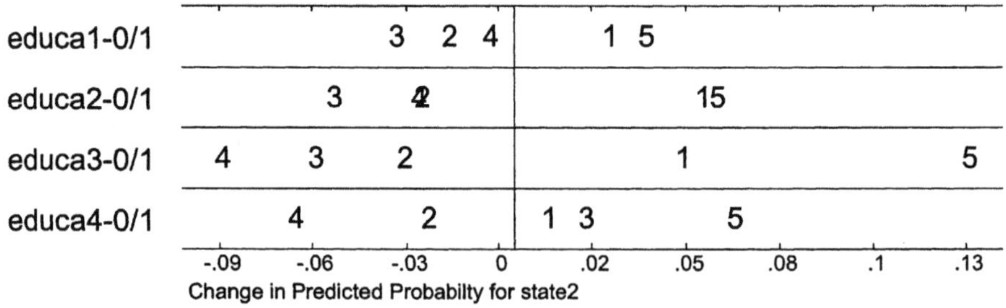

Source: "Monthly Labor Survey (PME) (1999), own calculations"
Covariates: educa1: first part primary school completed, educa2: second part primary school completed, educa3: high school completed, educa4: superior education completed
Outcome categories: (1) new state: formal employment, (2) new state: informal employment, (3) new state: self-employed, (4) new state: inactive, (5) new state: searching

Figure 15.12: Discrete change plots for different educational levels.

This strange pattern reflects the heterogeneity of self-employment, with petty trade and street vendors on one end of the spectrum and the highly educated free-lancer at the other end. Another interesting fact is that the transitions into informal employment and into inactivity follow a pattern that is similar, but weaker, to that for self-employment. The odds to take up informal employment or to become inactive versus remaining searching decline with increasing schooling level, but increase somewhat (while remaining negative) for the group of superior education.

The discrete change plots support most of the patterns of the odds ratios but show even larger negative impacts of the both highest educational levels for a transition into inactivity. The discrete changes also show that higher schooling increases the effect of remaining unemployed, with a very large effect for high school diploma.

Chapter 16

Conclusion

In the first line of empirical analysis in this part of my thesis, I have investigated the impact of the labor history on the search process, especially the choice of search channels. Estimation results show that former formally employed workers are less likely to use the informal search channel 'asked friend and family' than are all the other occupational groups. This finding is in line with my hypothesis that 'friends and family' is a channel primarily perceived as one leading to informal jobs (individuals having been self employed are twice as likely to use this channel) and is therefore probably chosen less by those formerly formally employed. A second explanation is the 'method of last resort'-character of this channel, being mostly used and perceived as important when other possible channels fail. Estimates of the impact of this search channel on the outcome of the search process show that individuals reporting this search channel are more likely to transit into self-employment or informal employment, and about 25% more likely to remain searching than to transit into formality. Of all the exit states, transiting into inactivity has the highest odds ratio.

The channel 'agency or union', although open to all searching individuals, is about 25% more likely to be used by searchers with a formal labor history. In part, this may be explained simply by an information deficit on the side of those without formal work experience. Many job searchers simply do not know that a public employment service exists, and many more may assume that it only services the former formally employed. The only significant effect this channel shows on the transition into other occupational states is that those using it are about one third less likely to transit into inactivity relative to remaining searching. This result reflects the low matching rate already reported by special evaluations of the SINE.

For another formal channel, 'tests', there is no significant pattern discernable and the use of this channel does not have any significant impact on the exit into work. Labor history does not seem to have an impact on the choice of the last of the formal channels considered, 'advertisement', but individuals using this channel versus 'asked employer' are less likely to take up informal employment than to remain searching. However, the impact on the transition into formal employment is far from significant.

Summarizing these results, it seems that the former occupational state does not automatically lead to a determined search behavior. This result can be interpreted in two ways: First, it could be assumed that there is no difference in the effects of different search channels on the outcome of the search process. Each search method may lead to jobs in each of the different labor market segments. The only difference between search methods lies in their specific hit rate (producing offers that lead to acceptances) and different requirement of search effort, measured in time and money spent. A second assumption could be that different search methods do lead to jobs in different segments. If this assumption holds, the results pose a larger puzzle. Either the workers in this sample have found their former job by using a special channel, and if there are different channels for finding jobs in different labor market segments, then the involved individuals did not learn by their former search process. Alternatively, measurement errors are involved, as individuals can only report one search method in the PME questionnaire; they may have reported one method but found the job via another channel. Cross tabulation of 'former occupational state', 'education' and 'search method used' reveals that search patterns for former informally employed workers, and those who held formal jobs, do not differ in proportions, with the exception of a slightly higher use of the 'friends and family' channel by former informally employed individuals.

The data reveal two facts: first, there exists a relation between the former occupational state and the search method chosen to look for the next job, but there is no discernable pattern for channels predestinated to lead to formal employment like 'test' and 'advertisement'. Second, effects of different search channels on exit rates into different occupational states can be distinguished, but none of the search channels seems to have a positive impact on taking up formal employment.

These results show that most of the job searchers in Brazil use channels that involve directly asking either an employer or friends and family. Search channels that provide collection of information on vacancies are only used by a small proportion of workers. There is potential for the public employment service to improve the allocation of workers by setting incentives for employers to post their openings with the agencies. Plans to turn the SINE agencies the only place for unemployed workers to collect their unemployment insurance benefits (instead of getting them at the local bank office) would bring more workers into contact with the agencies and so increasing the proportion of higher skilled job searchers.

Finally, one other result of this study should not be forgotten: education has a highly significant impact in both regressions performed. In the long run, the best instrument to improve the proportion of formal work will be the improvement of the educational system and access to education in Brazil. The improvement of the SINE agencies will be only a short-term solution to the deficits that result from the poor performance of the educational system and from the unequal distribution of access to good education.

Appendix A

Description of the Data Used in Part II

Table A.1: Covariates used in the estimation in chapter 8

Covariate	Mean	Std. Dev.	Minimum	Maximum
last job formal	0.3179593	0.4657436	0	1
last job informal	0.4511724	0.4976743	0	1
newcomer	0.1718629	0.3773099	0	1
last self employed	0.0590054	0.2356652	0	1
time worked before	8.572289	11.31041	0	49
male	0.5465086	0.4978964	0	1
head of household	0.1984025	0.3988482	0	1
age	21.32208	3.962823	15	29
age squared	470.3311	173.9863	225	841
no education	0.1221335	0.3274821	0	1
first primary	0.605514	0.488803	0	1
second primary	0.2723525	0.4452277	0	1
per capita househ. income	72.93238	96.95007	0	1637.955
winter	0.164133	0.3704439	0	1
spring	0.3305849	0.4704844	0	1
summer	0.1484154	0.355557	0	1
fall	0.3568668	.4791368	0	1

Source: Monthly Labor Survey (PME) (1999)," own calculations"

Table A.2: List of professions and proportions of formal and informal employment (in %) used in the estimation in Chapter 8

Profession	formal	informal	**Profession**	formal	informal
63 recepcionistas	21.93	78.07	604 reposit. de mercad.	11.33	88.67
424 mecânico veh'ic.	44.38	55.62	605 demonstradores	38.14	61.86
425 mecânicos	20.05	79.95	631 pracista, viajante	54.89	45.11
426 soldadores	17.82	82.18	632 repr. comercial	58.21	41.79
429 ferreiros/serralh.	51.14	48.86	641 corretor seguros	49.70	50.30
431 lanterneiros	60.80	39.20	643 corr. títulos e val.	29.27	70.73
470 alfaiate costureiro	42.26	57.74	645 outr. agentes corr.	41.43	58.57
471 auxiliar de costura	39.42	60.58	752 trocadores	16.11	83.89
473 modelistas cort.	35.59	64.41	774 telefonistas	17.56	82.44
474 bordadeiras/cerzid.	51.35	48.65	775 carteiros	8.15	91.85
478 trab. fabric. sapato	21.77	78.23	802 Babás	75.46	24.54
479 bolseiro/cinteiro	45.95	54.05	803 cozinheiras	37.74	62.26
481 marceneiro	51.69	48.31	804 faxineiras	81.86	18.14
482 carpinteiro	30.40	69.60	805 lavadeiras	85.60	14.40
487 estofador capoteiro	43.81	56.19	807 empregado dom.	55.30	44.70
503 reparador eq. elétr.	21.32	78.68	808 outr. ocup. dom.	52.35	47.65
506 eletricistas de inst.	30.80	69.20	812 camareiros	9.78	90.22
512 pedreiros	44.94	55.06	813 cozinheiros	33.86	66.14
513 servente de pedreiro	77.48	22.52	814 garçons	41.72	58.28
514 pintor caiador	58.48	41.52	815 atendente de bar	41.61	58.39
515 estucador	49.12	50.88	821 cabeleireiros	75.00	25.00
516 ladrilheiro taq	43.24	56.76	823 maquiladores	41.07	58.93
517 encanadores	25.83	74.17	824 manicuro, pedicuro	70.77	29.23
518 vidraceiro	43.84	56.16	825 lavadeira, passad.	23.75	76.25
519 calceteiro asfal	37.84	62.16	834 técnico de esp.	50.68	49.32
521 op máq constr. civil	17.48	82.52	841 porteiros	10.58	89.42
535 doceiro, confeiteiro	24.72	75.28	842 ascensoristas	11.59	88.41
537 padeiros	27.10	72.90	843 vigias	27.24	72.76
556 encadernador car	25.19	74.81	844 serventes	20.95	79.05
557 outr. ocup ind gráfica	30.68	69.32	845 contínuos	29.98	70.02
577 vassoureiros	34.62	65.38	869 guarda particular	10.75	89.25
578 marmoristas	23.08	76.92	917 guarda sanitár.	63.94	36.06
581 pintores a pistola	40.72	59.28	918 inspetor fiscais	30.98	69.02
584 emb mercadorias	18.06	81.94	919 jardineiro exc lav.	34.68	65.32
586 ocup ind art borracha	16.46	83.54	920 lixeiros	22.80	77.20
602 vendedores	29.59	70.41	921 lubrificadores	17.78	82.22
603 operador de caixa	14.38	85.62	922 operador trat. água	25.00	75.00

Source: Monthly Labor Survey (PME) (1999), own calculations.

Appendix B

Description of the Data Used in Part III

Table B.1: Cross tabulation of sex and former labor market state

sex	former occupational state				Total
	former formally employed	former informally employed	newcomer	self employed	
male	2220	1561	424	630	4835
	45.92	32.29	8.77	13.03	100.00
	57.05	50.06	42.57	70.47	54.33
female	1671	1557	572	264	4064
	41.12	38.31	14.07	6.50	100.00
	42.95	49.94	57.43	29.53	45.67
Total	3891	3118	996	894	8899
	43.72	35.04	11.19	10.05	100.00
	100.00	100.00	100.00	100.00	100.00

Source: Monthly Labor Survey (PME) (1999), own calculations
first row: absolute numbers
second row: row percentages
third row: column percentages

Table B.2: Covariates used in the estimations in Chapter 14

Covariate	Obs.	Mean	Std. Dev.	Minimum	Maximum
last job formal	8899	0.4372401	0.4960734	0	1
last job informal	8899	0.3503764	0.4771146	0	1
newcomer	8899	0.1119227	0.315289	0	1
last self employed	8899	0.1004607	0.3006302	0	1
male	8899	0.5433195	0.4981479	0	1
head of household	8899	0.3271154	0.4691862	0	1
age	8899	29.25306	10.68732	10	78
test	8899	0.0058434	0.0762224	0	1
agency or union	8899	0.090572	0.2870156	0	1
advertisement	8899	0.0745028	0.2626021	0	1
friends and family	8899	0.1473199	0.3544445	0	1
other	8899	0.0112372	.1054144	0	1
asked employer	8899	0.6705248	.4700491	0	1
no benefit	6965	0.5928212	0.491344	0	1
3 months benefit	6965	0.0854271	0.2795363	0	1
4 months benefit	6965	0.1132807	.3169584	0	1
5 months benefit	6965	0.2084709	.4062444	0	1
months of unemployment	8663	13.26365	15.89165	1	50
spell of last job	7969	14.55314	16.08434	0	49
no education	8899	0.0979885	0.491344	0	1
first primary	8899	0.3165524	0.4651573	0	1
second primary	8899	0.2481178	0.4319448	0	1
high school	8899	0.3373413	0.472829	0	1
superior	8899	0.045286	0.2079424	0	1
per capita househ. income	8899	127.4013	225.7776	0	3868.238

Source: Monthly Labor Survey (PME) (1999)", own calculations"

Appendix C

More Estimation Results for Part III

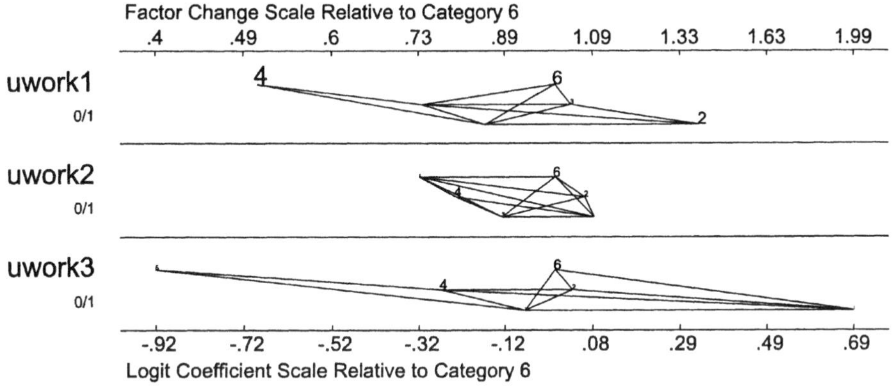

Source: "Monthly Labor Survey (PME) (1999), own calculations"
Covariates: uwork1: former formally employed, uwork2: former informally employed, uwork3: newcomer
Outcome categories: (1) search method: participated in test, (2) search method: contacted agency, (3) search method: answered to an advertisement, (4) search method: asked friends and family, (5) search method: other, (6) search method: asked employer

Figure C.1: Odds ratio plots with discrete change for the type of previous job: former formally employed, former informally employed, newcomer.

Table C.1: Odds ratios of the impact of benefit payments on the choice of search methods

Covariate	(1)	(2)	(3)	(4)	(5)
3 months benefits	1.1320	0.9217	0.8720	0.9869	1.1943
	(0.171)	(0.483)	(0.685)	(0.080)	(0.388)
4 months benefits	0.6917	0.8407	0.9060	0.8686	0.4937
	(0.513)	(1.107)	(0.563)	(0.910)	(1.325)
5 months benefits	0.6369	0.9547	0.9172	0.8605	1.4716
	(0.779)	(0.340)	(0.573)	(1.106)	(1.082)
male	0.9961	0.9060	1.1044	1.0401	1.0120
	(0.008)	(0.870)	(0.768)	(0.344)	(0.039)
head of household	0.5399	0.8577	0.8073	0.9252	0.7034
	(0.984)	(1.142)	(1.422)	(0.605)	(0.929)
age	1.0421	0.9868	1.0204	1.0068	0.9904
	(1.491)	(1.987)*	(2.899)**	(1.121)	(0.531)
first primary	0.0000	1.2774	1.2812	0.9944	1.0243
	(0.000)	(0.991)	(0.803)	(0.030)	(0.030)
second primary	1.7371	1.4156	1.6842	0.6295	1.4289
	(0.481)	(1.381)	(1.671)	(2.222)*	(0.451)
high school	2.0369	1.6170	3.3560	0.8392	2.6394
	(0.638)	(1.946)*	(4.078)**	(0.887)	(1.284)
superior education	8.1879	0.8145	1.6674	0.9693	2.0738
	(3.598)**	(0.713)	(2.420)**	(0.110)	(1.572)
per capita	1.0001	1.0003	1.0003	0.9999	1.0007
household income	(0.076)	(1.245)	(1.574)	(0.244)	(1.665)*

Base category: (6) asked employer. Absolute value of z statistics in parentheses
significant at 5%; ** significant at 1%

(1) search method: participated in test versus asked employer, (2) search method: contacted agency or union versus asked employer, (3) search method: answered to an advertisement versus asked employer, (4) search method: asked friends and family versus asked employer, (5) search method: other versus asked employer

Table C.2: Discrete changes of the impact of benefit payments on the choice of search methods

Covariate	(1)	(2)	(3)	(4)	(5)	(6)
3 months	5.41e-08	-0.0066	-0.0088	0.0005	0.0023	0.0126
benefits†	(0.00)	(0.44)	(0.68)	(0.03)	(0.41)	(0.54)
4 months	-1.06e-07	-0.0129	-0.0040	-0.0100	-0.0060	0.0329
benefits†	(0.00)	(0.95)	(0.33)	(0.71)	(1.52)	(1.56)
5 months†	-1.48e-07	-0.0024	-0.0048	-0.0139	0.0047	0.0163
benefits	(0.00)	(0.19)	(0.46)	(1.07)	(1.10)	(0.86)
male†	-1.99e-09	-0.0106	0.0075	0.0041	0.0001	-0.0011
	(.)	(1.00)*	(0.84)	(0.38)	(0.03)	(0.07)
head of	-1.97e-07	-0.0114	-0.0129	-0.0036	-0.0032	0.0311
household†	(0.00)	(0.93)	(1.26)	(0.30)	(0.85)	(1.72)*
age	1.47e-08	-0.0148	0.0015	0.0007	-0.0001	-0.0006
	(1.00)	(2.40)*	(3.09)**	(1.13)	(0.58)	(0.63)
first primary†	-0.0040	0.0222	0.0165	-0.0052	0.0002	-0.0292
	(2.26)*	(0.89)	(0.70)	(0.29)	(0.02)	(0.89)
second primary†	2.11e-07	0.0345	0.0418	-0.0489	0.0036	-0.0310
	(0.00)	(1.28)	(1.51)	(2.77)**	(0.37)	(0.87)
high school†	2.14e-07	0.0351	0.0950	-0.0345	0.0098	-0.1054
	(0.00)	(1.43)	(3.45)**	(1.83)	(0.96)	(3.02)**
superior	2.24e-06	-0.0230	0.0456	-0.0072	0.0104	-0.0257
education†	(0.00)	(1.05)	(2.13)*	(0.29)	(1.14)	(0.70)
household in-	-1.60e-12	0.0000	0.0000	-0.00010	6.46e-06	-0.0000
come per capita	(.)	(1.15)	(1.47)	(0.51)	(1.54)	(1.12)

† dy/dx is for discrete changes of the dummy variable from 0 to one. Values without † are for continuous variables. Absolute value of z statistics in parentheses

* significant at 5%; ** significant at 1%

(1) search method: participated in test, (2) search method: contacted agency, (3) search method: answered to an advertisement, (4) search method: asked friends and family, (5) search method: other, (6) search method: asked employer

Table C.3: Odds ratios of the impact of benefit payments on the transition into employment

Covariate	(1)	(2)	(3)	(4)
search channels				
test	0.1304	0.9670	1.0107	1.0003
	(0.000)	(0.454)	(1.190)	(0.008)
agency	0.9735	1.0467	0.9713	0.9603
	(0.382)	(0.859)	(0.448)	(0.972)
advertisement	1.1229	0.8545	1.0315	1.0479
	(1.896)*	(2.120)*	(0.505)	(1.164)
friends and family	0.9339	1.0007	1.0515	1.1289
	(0.859)	(0.012)	(0.857)	(3.091)**
other channels	0.9287	0.9340	0.9183	0.9926
	(0.880)	(0.978)	(1.011)*	(0.193)
unemployment benefits				
three months	0.9012	0.9980	0.9767	0.9073
benefits	(1.250)	(0.031)	(0.353)	(2.072)*
four months	0.9288	1.1327	0.9405	0.9802
benefits	(0.870)	(1.916)*	(0.851)	(0.424)
five months	1.0804	1.0254	0.8922	0.9422
benefits	(0.925)	(0.342)	(1.509)	(1.202)
personal characteristics				
male	1.0476	1.0355	1.4308	0.7103
	(0.633)	(0.574)	(4.908)**	(8.044)**
head of household	1.0788	1.1487	1.0749	0.7876
	(0.939)	(2.096)*	(1.017)	(4.801)**
age	0.8843	0.8159	1.1716	1.1565
	(1.454)	(2.895)**	(2.350)**	(3.054)**
per capita	0.9186	0.9310	0.9515	1.0830
household income	(0.972)	(0.933)	(0.629)	(2.069)*
education				
first primary	1.0592	0.8088	0.7398	0.9581
	(0.390)	(2.210)*	(3.415)**	(0.557)
second primary	1.1891	0.7950	0.7012	0.9041
	(1.256)	(2.445)**	(3.944)**	(1.355)
high school	1.0495	0.7624	0.5969	0.8189
	(0.307)	(2.601)**	(5.044)**	(2.416)*
superior education	1.0103	0.8925	1.0480	0.9110
	(0.143)	(1.469)	(0.725)	(2.106)*

Base category: (5) 'searching'. Absolute value of z statistics in parentheses
significant at 5%; ** significant at 1%
(1) new state: formal employment, (2) new state: informal employment, (3) new state: self-employed, (4) new state: inactive

Table C.4: Discrete change of the impact of benefit payments on the transition into employment

Covariate	(1)	(2)	(3)	(4)	(5)
search channels					
test†	-0.0633	-0.0317	0.0214	0.0248	0.0488
	(15.14)**	(0.49)	(0.31)	(0.23)	(0.42)
agency†	-0.0032	0.0187	-0.0051	-0.0249	0.0145
	(0.00)	(0.00)	(0.00)	(0.00)	(0.00)
advertisement†	0.0247	-0.0470	0.0061	0.0347	-0.0185
	(0.00)	(0.00)	(0.00)	(0.00)	(0.00)
friends and family†	-0.0161	-0.0103	0.0040	0.0774	-0.0550
	(0.00)	(0.00)	(0.00)	(3.01)**	(0.00)
other channels†	-0.0223	-0.0368	-0.0362	0.0190	0.0762
	(0.00)	(0.00)	(0.00)	(0.00)	(0.00)
unemployment benefits					
three months	-0.0110	0.0080	0.0015	-0.0437	0.0448
benefits †	(0.00)	(0.00)	(0.00)	(0.00)	(0.00)
four months	-0.0096	0.0337	-0.0115	-0.0123	-0.0002
benefits †	(0.00)	(0.01)	(0.00)	(0.00)	(0.00)
five months	0.0110	0.0086	-0.0155	-0.0220	0.0178
benefits †	(0.00)	(0.00)	(1.48)	(0.00)	(0.00)
personal characteristics					
male†	0.0112	0.0178	0.0628	-0.1495	0.0577
	(0.00)	(0.00)	(0.00)	(0.00)	(0.00)
head of household†	0.0126	0.0360	0.0172	-0.1007	0.0349
	(0.00)	(0.00)	(0.00)	(0.00)	(0.00)
age	-0.0008	-0.0022	0.0011	-0.0030	0.0011
	(0.00)	(0.00)	(0.00)	(0.00)	(0.00)
per capita	-0.0000	-0.0000	-0.0000	0.0001	-0.0000
household income	(0.00)	(0.00)	(0.00)	(2.70)**	(0.00)
education					
first primary†	0.0133	-0.0329	-0.0391	0.0031	0.0556
	(0.00)	(0.00)	(0.00)	(0.00)	(0.00)
second primary†	0.0347	-0.0359	-0.0463	-0.0245	0.0720
	(0.00)	(0.01)	(0.01)	(0.00)	(0.00)
high school†	0.0186	-0.0315	-0.0606	-0.0451	0.1186
	(0.00)	(1.86)	(0.00)	(0.00)	(0.00)
superior education†	0.0095	-0.0334	0.0298	-0.0975	0.0617
	(0.00)	(0.00)	(0.00)	(0.00)	(0.00)

† dy/dx is for discrete changes of the dummy variable from 0 to one. Values without † are for continuous variables. Absolute value of z statistics in parentheses. * significant at 5%; ** significant at 1%. (1) new state: formal employment, (2) new state: informal employment, (3) new state: self-employed, (4) new state: inactive, (5) new state: searching

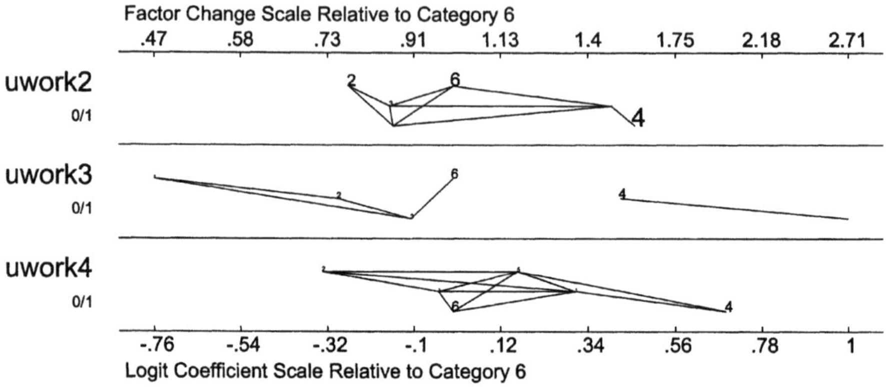

Source: "Monthly Labor Survey (PME) (1999), own calculations"
Covariates: uwork1: former formally employed, uwork2: former informally employed, uwork3: newcomer
Outcome categories: (1) search method: participated in test, (2) search method: contacted agency, (3) search method: answered to an advertisement, (4) search method: asked friends and family, (5) search method: other, (6) search method: asked employer

Figure C.2: Odds ratio plots with discrete change for the type of previous job former informally employed, newcomer, self employed.

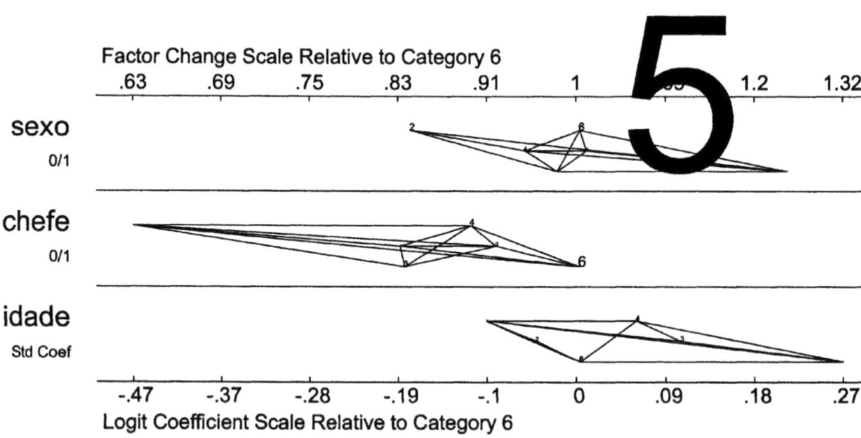

Source: "Monthly Labor Survey (PME) (1999), own calculations"
Covariates: sexo: sex, chefe: head of household, idade: age
Outcome categories: (1) search method: participated in test, (2) search method: contacted agency, (3) search method: answered to an advertisement, (4) search method: asked friends and family, (5) search method: other, (6) search method: asked employer

Figure C.3: Odds ratio plots for sex, head of household and age.

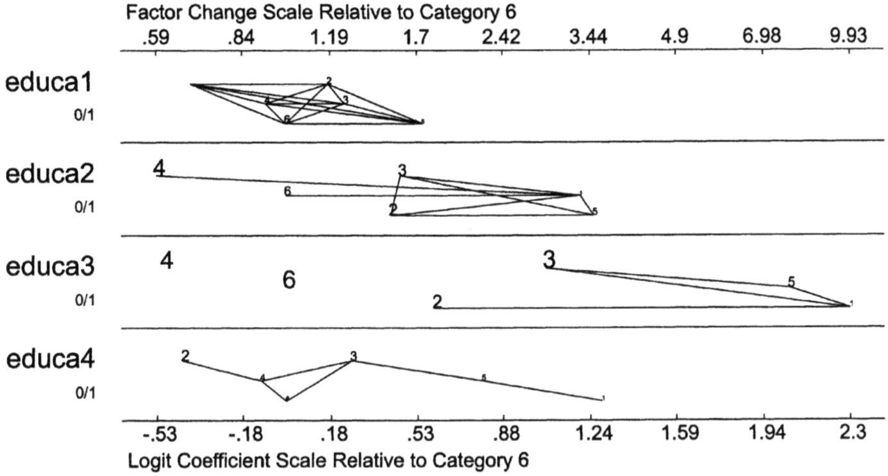

Source: "Monthly Labor Survey (PME) (1999), own calculations"
Covariates: educa1: first part primary school completed, educa2: second part primary school completed, educa3: high school completed, educa4: superior education completed
Outcome categories: (1) search method: participated in test, (2) search method: contacted agency, (3) search method: answered to an advertisement, (4) search method: asked friends and family, (5) search method: other, (6) search method: asked employer

Figure C.4: Odds ratio plots with discrete change for different levels of education.

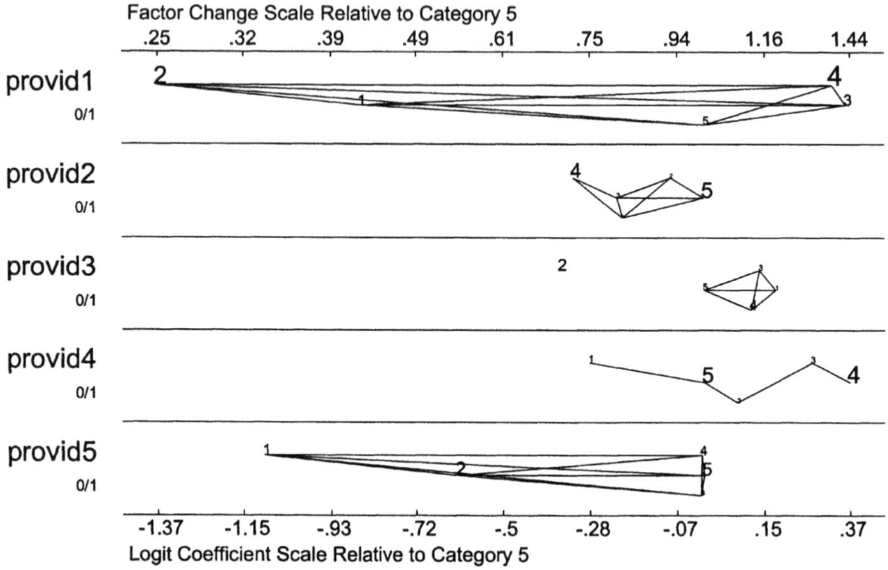

Source: "Monthly Labor Survey (PME) (1999), own calculations"
Covariates: provid1: test, provid2: agency, provid3: advertisement, provid4: friends and family, provid5: other channels
Outcome categories: (1) new state: formal employment, (2) new state: informal employment, (3) new state: self-employed, (4) new state: inactive, (5) new state: searching

Figure C.5: Odds ratio plots with discrete change for different search channels.

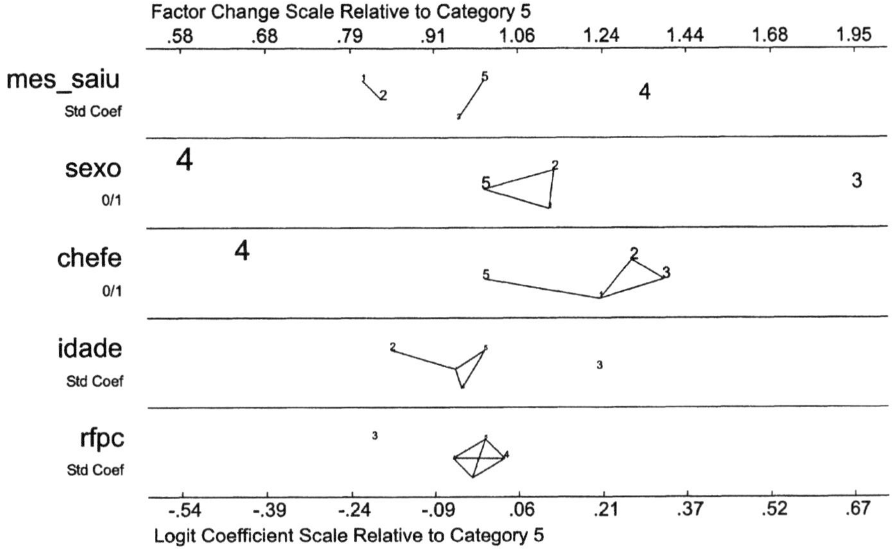

Source: "Monthly Labor Survey (PME) (1999), own calculations"
Covariates: mes_saiu: duration of unemployment, sexo: sex, chefe: head of household, idade: age, rfpc: per capita household income
Outcome categories: (1) new state: formal employment, (2) new state: informal employment, (3) new state: self-employed, (4) new state: inactive, (5) new state: searching

Figure C.6: Odds ratio plots with discrete change for the duration of unemployment and personal characteristics.

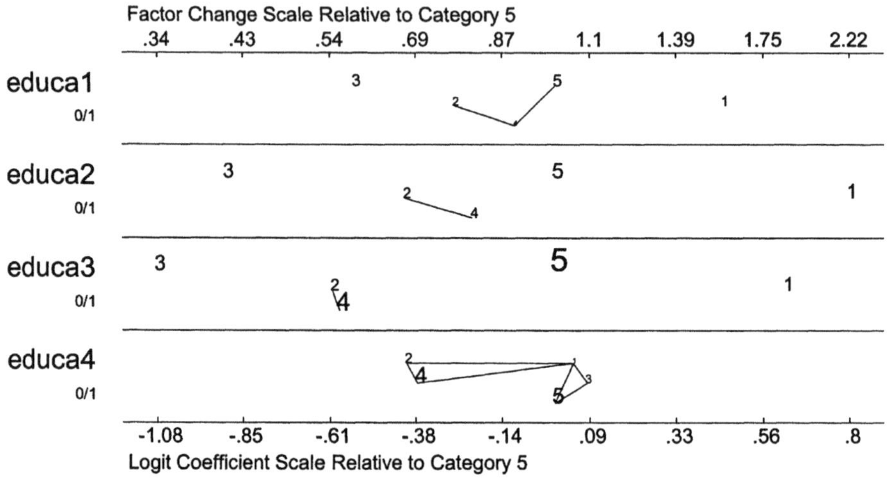

Source: "Monthly Labor Survey (PME) (1999), own calculations"
Covariates: educa1: first part primary school completed, educa2: second part primary school completed, educa3: high school completed, educa4: superior education completed
Outcome categories: (1) new state: formal employment, (2) new state: informal employment, (3) new state: self-employed, (4) new state: inactive, (5) new state: searching

Figure C.7: Odds ratio plots with discrete change for different educational levels.

Bibliography

Addison, John T., and Pedro Portugal. 2002. "Job search methods and outcomes." *Oxford Economic Papers* 54 (3): pp. 505–533.

———. 2003. "Unemployment duration." *The Journal of Human Resources* 38 (1): pp. 156–191.

Aigner, Dennis J., and Glen G. Cain. 1977. "Statistical theories of discrimination in labor markets." *Industrial and Labor Relations Review* 30 (2): pp. 175–187.

Akerlof, George A. 1982. "Labor contracts as partial gift exchange." *Quarterly Journal of Economics* 97 (November): pp. 543–569.

Akerlof, George A., and Janet L. Yellen. 1986. "Introduction." In *Efficiency Wage Models of the Labor Market*, edited by George A. Akerlof and Janet L. Yellen. Cambridge and others: Cambridge University Press.

Albrecht, J.W., B. Holmlund, and H. Lang. 1991. "Comparative statistics in dynamic programming models with an application to job search." *Journal of Economic Dynamics and Control* 15:pp. 755–769.

Allison, Paul D. 1995. *Survival Analysis Using the SAS System: A Practical Guide.* Cary, NC, USA: SAS Institute Inc.

———. 1999. *Logistic Regression Using the SAS System: Theory and Application.* Cary, NC, USA: SAS Institute Inc.

Amadeo, Edward J., and José M. Camargo. 1997. "Brazil: Regulation and Flexibility in the Labor Market." In *Labor Markets In Latin America – Combining Social Protection with Market Flexibility*, edited by Sebastian Edwards and Nora Lustig. Washington: The Brookings Institution Press.

Amadeo, Edward J., Indermit S. Gill, and Marcelo C. Neri. 2002. "Assessing the Impact of Regulations on Informal Workers in Brazil." In *Crafting Labor Policy*, edited by Indermit S. Gill, Claudio E. Montengro, and Dörte Dömeland. Washington and New York: World Bank and Oxford University Press.

Arbache, Jorge S. 1999. "Do unions always decrease wage dispersion? The case of Brazilian manufacturing." *Journal of Labor Research* 20 (5): pp. 425–436.

Atkinson, A., and J. Micklewright. 1991. "Unemployment compensation and labor market transitions: A critical review." *Journal of Economic Literature* 29 (December): pp. 1679–1727.

Beck, Ulrich. 1999. *Schöne neue Arbeitswelt: Vision: Weltbürgergesellschaft.* Frankfurt/Main, New York: Campus Verlag.

Becker, Gary, S. 1957. *The Economics of Discrimination.* Chicago: University of Chicago Press.

———. 1962. "Investment in human capital: A theoretical analysis." *Journal of Political Economy* 70 (5, Part 2): pp. 9–49.

———. 1964. *Human Capital: A Theoretical and Empirical Analysis, with Special Reference to Education.* New York: National Bureau of Economic Reserach. General Series No. 80.

Behrmann, Jere R. 1999. "Labor Markets in Developing Countries." In *Handbook of Labor Economics. Volume 3B*, edited by Orley C. Ashenfelter and David Card. Amsterdam and others: Elsevier Science B.V.

Bellman, R. 1957. *Dynamic Programming.* Princeton, N.J.: Princeton University Press.

Belman, Dale, and John Heywood. 1991. "Sheepskin effects in the returns to education: An examination of women and minorities." *Review of Economics and Statistics* 73 (4): pp. 720–724.

Belzil, Christian. 2001. "Unemployment insurance and subsequent job duration: Job matching versus unobserved heterogeneity." *Journal of Applied Econometrics* 16:pp. 619–636.

Berger, Marguerite, and Myra Buvinic. 1989. *Women's Ventures: Assistance to the Informal Sector in Latin America.* Hartford: Kumarian Press.

Bienefeld, Manfred A., and E.M. Godfrey. 1975. "Measuring unemployment and the informal sector." *Institute of Development Studies Bulletin* 7:pp. 4–10.

Blanchard, Olivier, and Augustin Landier. 2002. "The perverse effects of partial labour market reform: fixed–term contracts in France." *The Economic Journal* 112 (June): pp. F214–F244.

Blau, D.M., and P.K. Robins. 1990. "Job search outcomes for the employed and unemployed." *Journal of Political Economy* 98:pp. 637–655.

Böheim, René, and Mark P. Taylor. 2002, July. Job search methods, intensity and success in Britain in the 1990s. Johannes Kepler University of Linz, Working Paper No. 206.

Booth, Alison L., Marco Francesconi, and Jeff Frank. 2002. "Temporary jobs: Stepping stones or dead ends?" *The Economic Journal* 112 (480): pp. F189–F213.

Borjas, Georg, and Matthew Goldberg. 1978. "Biased screening and discrimination in the labor market." *American Economic Review* 68 (December): pp. 918–922.

Bover, Olympia, Manuel Arellano, and Samuel Bentolila. 2002. "Unemployment duration, benefit duration and the business cycle." *The Economic Journal* 112 (April): pp. 223–265.

Brown, Charles. 1999. "Minimum wages, employment, and the distribution of income." In *Handbook of Labor Economics. Volume 3B*, edited by Orley C. Ashenfelter and David Card. Amsterdam and others: Elsevier Science B.V.

Bulow, Jeremy I., and Lawrence H. Summers. 1986. "A Theory of dual labor markets with application to industrial policy, discrimination and Keynesian unemployment." *Journal of Labor Economics* 4 (June): pp. 376–414.

Burdett, Kenneth. 1979. "Search, Leisure, and Individual Labor Supply." In *The Economics of Job Search*, edited by Steven A. Lippman and John J. McCall, pp. 157–170. Amsterdam and New York and Oxford: North Holland Publishing Company.

Burdett, Kenneth, Nicholas M. Kiefer, and Sunil Sharma. 1985. "Layoffs and duration dependence in a model of turnover." *Journal of Econometrics* 28:pp. 51–69.

Cain, Glenn. 1976. "The Challenge of Segmented Labor Market Theories to Orthodox Theory." *Journal of Economic Literature* 14:pp. 1215–1257.

Calderón-Madrid, Angel. 2000. Job-stability and labor mobility in urban Mexico: A study based on duration models and transition analysis. Inter-American Development Bank, Research Network Working Paper No. R-419.

Camargo, José Márcio. 1997. "Brazil: Labour market flexibility and productivity, with many poor jobs." In *Labour Productivity and Flexibility*, edited by Edward J. Amadeo and Susan Horton. New York: Palgrave Macmillan.

Card, David. 1999. "The causal effect of education on earnings." In *Handbook of Labor Economics. Volume 3B*, edited by Orley C. Ashenfelter and David Card. Amsterdam and others: Elsevier Science B.V.

Cardoso, Júnior, José Celso Pereira. 2000. Desestruturação do mercado de trabalho brasileiro e limites do seu sistema público de emprego. Instituto de Pesquisa Econômica Aplicada (IPEA) Discussion Paper No. 751.

Carneiro, Francisco G. 1997. "The changing informal labour market in Brazil: Cyclicality versus excessive intervention." *Review of Labour Economics and Industrial Relations* 11 (1): pp. 3–22.

Carneiro, Francisco G., and Andrew Henley. 1998. "Wage determination in Brazil: The growth of union bargaining power and informal employment." *The Journal of Development Studies* 34 (4): pp. 117–138.

Chahad, Jose P.Z. 2000a. Brazilian unemployment insurance: Its history, current status and challenges for the future. Paper presented at the conference 'Learning from Foreign Models in Latin American Policy Reform' on 14th of September 2000 at the Woodrow Wilson International Center in Washington D.C.

———. 2000b. Um novo desenho para as políticas públicas na área trabalho no Brasil. Mimeo.

Chahad, Jose P.Z., and Reynaldo Fernandez. 2000. Unemployment insurance and transitions in the labor market: An evaluation of Brazil's Program. Research Report.

Chahad, Jose P.Z., Veronica Orellano, and Paulo Picchetti. 2001. A Bi-Variate Probit Analysis of Job Turnover in Brazil. Anais do XXIII Encontro Brasileiro de Econometria. Salvador: SBE.

Charmes, Jacques. 1990. "A Critical Review of Concepts, Definitions and Studies in the Informal Sector." In *The Informal Sector Revisited*, edited by David Turnham, Bernard Salomé, and Antoine Schwarz. Paris: OECD.

Chiswick, Barry. 1973. "Schooling, screening and income." In *Does College Matter?*, edited by Lewis Solomon and Paul Taubman. New York: Academic Press.

Chow, Y.S., Herbert Robbins, and David Siegmund. 1971. *Great Expectations: The Theory of Optimal Stopping.* New York: Houghton–Mifflin.

Christensen, R. 1997. *Log–Linear Models and Logistic Regression, Springer Texts in Statistics.* Second Edition. New York: Springer–Verlag.

Cleves, Mario A., William W. Gould, and Roberto W. Gutierrez. 2002. *An Introduction to Survival Analysis Using Stata.* College Station, Texas, U.S.A.: Stata Press.

Cocks, Bart L. W. 1997. "Analysis of transition data by minimum-chi square method: An application to welfare spells in Belgium." *Review of Economics and Statistics* 15 (31): pp. 392–405.

Corseuil, Carlos Henrique, and Miguel N. Foguel. 2002, June. Uma sugestão de deflatores para rendas obtidas a partir de algumas pesquisas domiciliares do IBGE. Instituto de Pesquisa Econômica Aplicada (IPEA) Discussion Paper No. 897.

Corseuil, Carlos Henrique, Eduardo Pontual Ribeiro, and Daniel D. Santos. 2002, January. Criação, destruição e realocação do emprego no Brasil. Instituto de Pesquisa Econômica Aplicada (IPEA) Discussion Paper No. 855.

Cox, D.R. 1972. "Regression models and life-tables (with discussion)." *Journal of the Royal Statistical Society* Series B 30:pp. 187–220.

Cunningham, Wendy V. 1997, March. Unemployment in a Multi-Sectoral Labor Market: The Case of Brazil. Extract of the Ph.D. thesis, unpublished in this form.

De Groot, Morris H. 1970. *Optimal Statistical Decision.* New York: McGraw–Hill.

Devine, Theresa J., and Nicholas M. Kiefer. 1991. *Empirical Labor Economics - The Search Approach.* Oxford: Oxford University Press.

Dickens, W.T., and Lawrence F. Katz. 1987. Interindustry wage differences and industry characteristics. NBER Working Paper No.

Dickens, W.T., and K. Lang. 1985. "A test of dual labor market theory." *American Economic Review* 75 (September): pp. 792–805.

———. 1987. A goodness of fit test of dual labor market theory. NBER Working Paper No. 2350.

———. 1988. "The reemergence of segmented labor market theory." *American Economic Review* 78 (2): pp. 129–134.

Di Tella, Rafael, Robert J. MacCulloch, and Andrew Oswald. 2003. "The macroeconomics of happiness." *Review of Economics and Statistics. Forthcoming.*

Doeringer, P.B., and M.J. Piore. 1971. *Internal Labor Markets and Manpower Analysis.* Heath, Lexington, Massachusetts.

Dolado, Juan J., Carlos García-Serrano, and Juan F. Jimeno. 2002. "Drawing lessons from the boom of temporary jobs in Spain." *The Economic Journal* 112 (June): pp. F270–F295.

Efron, B. 1977. "The efficiency of Cox's likelihood function for censored data." *Journal of the American Statistical Association* 72:pp. 557–565.

Ehrenberg, Ronald G., and Robert S. Smith. 1991. *Modern Labor Economics: Theory and Public Policy.* 7th Edition. Reading, MA: Addison Wesley Longman, Inc.

Fajnzylber, Pablo. 2001. Minimum wage effects throughout the wage distribution: Evidence from Brazil's formal and informal sectors. Texto para Discussão No. 151. Universidade Federal de Minas Gerais, Faculdade de Ciências Econômicas, and Centro de Desenvolvimento e Planejamento Regional, Belo Horizonte.

Ferreira, Francisco H.G., and Ricardo Paes De Barros. 1999, April. The slippery slope: explaining the increase in extreme poverty in urban Brazil, 1976–1996. Pontífica Universidade Católica (PUC) Rio de Janeiro, Discussion Paper No. 404.

Ferrer, Ana M., and W. Craig Riddell. 2002. "The role of credentials in the Canadian labour market." *Canadian Journal of Economics* 35 (4): pp. 879–905 (November).

Fields, Gary S. 1990. "Labour market modelling and the urban informal sector: Theorie and evidence." In *The Informal Sector Revisited,* edited by David Turnham, Bernard Salomé, and Antoine Schwarz. Paris: OECD.

Foster, James, and Henry Wan. 1984. "Involuntary unemployment as a principal-agent equilibrium." *American Economic Review* 74:pp. 476–484.

Fougère, Denis, Jaqueline Pradel, and Muriel Roger. 2002, May. The influence of the public employment service on the search effort and on the probability of leaving unemployment. Mimeo, CREST-INSEE, Paris, revised version.

Fox, M. Louise, Edward Amadeo, and José M. Camargo. 1994. "Brazil." In *Labor Markets in an Era of Adjustment,* edited by Susan Horton, Ravi Kanbur, and Dipak Mazdumar. Washington, D.C.: EDI Development Studies. The World Bank.

Franz, Wolfgang. 2003. *Arbeitsmarktökonomik.* Berlin and others: Springer Verlag.

Gallaway, Julie H., and Alexandra Bernasek. 2002. "Gender and informal sector employment in Indonesia." *Journal of Economic Issues* 36 (2): pp. 313–321 (June).

Gill, Indermit, Amit Dar, and Mark Thomas. 1999, November. Financing unemployment insurance: International experience and lessons for Brazil. Seminário: O Sistema Brasileiro de Proteção Social ao Desempregado, Ministry of Labor and employment, São Paulo.

Gordon, D.M. 1972. *Theories of Poverty and Underemployment: Orthodox, Radical and Dual Labor Market Perspectives.* Lexington, Massachusetts: Lexington Books.

Gottfries, N., and B. McCormick. 1995. "Discrimination and open unemployment in a segmented labour market." *European Economic Review* 39:pp. 1–15.

Gregg, P., and J. Wadsworth. 1996. "How effective are state employment agencies? Jobcentre use and job matching in Britain." *Oxford Bulletin of Economics and Statistics* 58:pp. 43–67.

Guell-Rotllan, Maia, and Barbara Petrongolo. 2000, January. Workers' transitions from temporary to permanent employment: The Spanish case. London School of Economics, Discussion Paper No. 438.

Harris, John R., and Michael P. Todaro. 1970. "Migration, unemployment, and development: A two sector-analysis." *American Economic Review* 60 (1): pp. 126–142.

Hart, Keith. 1973. "Informal income opportunities and urban employment in Ghana." *Journal of Modern African Studies* 2:pp. 61–89.

Heckman, James J., and Joseph V. Hotz. 1986. "An investigation of the labor market earnings of panamanian males: Evaluating the sources of inequality." *Journal of Human Resources* 21:pp. 507–542.

Heckman, James J., and Carmen Pagés. 2000, August. The cost of job security regulation: Evidence from Latin American labor markets. Inter-American Development Bank Working Paper No. 430.

Heckman, James J., and Guilherme Sedlacek. 1985. "Heterogeneity, aggregation and market wage functions: An empirical model of self-selection in the labor market." *Journal of Political Economy* 93 (December): pp. 1077–1125.

Hoek, Jasper. 2002, July. Labor market institutions and restructuring: Evidence from regulated and unregulated labor markets in Brazil. William Davidson Working Paper No. 484.

Holen, Arlene. 1977. "Effects of unemployment insurance entitlement on duration and job search outcome." *Industrial and Labor Relations Review* 30 (4): pp. 445–450.

Holmlund, Bertil. 1998. "Unemployment insurance in theory and practice." *Scandinavian Journal of Economics* 100 (1): pp. 113–141.

Holmlund, Bertil, and Donald Storrie. 2002. "Temporary work in turbulent times: the Swedish experience." *The Economic Journal* 112 (June): pp. F245–F269.

Holzer, H.J. 1988. "Search methods used by the unemployed youth." *Journal of Labor Economics* 6:pp. 1–20.

Hosmer, Jr., David W., and Stanley Lemeshow. 1991. *Empirical Labor Economics – The Search Approach.* Oxford: Oxford University Press.

Hungerford, Thomas, and Gary Solon. 1987. "Sheepskin effects in the returns to education." *Review of Economics and Statistics* 69 (1): pp. 175–177.

IDB. 2003. *Good jobs wanted: Labor markets in Latin America. 2004 Economic and Social Progress Report.* Inter-American Development Bank. The Johns Hopkins University Press. Washington, DC: IDB.

ILO. 1972. *Employment, incomes and equality: A strategy for increasing productive employment in Kenya.* Geneva: ILO.

———. 2003. *The National Worker Qualification Plan – PLANFOR – Brazil.* http://www.logos-net.net/ilo/150_base/en/init/bra_5.htm, date: Dec. 12, 2003: ILO.

Joll, Caroline, et al. 1983. *Developments in Labor Market Analysis.* London: George Allen & Unwin.

Kassouf, Ana L. 1998. "Wage gender discrimination and segmentation in the Brazilian labour market." *Economia Aplicada* 2 (Abril – Junho): pp. 243–269.

Kaufman, R.L. 1996. "Comparing effects in dichotomous logistic regressions: A variety of standardized coefficients." *Social Science Research* 77:pp. 90–109.

Koning, Pierre, Gerard J. van den Berg, and Geert Ridder. 1997, June. A structural analysis of job search methods and subsequent wages. Research Memorandum No. 1997-36, Free University of Amsterdam.

Kröger, Martin, and Ulrich van Suntum. 1999. *Mit aktiver Arbeitsmarktpolitik aus der Beschäftigungsmisere? Ansätze und Erfahrungen in Großbritannien, Dänemark, Schweden und Deutschland.* Gütersloh: Verlag Bertelsmann Stiftung.

Krueger, Alan, and Lawrence Summers. 1988. "Efficiency wages and the inter-industry wage structure." *Econometrica* 56 (2): pp. 259–393 (March).

Lancaster, Tony. 1992. *The Econometric Analysis of Transition Data.* New York: Cambridge University Press.

Latinobarometer. 2001. *Chart: The most pressing problem in the region. Cited by IDB: Good jobs wanted: Labor markets in Latin America. 2004 Economic and Social Progress Report. Inter-American Development Bank. The Johns Hopkins University Press. Washington, D.C.: IDB.* Latinobarometer.

Leblanc, G. 1995. "Discrimination in the Labour Market." *Canadian Journal of Economics* 28:pp. 702–717.

Leibenstein, Harvey. 1963. "The Theory of Underemployment in Densely Populated Backward Areas." In *Economic Backwardness and Economic Growth*, edited by Harvey Leibenstein. New York: John Wiley & Sons, Inc.

Lindbeck, A., and D.J. Snower. 1988. *The Insider-Outsider Theory of Employment and Unemployment.* Cambridge, Massachusetts.

———. 2001. "Insiders versus Outsiders." *Journal of Economic Perspectives* 15:pp. 165–188.

Lippmann, Steven A., and John J. McCall. 1976a. "The economics of job search: A survey. Part I,II." *Economic Inquiry* 14:pp. 155–189.

———. 1976b. "The eEconomics of job search: A survey. Part II." *Economic Inquiry* 14 (September): pp. 347–368.

Long, J. Scott. 1997. *Regression Models for Categorical and Limited Dependent Variables.* Thousand Oaks, London, New Delhi: Sage Publications.

———. 2001. *Regression Models for Categorical Dependent Variables Using Stata.* College Station, Texas, U.S.A.: Stata Press.

Lyra, José Augusto. 1999. *Direito do Trabalho.* Brasília: Editora Vestcon.

Malcomson, James. 1981. "Unemployment and the efficiency wage hypothesis." *Economic Journal* 91:pp. 848–866.

Malliaris, A.G., and W.A. Brock. 1981. *Stochastic Methods in Economics and Finance.* Amsterdam and others: Elsevier Science Publishers B.V.

Maloney, William F. 1997, May. Labor market structure in LDCs - Time series evidence on competing views. The World Bank, Working Paper No. 1940.

———. 1999. "Does informality imply segmentation in urban labor markets? Evidence from sectoral transitions in Mexico." *World Bank Economic Review* 13:pp. 275–302.

McDonald, Ian M., and Robert M. Solow. 1985. "Wages and employment in a segmented labor market." *Quarterly Journal of Economics* 100 (Fall): pp. 1115–1141.

McNabb, R. 1987. "Labour Market Theories and Education." In *Economics of Education: Research and Studies*, edited by George Psacharopoulos. Oxford and others: Pergamon Press.

Menezes Filho, Naercio, Helio Zylberstajn, José Z. Chahad, and Elaine Pazello. 2002. Unions and the economic performance of Brazilian establishments. Research Network Working Paper No. R-464. Inter-American Development Bank, Washington, D.C.

Mincer, Jacob. 1962. "On-the-job training: Costs, returns and some implications." *Journal of Political Economy* 70 (supplement): pp. 50–79.

Ministério de Trabalho e Emprego (MTE). 1999. *Relatório de Avaliação do Sistema Nacional de Emprego, Exercício 1998.* Ministério de Trabalho e Emprego (MTE).

———. 2003a. *Brasil - evolução do emprego, CAGED, various years.* http://www.mte.gov.br/Temas/CAGED/Estatistica/Planilhas/1999/Janeiro/Atividade.pdf, date: Sept. 18, 2003: Ministério de Trabalho e Emprego (MTE).

———. 2003b. *Histórico do seguro-desemprego.* http://www.mte.gov.br/Temas/SeguroDesemp/Estatistica/Conteudo/2040.pdf, date: Sept. 18, 2003: Ministério de Trabalho e Emprego (MTE).

———. 2003c. *Movimentação da Intermediação de mão-de-obra, setor formal SINE/Brasil, Resultados e Indicadores - Ano 2000.* http://www.mte.gov.br/Temas/SINE/Imagens/Tabelas/Rel2000.asp, date: Sept. 18, 2003: Ministério de Trabalho e Emprego (MTE).

Montgomery, J.D. 1991. "Social networks and labor-market outcomes: Towards an economic analysis." *American Economic Review* 81 (5): pp. 1408–1418.

Monthly Labor Survey (PME), Instituto Brasileiro de Geografia e Estatística (IBGE). 1999. Pesquisa Mensal de Emprego (PME).

Mortensen, Dale T. 1977. "Unemployment and job search decisions." *Industrial and Labor Relations Review* 30 (4): pp. 505–517.

———. 1986. "Job Search and Labor Market Analysis." In *Handbook of Labor Economics. Volume II,* edited by Orley C. Ashenfelter and Richard Layard. Amsterdam and others: Elsevier Science Publishers BV.

Mortensen, Dale T., and Christopher A. Pissarides. 1999. "New Developments in Models of Search in the Labor Market." In *Handbook of Labor Economics. Volume 3B,* edited by Orley C. Ashenfelter and David Card. Amsterdam and others: Elsevier Science B.V.

Narendranathan, W., and S. Nickell. 1985. "Modeling the process of job search." *Journal of Econometrics* 28:pp. 29–49.

National Household Survey PNAD, Instituto Brasileiro de Geografia e Estatística (IBGE). 1999. Pesquisa Nacional por Amostra de Domicílios, (PNAD).

Navarro-Lozano, Salvador. 2002, May. The importance of being formal: Testing for segmentation in the Mexican labor market. Paper presented at the conference of the LACEA in Madrid, Spain, 11-13 of October 2002.

Neri, Marcelo, Gustavo Gonzaga, and José M. Camargo. 2001. "Salário mínimo, efeito-farol e pobreza." *Revista de Economia Política* 21 (2): pp. 78–90.

OECD. 1994. *The OECD Jobs Study. Part II – The Adjustment Potential of the Labour Market.* Paris: OECD.

———. 1999. *Standardizes employment rates - Archives.* http://www.oecd.org/dataoecd/59/11/2663936.pdf: OECD.

O'Higgins, Niall. 2001. *Youth Unemployment and Employment Policy – A Global Perspective.* Geneva: ILO.

Oi, W.Y. 1962. "Labor as a quasi-fixed factor of production." *Journal of Political Economy* 70:pp. 538–555.

O'Reilly, Jaqueline, and Silke Bothfeld. 2002. "What happens after working part time? Integration, maintenance or exclusionary transitions in Britain and western Germany." *Cambridge Journal of Economics* 26 (4): pp. 409–439.

Oswald, Andrew. 1997. "Happiness and economic performance." *Economic Journal* 107:pp. 1815–1831.

Paes De Barros, Ricardo, Carlos Henrique Corseuil, and Miguel Foguel. 1999, November. Os incentivos adversos e a focalisação dos programas de proteção ao trabalhador no Brasil. Seminário: O Sistema Brasileiro de Proteção Social ao Desempregado, Ministry of Labor and employment, São Paulo.

Paes De Barros, Ricardo, Carlos Henrique Corseuil, and Gustavo Gonzaga. 1999b, June. Labor market regulations and the demand for labor in Brazil. Instituto de Pesquisa Econômica Aplicada (IPEA) Discussion Paper No. 656.

Paes De Barros, Ricardo, Carlos Henrique Corseuil, and Phillippe G. Leite. 2000, May. Labor market and poverty in Brazil. Instituto de Pesquisa Econômica Aplicada (IPEA) Discussion Paper No. 723.

Piore, Michael J. 1972. Notes for a theory of labor market stratification. MIT Working Paper No. 95.

———. 1975. "Notes for a Theory of Labor Market Segmentation." In *Labor Market Segmentation*, edited by Richard C. Edwards et al. Lexington: D.C. Heath.

Programa Regional del Empleo para América Latina y el Caribe PREALC, ILO. 1991. *Retrospectiva del sector informal urbano en América Latina: Una bibliografía anotada.* ILO, Geneva: Programa Regional del Empleo para América Latina y el Caribe PREALC, ILO.

Ramos, Carlos Alberto, and Paulo Springer de Freitas. 1998, July. Sistema público de emprego: Objetivos, eficiência e eficácia (Notas sobre os países da OCDE e o Brasil). Instituto de Pesquisa Econômica Aplicada (IPEA) Discussion Paper No. 568.

Ramos, Lauro. 2002, November. A evolução da informalidade no Brasil metropolitano 1991 - 2001. Instituto de Pesquisa Econômica Aplicada (IPEA) Discussion Paper No. 914.

Røed, Knut, and Tao Zhang. 2003. "Does unemployment compensation affect unemployment duration?" *The Economic Journal* 113 (January): pp. 190–206.

Sachs, J., and A.A. Zini. 1996. "Brazilian inflation and the Plano Real." *World Economy* 19 (1): pp. 13–37.

Salm, Claudio. 1998. "Novos requisitos educacionais do mercado de trabalho." In *Economia & trabalho: textos básicos,* edited by Marco Antonio de Oliveira. Campinas, SP, Brazil: UNICAMP.IE.

Salop, Steven C. 1979. "A model of the natural rate of unemployment." *American Economic Review* 69 (March): pp. 117–125.

Schlicht, Ekkehart. 1978. "Labor turnover, wage structure and natural unemployment." *Zeitschrift für die gesamte Staatswissenschaft* 134:pp. 337–346.

Schneider, Friedrich. 2002. The size and development of the shadow economies of 22 transition and 21 OECD countries. IZA Discussion Paper No. 514.

Schultz, Theodore W. 1961. "Investment in human capital." *American Economic Review* 51 (March): pp. 1–17.

Sesselmeier, Werner, and Gregor Blauermel. 1997. *Arbeitsmarkttheorien: Ein Überblick.* Heidelberg: Physika-Verlag.

Shapiro, Carl, and Joseph Stiglitz. 1984. "Equilibrium unemployment as a worker discipline device." *American Economic Review* 74:pp. 433–444.

Soares, Sergei, Luiza Carvalho, and Bernardo Kipnis. 2003, June. Os jovens adultos de 18 a 25 anos: Retrato de uma dívida da política educacional. Instituto de Pesquisa Econômica Aplicada (IPEA) Discussion Paper No. 754.

Soares, Sergei, and Rejane Sayuri Izaki. 2002, December. A participação feminina no mercado de trabalho. Instituto de Pesquisa Econômica Aplicada (IPEA) Discussion Paper No. 923.

Solow, Robert. 1979. "Another possible source of wage stickiness." *Journal of Macroeconomics* 1:pp. 79–82.

Spence, Michael. 1973. "Job market signalling." *Quarterly Journal of Economics* 87 (3): pp. 355–374.

Stigler, George J. 1961. "The economics of information." *Journal of Political Economy* 69 (June): pp. 213–225.

———. 1962. "Information in the labor market." *Journal of Political Economy* 70 (October): pp. 94–104.

Stiglitz, Joseph. 1974. "Wage determination and unemployment in L.D.C.s: The labor turnover model." *Quarterly Journal of Economics* 88:pp. 194–227.

———. 1976, August. Prices and queues as screening devices in competitive markets. IMSSS Technical Report No. 212, Stanford University.

———. 2002. "Information and the change in the paradigm in economics." *American Economic Review* 92 (3): pp. 460–501.

Theodoro, Mario. 2002, December. Participação social e políticas públicas: Os conselhos federais de política social – O caso CODEFAT. Instituto de Pesquisa Econômica Aplicada (IPEA) Discussion Paper No. 931.

Thomas, J.J. 1992. *Informal Economic Activity. - (LSE Handbooks in Economics)*. New York and others: Harvester Wheatsheaf.

Todaro, Michael P. 1969. "A model of labor migration and urban unemployment in less developed countries." *American Economic Review* 59 (1): pp. 138–148.

Tokman, Victor E. 1990. "The Informal Sector in Latin America: Fifteen Years Later." In *The Informal Sector Revisited*, edited by David Turnham, Bernard Salomé, and Antoine Schwarz. Paris: OECD.

Urani, André. 1998. "The effects of macroeconomic adjustment on the labor market and on income distribution in Brazil." In *Poverty, Economic Reform & Income Distribution in Latin America*, edited by Albert Berry. Boulder and London: Lynne Rienner Publishers.

Van Den Berg, Gerard J. 1990. "Nonstationarity in job search theory." *Review of Economic Studies* 57:pp. 255–277.

Van Den Berg, Gerard J., Arjan Heyma, and Marloes Zijl. 2003, February. Stepping stones for the unemployed? Effects of temporary jobs on job search duration of the unemployed. Paper presented at the 15th Annual Conference of the European Association of Labour Economists (EALE) at Seville, Spain from 18-21 September, 2003.

Van Den Berg, Gerard J., Anders Holm, and Jan C. Van Ours. 1999, May. Do stepping-stone jobs exist? Early career paths in the medical profession. Tinbergen Institute Discussion Paper, forthcoming in Journal of Population Economics 4/2002.

Van Den Berg, Gerard J., and Bas Van Der Klaauw. 2001, October. Counseling and monitoring of unemployed workers: Theory and evidence from a controlled social experiment. IZA Discussion Paper No. 374.

Weiss, Andrew. 1980. "Job Queues and Layoffs in Labor Markets with Flexible Wages." *Journal of Political Economy* 88 (June): pp. 526–538.

———. 1990. *Efficiency Wages. Models of Unemployment, Layoffs, and Wage Dispersion.* Princeton: Princeton University Press.

Winkelmann, Rainer, and Liliana Winkelmann. 1998. "Why are the unemployed so unhappy." *Economica* 65 (257): pp. 1–15.

Yellen, Janet L. 1984. "Efficiency wage models of unemployment." *American Economic Review P+P* 74:pp. 200–205.

Göttinger Studien zur Entwicklungsökonomik
Göttingen Studies in Development Economics

Herausgegeben von / Edited by Hermann Sautter

Die Bände 1-8 sind über die Vervuert Verlagsgesellschaft (Frankfurt/M.) zu beziehen.

Bd./Vol. 9 Hermann Sautter / Rolf Schinke (eds.): Social Justice in a Market Economy. 2001.

Bd./Vol. 10 Philipp Albert Theodor Kircher: Poverty Reduction Strategies. A comparative study applied to empirical research. 2002.

Bd./Vol. 11 Matthias Blum: Weltmarktintegration, Wachstum und Innovationsverhalten in Schwellenländern. Eine theoretische Diskussion mit einer Fallstudie über »Argentinien 1990-1999". 2003.

Bd./Vol. 12 Jan Müller-Scheeßel: Die Privatisierung und Regulierung des Wassersektors. Das Beispiel Buenos Aires/Argentinien. 2003.

Bd./Vol. 13 Ludger J. Löning: Economic Growth, Biodiversity Conservation, and the Formation of Human Capital in a Developing Country. 2004.

Bd./Vol. 14 Silke Woltermann: Transitions in Segmented Labor Markets. The Case of Brazil. 2004.